THE TRIUMPH
of
ECONOMIC FREEDOM

THE TRIUMPH

of

ECONOMIC FREEDOM

DEBUNKING THE SEVEN GREAT MYTHS
OF AMERICAN CAPITALISM

———

PHIL GRAMM *and*
DONALD J. BOUDREAUX

ROWMAN & LITTLEFIELD
Lanham • Boulder • New York • London

Published by Rowman & Littlefield

Bloomsbury Publishing Inc, 1385 Broadway, New York, NY 10018, USA

Bloomsbury Publishing Plc, 50 Bedford Square, London, WC1B 3DP, UK

Bloomsbury Publishing Ireland, 29 Earlsfort Terrace, Dublin 2, D02 AY28, Ireland

www.rowman.com

British Library Cataloguing in Publication Information Available

Library of Congress Cataloging-in-Publication Data
Names: Gramm, Phil, author. | Boudreaux, Donald J., author.
Title: The triumph of economic freedom : debunking the seven great myths of
    American capitalism / Phil Gramm and Donald J. Boudreaux.
Description: Lanham, Maryland : Rowman & Littlefield, [2025] | Includes
    bibliographical references and index.
Identifiers: LCCN 2024053957 (print) | LCCN 2024053958 (ebook) |
    ISBN 9798881808365 (cloth) | ISBN 9798881808372 (epub)
Subjects: LCSH: Capitalism—United States—History. | Free enterprise—
    United States—History. | United States—Economic conditions.
Classification: LCC HB501 .G62758 2025 (print) | LCC HB501 (ebook) |
    DDC 330.12/20973—dc23/eng/20250226
LC record available at https://lccn.loc.gov/2024053957
LC ebook record available at https://lccn.loc.gov/2024053958

For product safety related questions contact productsafety@bloomsbury.com.

♾️™ The paper used in this publication meets the minimum requirements of
American National Standard for Information Sciences—Permanence of Paper for
Printed Library Materials, ANSI/NISO Z39.48-1992.

We dedicate this book to America—not the idealized shining city on a hill but, rather, an unfinished work of a free people who strive and often fail to live up to their high principles but who then learn from their mistakes and perpetually rededicate themselves to the task.

CONTENTS

———

PREFACE AND INTRODUCTION

*How the Lessons We Learn from History
Affect Our Political Values*

———

THOMAS JEFFERSON BELIEVED THAT good men with the same facts are prone to disagree, but it seems hardly a coincidence that people who hold different opinions about public policy almost invariably have very different perceptions of what is happening in the world around them.[1] People's opinions are molded not just by the evidence they have but, based on their knowledge and experience, how they interpret that evidence. Economist Thomas Sowell sees differences in political opinion springing from the fact that people "reasoning from fundamentally different premises . . . have different visions of how the world works."[2] From their visions, which frequently are nothing more than "gut feelings," people build their theories, which can be weighed against new evidence.[3] Crucial to forming our values is how we interpret the facts concerning the contemporary state of affairs, as well as the lessons we have learned from history.

Chuck Schumer, the current Democrat leader in the Senate, and John Thune, the current Republican leader of the Senate, hold very different views concerning key public policy issues and the role of government. It is tempting to say they differ in opinion simply because Thune is a modern conservative and Schumer is a twenty-first-century American progressive. But if we asked them to give us their perception of what happened in the Industrial Revolution, the causes of the Great Depression, or what triggered the 2008 financial crisis, they would have totally different interpretations of each historical event. The same would be true if we asked them for their assessments of income inequality and poverty in America.

Scientific propositions are the bases for formal theories, which can then be tested using empirical observations. While empirical evidence is important in validating or rebutting political views, historical evidence is seldom definitive, as it is not the result of controlled experiments and, therefore, is subject to different interpretations. The problem is compounded by the level of commitment with which many people hold their social values.

The initial lessons we draw from our experiences lead us to tentatively form our values, which are often based on very limited information. But accumulating more in-depth knowledge can profoundly affect what we believe and the confidence we have in those beliefs. As Sowell concludes, what ultimately divides people is "their different empirical assumptions as to human nature and social cause and effect."[4] In studying the impact of history on public opinion, Nobel laureate economist Friedrich Hayek found that "past experience is the foundation on which our beliefs about the desirability of different policies and institutions are mainly based."[5]

Our national experience, public perception of events, and conclusions about their causes and effects have molded public opinion and public policy. In this way, he who writes history determines the future. Schooled in the corruption of monarchs, the history of the British Parliament, the rise and fall of the Roman Republic, and the virtues of British property rights and the rule of law, the American founders saw self-interest as inherent in human nature and, therefore, in the governments that humans institute. According to Alexander Hamilton, government must be limited and its power checked, as "it is the lot of all human institutions, even those of the most perfect kind, to have defects as well as excellencies—ill as well as good propensities. This results from the imperfection of the Institutor, Man."[6]

In the founders' view, the best that society can do is discover and enforce rules of law that generally allow individuals to pursue their diverse interests in ways that minimize conflict and maximize social cooperation. Adam Smith famously explained how the pursuit of private interest could promote the public interest: "It is not from the benevolence of the butcher, the brewer, or the baker, that we expect our dinner, but from their regard to their own interest."[7] While the result would always be far from heaven on earth, at its best, it would bring peace, prosperity, and progress. As summed up by Lord Macaulay, government officials "will best promote the improvement of the nation by strictly confining themselves to their own legitimate duties, by leaving capital to find its most lucrative course, commodities their fair price, industry and intelligence their natural reward, idleness and folly their natural punishment, by maintaining peace, by defending property, by diminishing the price of law, and by observing strict economy in every department of the state. Let the Government do this: the People will assuredly do the rest."[8] Beyond establishing the rule of law and the powers required to enforce that rule of law, the founders were skeptical of a powerful government not just because they questioned its competency but because they also feared its unchecked power. Milton and Rose Friedman expressed that same fear when they warned that "force, introduced for good purposes, will end up in the hands of people who will use it to promote their own interests."[9]

At its founding, the American government was small, and its powers were constrained. The government expanded during times of war, and some of those expansions carried over into the ensuing peacetime.[10] The Industrial Revolution gave rise to levels of prosperity that, for the first time in history, made it thinkable that child labor and abject poverty could be banned. Populist demands that government regulate large industries gave rise to government involvement in the functioning of the economy. The Great Depression profoundly changed public opinion concerning the reliability of the free market system and the role of government. The magnitude and the length of the Depression—during a time without a government social safety net—traumatized Americans and ushered in a massive expansion in the government's power to provide benefits to its citizens and exert greater influence over the functioning of the economy. The end of America's global dominance in manufacturing as the world recovered from World War II and the subsequent decline in manufacturing employment has increasingly been viewed as evidence that foreign trade is bad for America. That change in public opinion, powered by the fact that blue-collar industrial workers are now the swing voters in national elections, is reversing eighty years of public policy committed to expanding world trade. With the growth in postwar prosperity, the consensus grew that government should do more to help the nation's poor. The War on Poverty significantly expanded government expenditures as the government sought to alleviate poverty in the nation. And the 2008 financial crisis undercut public confidence in the financial sector, further expanding federal power over the banking and securities industries.

Today governments at the local, state, and federal levels direct the flow of 33.4 percent of the nation's gross domestic product (GDP). Almost half of Americans receive more benefits, at least valued in terms of their costs, from the government than these citizens pay in taxes. And the government regulates, mandates, subsidizes, and controls a growing share of the American economy.

In this book we focus our attention on the evidence that profoundly changed public opinion and gave rise to the dramatic expansion in the role of government. We look specifically at the evidence on the Industrial Revolution, the Progressive antitrust era, the Great Depression, the decline in the level of employment in manufacturing starting in the late 1970s, and the Great Recession. In addition, we look at two contemporary issues: income inequality and poverty in America. For most Americans, their interpretations of these five defining periods of American history and the contemporary issues of income inequality and poverty largely determine their views of the proper role of government.

There are at least two sides to every story, and as John Stuart Mill has observed, "He who knows only his side of the case knows little of that."[11] But we hope to convince you, the readers of this book, that the preponderance of evidence about the most disputed periods of American history and the most contentious contemporary issues support those who would limit the power of government. We also believe that by getting the facts straight, we can enhance the development of political consensus and compromise and, in the process, strengthen the ability of our political system to better deal with our nation's many problems. This reassessment of the facts is especially timely—and important—because, today, conventional wisdom firmly holds that these five periods of American history, along with the existing levels of income inequality and poverty, constitute strong evidence for further expanding the government's role. In this book we use hard facts to dispel that myth.

In each of the five historic periods and in the analysis of income inequality and poverty, we introduce the era or the issue with a simple factual description. We attempt to give what we define as the myth a full and fair presentation, citing views that are expressed by many of the world's greatest historians, as well as through unforgettable descriptions found in literature's most acclaimed works, words that are burned into our memories and hearts. We focus special attention on the facts presented in support of the supposed myths. We then present the evidence in our effort to debunk these myths. At its best, we hope that each chapter will demonstrate that conventional wisdom on these seven myths of American capitalism is wrong. But even if you are not convinced, we hope that a review of the evidence will make it clear that conventional wisdom is at least overstated and deserving of more skepticism. Public policy, the power of government, and ultimately, our freedom and happiness depend on getting the facts straight. The truth can make us free only if we know the truth. In this book we seek the truth and leave it to your better judgment to determine how close we have come to finding it.

ACKNOWLEDGMENTS

THIS BOOK COULD NOT have been written without the help of Mike Solon. He has researched, documented, proofread, and enriched every part of the book. John Early has provided documentation and source materials that were only possible to obtain with his in-depth knowledge of how the government collects and reports economic data. Mariel Peterson's contributions in assisting with writing each part of the book and proofing and correcting each of its many drafts have been indispensable. We extend our gratitude also to the skilled editors and production team at Bloomsbury—Jenna Dutton, Kate Genn, Charles Harmon, Mikayla Lindsay, and Jon Sisk.

We, the authors of this book, see eye to eye on all fundamental issues involving economics, history, and public policy. But as with all coauthored projects, along the way, there naturally arose a handful of minor disagreements on inessential matters. Fortunately, these were few, and both of us are happy with the compromises we reached to settle them.

During the writing of this book, we received generous and detailed feedback from many friends who, thankfully, did not hesitate to offer frank criticism when criticism was called for and, in many cases, provided input that improved our focus and thus dramatically improved the book. We've done our best to incorporate their feedback and ideas into the text, which is far better than it would have been without their input. We are especially grateful for the help and comments we received from Karol Boudreaux, Charles Calomiris, John Cochrane, Burt Folsom,

ACKNOWLEDGMENTS

Vincent Geloso, Teresa Gramm, Robert Higgs, Douglas Irwin, Mark Koyama, Brian Mannix, Deirdre McCloskey, Steve McMillin, Mark Perry, Caleb Petitt, Veronique de Rugy, George Selgin, Amity Shlaes, and Robyn Weaving. Of course, none of these friends and scholars is responsible for any remaining oversights and errors, for which we take full responsibility.

One

THE GENESIS MYTH

The Industrial Revolution Impoverished Workers

N O ONE APPRECIATED THE power of capitalism more than its greatest antagonist, Karl Marx.[1] Born of the Enlightenment and embodied in the Industrial Revolution, capitalism, according to Marx and his coauthor and patron, Friedrich Engels, "accomplished wonders far surpassing Egyptian pyramids, Roman aqueducts, and Gothic cathedrals . . . achieving more massive and colossal productive forces than have all preceding generations together" in "scarce one hundred years."[2]

In the communal world of the Middle Ages, the worker owed fealty to the crown, church, guild, and village. Those "stakeholders," as they would be called today, extracted large shares of the output produced by the sweat of workers' brows and the fruits of their thrift. Rewards for effort and saving were thus leeched away. Unsurprisingly, the economic output was so sparse and economic growth so slow that they were noticeable only across the span of centuries. This dreary reality suddenly (in historical terms) changed in the seventeenth and eighteenth centuries. Starting in northwestern Europe, the Enlightenment of the era gave birth to liberalism, which—true to its name—liberated mind, soul, and property. Individuals were freed and empowered to think their own thoughts and, ultimately, have a voice in their government. Men and women secured the right to worship as they chose, as well as to own the fruits of their labor, thrift, risk-taking, and entrepreneurial creativity. In a passage carved on his gravestone, Scottish Enlightenment philosopher Adam Smith (1723–1790) observed, "The property which every man has in his own labor, as it is the original foundation of all property, so it is the most sacred and inviolable." This idea was new at that time and its liberating consequences immense.

In the mid-nineteenth century, the British Parliament started re-pealing royal charters, gradually permitting businesses to incorporate simply by meeting preset capital requirements. The common law evolved to more effectively govern contracting and competition. Parliamentary reforms widened the franchise, increasing representation of the towns and the middle class. Legislation was increasingly enacted through public votes following open deliberation. In this newly enlightened and liberated world, individuals were empowered to pursue their own private interests instead of being conscripted by law or tradition into assisting the elite in pursuing *their* private interests.[3] The economist W. H. Hutt described the change succinctly: "One of the main social re-sults of the factory regime seems to have been the evolution of the idea of a wage *contract*, replacing the former idea of servitude."[4] Laborers and savers, working in increasingly competitive markets to raise their own level of economic attainment, accomplished what no benevolent king's redistribution, no loving bishop's charity, no mercantilist's pro-tectionism, and no powerful guild ever did—namely, they delivered a massive increase in productive capacity that continues to enrich our world today.

Of course, even at the height of the acceptance of classical liberalism by the British in the mid-nineteenth century, the government per-formed some positive functions beyond providing public goods such as policing and infrastructure. For example, it arranged for government inspection of factories, legislatively controlled hours of work for chil-dren, and mandated minimum amounts of schooling.[5] But as argued by the Nobel laureate economist F. A. Hayek, such legislative interventions were themselves the children of capitalist enrichment. The agitation in nineteenth-century Britain for government efforts to improve the lot of the working classes was, according to Hayek, the product of how "the very essence of wealth and well-being which had been achieved raised standards and aspirations. What for ages had seemed a natural and inevitable situation, or even as an improvement upon the past, came to be regarded as incongruous with the opportunities which the new age appeared to offer. Economic suffering both became more conspicuous and seemed less justified, because general wealth was increasing faster than ever before."[6]

Even the harshest critics of capitalism have been forced to join Marx in conceding that, with the Industrial Revolution, capitalism ignited an explosion in productive capacity such as history had never before experienced.[7] The dispute was then, and is now, not about whether unprecedented economic growth occurred or not but, rather, about who benefited from this growth and who didn't.

THE MYTH

The nineteenth-century historian Arnold Toynbee, in his posthumously published *Industrial Revolution* (1884), rendered his influential judgment about Britain's Industrial Revolution:

> There were dark patches even in his [Adam Smith's] age, but we now approach a darker period—a period as disastrous and as terrible as any through which a nation ever passed; disastrous and terrible, because, side by side with a great increase of wealth was seen an enormous increase of pauperism; and production on a vast scale, the result of free competition, led to a rapid alienation of classes and to the degradation of a large body of producers. . . .
>
> The misery which came upon large sections of the working people at this epoch was often, though not always, due to a fall in wages. The effects of the Industrial Revolution prove that free competition may produce wealth without producing well-being.[8]

The Romantic View of the Industrial Revolution in Britain

Before empiricism became the primary basis of economic history, most historical analysis relied on contemporary accounts and romantic depictions of events. For example, British historians have often continued to repeat and embellish Toynbee's harsh assessment of the Industrial Revolution. Such historians are too numerous to count, but featured most prominently among them are Sidney and Beatrice Webb, J. L. and Barbara Hammond, Eric Hobsbawm, and E. P. Thompson. The last of these declared that the Industrial Revolution had a "truly catastrophic nature [that brought] intensified exploitation, greater insecurity and increasing human misery."[9] The belief remains widespread that the high living standards we enjoy today were purchased at the price of subjecting ordinary workers two hundred years ago to unprecedented brutal privation and toil.

Victorian literature paints a "worst of times" portrait of England amid the Industrial Revolution, with emotional novels and poems that cry out against the period's poverty, exploitation, and human want. Among the best-known examples are a novel and a poem, both published in December 1843.

Charles Dickens's *A Christmas Carol*, one of the most popular books ever written, tells the story of Ebenezer Scrooge, a coldhearted, wealth-hoarding financier who is visited by four apparitions on Christmas Eve night. The first is the ghost of his partner, Jacob Marley, condemned to wander the world, for he had shown so little compassion for his fellow human beings during his life. He comes to tell Scrooge of the horrors that await him in death. Scrooge is then visited by the ghosts of Christmas Past, Present, and Yet to Come. Scrooge awakens to a world of poverty in which the unemployed scavenge potatoes that have fallen off a wagon and people live in squalor, and to the danger of not recognizing the twin threats, personified by two small children, of Want and Ignorance. Their neglect would doom civilization.

Thomas Hood's poem "The Song of the Shirt," published in the 1843 Christmas issue of *Punch* magazine, portrays the conditions faced by women sewing in British sweatshops. This despairing poem is a plea to the privileged to understand the dire conditions workers endured in industrial workshops. The seamstress is compared to a slave, as she sewed from morning to night. The poet draws an analogy between the wearing out of men's shirts and other clothing and the wearing out of the seamstress's body:

Oh, Men, with Sisters dear!

Oh, men, with Mothers and Wives!

It is not linen you're wearing out,

But human creatures' lives![10]

Hood's poem contains one of the most moving lines ever written: "Oh God that bread should be so dear and flesh and blood so cheap."[11]

According to Dickens and Hood, the urban workplace was but a prison with rations of only bread crusts for food, threadbare rags for clothes, and rented hovels for shelter. So persuasive is this grimness in Victorian-era literature, with its vivid portrayals of poverty and misery, that twenty-first-century French academic Thomas Piketty cites *Germinal, Oliver Twist,* and *Les Misérables,* novels from the era, as empirical "evidence" that the Industrial Revolution was indeed a terrible time. In Piketty's view, the misery portrayed in these works is so vivid that it "did not spring from the imagination of their authors."[12]

Poets and writers contrasted the vileness of factory work with the virtues of rural life and the dignity of rural work. The theme of city life as a source of evil found voice in William Blake's poem "London":

I wander thro' each charter'd street,

Near where the charter'd Thames does flow.

And mark in every face I meet

Marks of weakness, marks of woe.[13]

Blake and William Wordsworth viewed rural life and nature as life affirming, filled with fresh air, sunshine, morality, and beauty, which contrasted with the dehumanizing evils of city living for poor workers.

In 1845 Friedrich Engels, whose father owned large textile mills in both England and Germany, published *The Condition of the Working Class in England.* In it he expressed nostalgia for rural life and claimed that people didn't have to work very hard in preindustrial bucolic settings. He wrote,

Workers vegetated throughout a passably comfortable existence, leading a righteous and peaceful life in all piety and probity; and their material position was far better than that of their successors. They did not need to overwork; they did no more than they chose to do, and yet earned what they needed. They had leisure for healthful work in garden or field, work which, in itself, was recreation for them, and they could take part besides in the recreations and games of their neighbours.[14]

Engels contrasted this pleasure and ease of rural life with the hell of factories in which "workers, treated as brutes, actually become such."[15] His bleak picture of mid-nineteenth-century industrial England carried over into the rallying cry of the *Communist Manifesto*, which he wrote with Karl Marx in 1848: "The proletarians have nothing to lose but their chains. They have a world to win. Workingmen of all countries, unite."[16]

Philosopher Bertrand Russell found "the Industrial Revolution caused unspeakable misery in both England and America."[17] This bleak assessment, often repeated in history textbooks and popular literature, dominates conventional wisdom and, therefore, public opinion to this day.

Remarkably, these historical and romantic critiques were written about a period that, by every available economic measure, was the beginning of a golden age of material well-being—especially for workers. The claim that the dawning of capitalism in Britain impoverished workers is the "Genesis myth" of capitalism, yet it is refuted by every major measure of material well-being. In a single century, from 1800 to 1900, wages, lifespan, and literacy expanded at rates never before experienced. The Industrial Revolution, beginning in Britain and then spreading to continental Europe, the United States, and eventually, most of the globe, ushered in a golden age for workers that continues to this day.

THE FACTS THAT DEBUNK THE MYTH

We can only fully appreciate the true achievements of Britain's Industrial Revolution during the Victorian era by understanding that from the fall of Rome in 476 to the Enlightenment of the seventeenth and eighteen centuries, economic growth, wages, and living conditions were not only largely stagnant but stagnant at very low levels. We must judge the improvement in worker conditions during the nineteenth century not by the standards of the twenty-first century but by those that prevailed prior to the nineteenth century.

The economic historian Deirdre McCloskey estimates that since the Industrial Revolution—what she calls the "Great Enrichment"—began just over two hundred years ago, living standards in countries such as Britain, the United States, Japan, and Finland have risen by *at least* 3,000 percent and perhaps—if improvements in product quality are more fully taken into account—by as much as 10,000 percent![18] Based on the available records of economic production and distribution, it would be no overstatement to say that the Industrial Revolution initiated the greatest concentration of material blessings ever experienced by ordinary men, women, and children. According to economic historian Carlo Cipolla, "no revolution has ever been as dramatically revolutionary."[19] The simple yet stunning graph (see figure 1.1) below, drawn from World Bank data of world GDP per capita, proves both his and McCloskey's point.

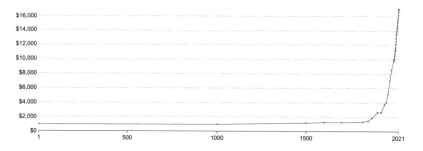

Figure 1.1. Inflation-Adjusted Gross per Capita Income Growth since the Year 1 CE (in 2017 USD). *Source:* World Bank Group, "Our World in Data, World Bank Development Indicators (2023)," updated 2024, https://databank.worldbank.org/source/world-development-indicators; Jutta Bolt and Jan Luiten van Zanden, "Maddison Style Estimates of the Evolution of the World Economy. A New 2020 Update," published October 2020, https://www.rug.nl/ggdc/historicaldevelopment/maddison/publications/wp15.pdf.

This astonishing rise in per capita output naturally enabled dramatic improvements in living standards. Before the modern age, infancy was an especially lethal period of human life, with the rest of childhood being only a little safer. University of California, Davis, economic historian Gregory Clark found that "in England from 1580 to 1800 18 percent of infants died within the first year. Only 69 percent of newborns made it to their fifteenth birthday."[20] It's notable that Queen Anne of England, who reigned from 1702 until her death in 1714 at the age of forty-nine, departed this vale childless despite getting pregnant at least seventeen times. Most of her pregnancies ended in miscarriages or stillbirths; Anne gave birth to a live infant only five times, four of whom died before the age of two. The fifth—William, Duke of Gloucester—died at the age of eleven, in 1700.[21] In the preindustrial world, a great deal of material deprivation was inescapable, even for the richest individuals.

One important reason for short lifespans, of course, was poor diet—what the late Nobel laureate economic historian Robert Fogel described as "chronic malnutrition."[22] According to Fogel, "the supply of food available to ordinary French and English families between 1700 and 1850 was not only meager in amount but also relatively poor in quality."[23] Although Fogel's figures show that calories per capita in both France and Britain rose throughout the eighteenth century—and that throughout, they were slightly higher in Britain—they remained low until the second half of the nineteenth century, the inflection point in economic growth during the Industrial Revolution.

Preindustrial housing was also, for all but the elites, no better than diets. Dwellings were decrepit and filthy. Medieval English villagers typically lived either in tiny one-room cottages or communally, in single-story, three-room "longhouses," which weren't especially long and were certainly not wide, at forty to fifty feet in length and fourteen feet across.[24] Whether it was a cottage or longhouse, its floor was typically made of dirt and covered with the waste from threshing grain. A barrier was placed at the base of each dwelling's doorway to prevent foot traffic from dragging this floor covering outside too quickly—thus the word *threshold*. Roofs were made of thatch, which, to modern eyes, appears quaint and charming but were likely viewed very differently by our many ancestors who slept beneath them. "Thatched roofs," as described by the historians Frances and Joseph Gies, "had formidable drawbacks; they rotted from alternations of wet and dry, and harbored a menagerie of mice, rats, hornets, wasps, spiders, and birds; and above all they caught fire. Yet even in London, they prevailed."[25]

The historian William Manchester paints a gruesome portrait of the home of a typical "prosperous peasant" in Europe during the sixteenth century:

> Lying at the end of a narrow, muddy lane, his rambling edifice of thatch, wattles, mud, and dirty brown wood was almost obscured by a towering dung heap in what, without it, would have been the front yard. The building was large, for it was more than a dwelling. Beneath its sagging roof were a pigpen, a henhouse, cattle sheds, corncribs, straw and hay, and, last and least, the family's apartment, actually a single room whose walls and timbers were coated with soot. According to Erasmus, who examined such huts, "almost all the floors are of clay and rushes from the marshes, so carelessly renewed that the foundation sometimes remains for twenty years, harboring, there below, spittle and vomit and wine of dogs and men, beer . . . remnants of fishes, and other filth unnameable. Hence, with the change of weather, a vapor exhales which in my judgment is far from wholesome."
>
> The centerpiece of the room was a gigantic bedstead, piled high with straw pallets, all seething with vermin. Everyone slept there, regardless of age or gender—grandparents, parents, children, grandchildren, and hens and pigs—and if a couple chose to enjoy intimacy, the others were aware of every movement. In summer they could even watch. If a stranger was staying the night, hospitality required that he be invited to make "one more" on the familial mattress.[26]

The average dwelling changed little until the beginning of the Industrial Revolution.

This poverty remained largely out of sight because it was predominantly rural. The poor lived in villages off the road or in the forests, and even a run-down mud shack looked picturesque when viewed at a distance from across the creek. But when huge numbers of relatively poor people flooded the cities in search of better lives for themselves and their children, they were painfully visible. Many authors of fiction, philosophy, and history in the Victorian era had apparently seen little of rural poverty, and what view they did have of the reality of life in rural areas appears to have come from the verandas of manor houses. But farm and village workers saw the poverty and hopelessness of rural life up close and personal, and they daily suffered the consequences.

Then came the liberation brought by the Enlightenment and liberalism. For the first time in history, entrepreneurship, shopkeeping, commercial innovation, and market activity generally came to be widely regarded as honorable and even dignified.[27] This freed labor and capital, enabling them to serve their owners. Human effort surged, capital accumulated, knowledge and productivity exploded, and the rate of what McCloskey describes as "market-tested innovation" skyrocketed.[28] Agrarian and handicraft production gave way to mechanization and mass production. People left rural areas for better lives in the cities. The movement of people began before the end of the eighteenth century and accelerated markedly by the 1830s. By the mid-nineteenth century, urban dwellers accounted for half the total population of England.

This migration to towns and cities was propelled by the rising wages found there. Using available data, Gregory Clark finds that the wages of craftsmen and apprentices in Britain were stagnant for centuries before the Industrial Revolution.[29] For at least six hundred years, the real (inflation-adjusted) wages of skilled craftsmen and their unskilled apprentices were basically unchanged, rising and falling based on the economic conditions of the times. Wages rose after the Black Death due to a reduced labor supply, but these receded over time. At the dawn of the nineteenth century, real wages were no higher than they had been at the dawn of the thirteenth. According to Clark, a revolution in economic production accelerated around the start of the 1800s, and the quality of life in Britain underwent more rapid improvement than had ever occurred in recorded human history. Wages that had largely stagnated for thirty generations began to rise rapidly (see figure 1.2). During the Victorian era, from 1840 to 1900, the real wages of skilled builder craftsmen increased by 113 percent, and the real wages of unskilled builder helpers rose by 124 percent.[30]

Figure 1.2. Real Wages of Builder Craftsmen in England, 1860s = 100, by Decade 1200–1900. *Source:* Constructed from data from table A-2 in Gregory Clark, "The Condition of the Working Class England, 1209–2004," *Journal of Political Economy* 113, no. 6 (2005): 1324–25, http://www.journals.uchicago.edu/t-and-c.

Professor N. F. R. Crafts of the London School of Economics found a similar result for real per capita annual income in England. Measured in 1970 US dollars, income rose from less than $500 in 1830 to over $1,200 in 1900.[31] A new era of human achievement had begun, with these increases in wages and incomes naturally translating into improved living standards.

Between 1841 and 1901, life expectancy for males rose by 20 percent, from 40.2 years to 48.5 years. For females, it rose by 24 percent, from 42.2 years to 52.4 years.[32] The literacy rate, which was 64 percent for men and 55 percent for women in 1851, improved to an almost-universal 97 percent for both by 1900.[33] "An Index of the Quality of Life for Victorian Children and Youths, the VICY Index," an article by Thomas Jordan, combined metrics for the mortality rate in the first five years of life, a body-mass index to measure adequacy of nutrition, a wage index, school enrollment, female literacy, and household size, finding that these numbers more than doubled from 40.9 in 1840 to 93.5 in 1900, and in 1914 equaled 100.[34]

Children had worked as field hands and servants since the beginning of settled agriculture, more than ten thousand years before. "Child labor," note economic historians Carolyn Tuttle and Simone Wegge, "did not begin during the Industrial Revolution of Great Britain but had existed for centuries across Europe."[35] Some of these jobs were dangerous and filthy, and nearly all would be unlawful today. Tuttle writes elsewhere that in preindustrial Britain, "boys as young as four would work for a master sweep who would send them up the narrow chimneys of British homes to scrape the soot off the sides" and that "around age twelve[,] many girls left home to become domestic servants in the homes of artisans, traders, shopkeepers and manufacturers. They received a low wage, and room and board in exchange for doing household chores (cleaning, cooking, caring for children and shopping)."[36]

With the advent of factories, many parents found employment opportunities for their children there. Early factories employed large numbers of children, and there is some evidence, as found by economic historian Jane Humphries, "that the classic era of industrialization, 1790–1850, saw an upsurge in child labour."[37] The surge of material well-being and the visibility of children working in factories prompted enough agitation for reform that Parliament, starting earnestly in 1833, passed a series of Factory Acts designed to reduce child labor in factories. Nevertheless, most young working children did not toil in factories or mines. Agriculture, services, trades, and clerical duties together employed far more children than did factories and mines, and the Factory Acts did not apply to child labor economy-wide.[38] Furthermore, the economist Clark Nardinelli of the University of Virginia found that the employment of children in factories was declining before the Factory Acts were passed: "Technological change reduced the demand for child labor and increasing income reduced the supply. The Factory Acts, then, did not cause the long-term decline in child labor."[39] The Factory Acts codified the market process that was already underway. In closing the ugly ten-millennial chapter of child labor by the end of 1900, the Industrial Revolution had ushered in a new chapter of more intense childhood nurturing and learning. Whether it was the market or government policy that ultimately had the greater impact is debatable, but prior to the exploding prosperity produced by the Industrial Revolution, ending child labor would have been both unthinkable and unachievable.

Even within the existing city population, the arrival of factories and the opportunities they produced were liberating influences. In 1851 one-third of the young women living in London were employed as servants in rich and middle-class households.[40] Life "below stairs" was generally miserable, with hard work, long hours, low pay, and physical punishment. The basement environment even in the finest homes was often damp, infested with vermin, and generally unhealthy. The factories offered higher pay, shorter hours, better working conditions, and even more fresh air.[41] As a result, in 1872 a Victorian complained that "it was now necessary . . . to allow their maids to go to bed at ten o'clock every night, and to give them an afternoon out every other Sunday, or no servant would stay."[42]

This extraordinary progress was described in the official statistics and published reports of the time. In May 1842, amid Britain's rapid industrialization, the public health advocate Edwin Chadwick submitted his paper, *Report on the Sanitary Conditions of the Labouring Population and on the Means of Its Improvement*. There he wrote, "I shall here only observe, as to the depressing effects assumed from the admitted tendencies of an increase of population, that the fact is, that hitherto, in England, wages, or the means of obtaining the necessaries of life for the whole mass of the labouring community, have advanced, and the comforts within the reach of the labouring classes have increased with the late increase of population."[43]

Using empirical evidence, modern historians increasingly reject the traditional, dismal view of the Industrial Revolution. The imminent economic historian T. S. Ashton observes that

> during the period 1790–1830 factory production increased rapidly. A greater proportion of the people came to benefit from it both as producers and as consumers. The fall in the price of textiles reduced the price of clothing. . . . Boots began to take the place of clogs, and hats replaced shawls, at least for wear on Sundays. Miscellaneous commodities, ranging from clocks to pocket handkerchiefs, began to enter the scheme of expenditure, and after 1820 such things as tea and coffee and sugar fell in price substantially.[44]

Ashton compares the experiences of England and Ireland:

An historian has written of "the disasters of the industrial revolution." If by this he means that the years 1760–1830 were darkened by wars and made cheerless by dearth, no objection can be made. But if he means that the technical and economic changes were themselves the source of calamity the opinion is surely perverse. The central problem of the age was how to feed and clothe and employ generations of children outnumbering by far those of any earlier time. Ireland was faced by the same problem. Failing to solve it, she lost in the 'forties about a fifth of her people by emigration or starvation or disease. If England had remained a nation of cultivators and craftsmen she could hardly have escaped the same fate, and, at best, the weight of a growing population must have pressed down the spring of her spirit. She was delivered, not by her rulers, but by those who, seeking no doubt their own narrow ends, had the wit and resource to devise new methods of production and new methods of administering industry.[45]

Professor McCloskey agrees:

The increase and redistribution of the [British] population was accompanied by its enrichment, contrary to all reasonable expectations. This is the conclusion of the second piece of counting, the counting of national income. It was a real increase, no monetary trick; the money income is measured in the prices of the 1850s. Because he produced two-and-a-half times more than his great-grandfather produced in 1780, the average person in 1860 could buy two-and-a-half times more goods and services.[46]

Peter Lindert and Jeffrey Williamson found evidence suggesting that a significant portion of that 2.5 times greater production of goods and services went to workers. Farm laborers' standard of living rose by about 64 percent, while blue-collar workers' standard of living nearly doubled, increasing by 99.2 percent. All workers, taken together, enjoyed a standard of living gain of almost 155 percent.[47] The acclaimed science writer Matt Ridley noted that this growth in workers' real incomes brought about greater equality in health: "In terms of both physical stature and number of surviving children, the gap narrowed between the richest and the poorest during industrialisation."[48] The same thing happened with the literacy rate.

Of course, there was still poverty and suffering—as there had always been. As the poor flooded the cities, London's population exploded from 1 million in 1800 to 6.7 million in 1900. The causes of many common diseases were not yet known, water and sewer systems were in their infancy, and housing was crowded. But by the time Dickens and Hood were writing, enormous improvements had already been made, and the unprecedented trend of continuing improvement and production of abundance had been set in place. These improvements could not have been possible without the enlightened spirit of liberalism and one of its fruits: the Industrial Revolution.

Ironically, in a period for which economic data show per capita income, with real wages, life expectancy, and the general condition of human life improving at never-before-seen rates, there was an unprecedented, incredible outpouring of passionate concern about the living and working conditions of the poor. It is important to recognize the sources of these attacks on industrialization and economic development. Their philosophical basis rests in writings that extolled a "return to nature" and a kind of perfectibility of human nature in rural settings. Yet actual, flesh-and-blood poor people in rural Britain sought greater prosperity and freedom, not an opportunity to commune with nature. Critics of industrialization never seemed to ask, "If life was so much better in the country, why did millions of workers choose to move to the cities?" Not only did they believe that their prospects were better in the cities, but any objective reading of the economic data of the Victorian era conclusively proves they were right.

It is worth observing that most novelists, poets, historians, and members of Parliament were either part of the landed gentry or supported by that privileged group.[49] Clearly, that entailed a significant potential for bias. The Industrial Revolution brought a new class of wealth, a British nouveau riche, as well as new opportunities for the masses. The workers who left rural England to seek employment in the cities had once worked, with few other options, for the landed gentry. Parliament had subsidized landowners with Britain's infamous Corn Laws, which limited grain imports and thus hurt consumers by raising the prices of foodstuffs, especially bread.

Starting in 1838, under the leadership of John Bright and Richard Cobden, a Manchester factory owner, the Anti–Corn Law League was founded to push for the repeal of this protectionist legislation. Hoping to neutralize agitation for repealing the corn laws, landowners attempted to sully the reputation of Cobden and other industrialists by spreading reports of the allegedly horrific conditions in the factories. Hayek writes

> It is evident that the belief about the "horrible" conditions prevailing among the manufacturing populations of the Midlands and the north of England was in the 1830s and 1840s widely held among the upper classes of London and the south. It was one of the main arguments with which the landowning class hit back at the manufacturers to counter the agitation of the latter against the Corn Laws and for free trade.[50]

Yet Cobden and Bright prevailed. These onerous tariffs were repealed in 1846.[51] The ordinary people of Britain were the principal beneficiaries of the resulting fall in bread prices that the repeal of the Corn Laws had brought about, as confirmed by recent research conducted by Dartmouth College economist Douglas Irwin and Purdue University's Maksym Chepeliev. These scholars "find that the top 10% of income earners lost while the bottom 90% of income earners gained."[52]

The hard evidence of the real and widespread benefits of Britain's industrialization is overwhelming. It is further supported by an original study carried out by historian Emma Griffin, a professor of modern British history at the University of East Anglia and former president of the Royal Historical Society. Griffin studied the writings of workers during the Industrial Revolution to determine whether or not they were happy with the unprecedented changes occurring in their lives.

From the evidence gathered by reading 350 autobiographical writings of ordinary workers of the era, Griffin concludes that "it is time to think the unthinkable: that these writers viewed themselves not as downtrodden losers, but as men and women in control of their destiny; that the industrial revolution heralded the advent not of a yet 'darker period', but of the dawn of liberty."[53]

More generally, in the autobiographical writings Griffin found more than enough evidence to conclude that "the downbeat narrative of working-class life during the industrial revolution may be cathartic for some. But it is not good history."[54] It is "not good history" in part because the workers themselves testified to the better lives they were experiencing. Griffin summarizes her findings:

> If wages were higher, what about the possibility that life was simpler and the poor happier back in the old [preindustrial] days? James Hawker [born in 1836; one of the workers who wrote an autobiographical essay] could not be more scathing about this proposition. He scoffed at the notion that the agricultural labourer "seemed a Deal Happier 60 years ago." In his opinion [back then], he "was merely a Serf." None of the autobiographers had time for those who fondly reminisced about the past. "When I hear people talk of the good old days," wrote George Mallard [born in 1835], "they must be ignorant of what did happen in those days. I know it was hard times where I was."[55]

The best evidence, which can be found both in statistics and in the written testimony of workers who lived during the Industrial Revolution, strongly suggests that the initial spark of the lavish material prosperity that we enjoy today was not struck at the expense of the first few generations of workers who toiled in Britain's water- and steam-powered factories. They, too, benefited, as the Great Enrichment made even those workers and their families richer, freer, and happier.

THE US GILDED AGE: AMERICA'S "INDUSTRIAL REVOLUTION"

A Genesis myth is also told about America's Industrial Revolution— the era known as the Gilded Age. As in Britain decades earlier, many journalists and social critics in post–Civil War America raged against the period's rapid change and what they viewed as the ruthless exploitation of the working class. The rich were accused of seizing their outsized fortunes unfairly or even cruelly. Many of these critics believed workers were being mistreated and driven to exhaustion while earning low wages, consumers were being robbed by exorbitantly high prices, and competitors were being hamstrung through unscrupulous business tactics. They seemed to be universally charging large firms and concentrated industries with seizing and abusing monopoly power. These critics called for much more detailed government control of industry, without which, they believed, monopolies would run rampant and deny ordinary people their fair share of the nation's growing prosperity.

This view still dominates the popular picture of America's Gilded Age, a pejorative term coined by Mark Twain and Charles Dudley Warner in their 1873 book, *The Gilded Age: A Tale of Today.* The *Encyclopedia Britannica* calls the Gilded Age an era of "gross materialism."[56] This picture was first painted by a torrent of magazine articles and books of the era, which described hapless citizens being pillaged by "robber barons." These years were, as American schoolchildren have long been taught, marked by extremes of wealth and poverty, with the rich getting fabulously richer and the poor getting frightfully poorer.

Washington's National Portrait Gallery has a room filled with paintings of the great titans of industry and finance, wherein also hangs a depiction of the economic journalist Henry George. Accompanying his portrait is a plaque that quotes his assessment of the Gilded Age, which he pronounced as material and technical progress advanced in the United States. He insisted that "the rich get richer, the poor grow helpless, the middle class is swept away." The many readers of Howard Zinn's popular high school history text, *A People's History of the United States*, encounter the same story: "Ordinary people who lived through the Gilded Age . . . experienced tremendous hardships and losses. . . . While they got poorer, the rich were getting richer. . . . And so it went, in industry after industry—shrewd, efficient businessmen building empires, choking out competition, maintaining high prices, keeping wages low."[57]

Among the most influential early writers to rage against the "robber barons" was the social critic Henry Demarest Lloyd. In his 1894 book, *Wealth Against Commonwealth*, he argued that the accumulation of massive private wealth through commerce not only impoverished the commonwealth but enslaved the masses to the masters of industry.[58] While still working on the book, Lloyd described his research as "poking about and scavengering in piles of filthy human greed and cruelty almost too nauseous to handle."[59] Popular accounts such as Lloyd's served as the basis for much of the later history of the Gilded Age in the work of, among others, Ray Ginger,[60] Richard Hofstadter,[61] and C. Vann Woodward.[62]

Such horrific accounts of the Gilded Age economy continue to appear today, particularly in television documentaries,[63] podcasts,[64] and school textbooks. French economist Thomas Piketty, never one to miss an opportunity to denounce capitalism, insists that America's poor and middle class "suffered a setback during the Gilded Age."[65]

But perhaps no one has done as much to portray the Gilded Age falsely—and to popularize the term "robber barons"—as the journalist Matthew Josephson. In his best-selling 1934 book, *Robber Barons*, Josephson blamed Thomas Jefferson's "laissez faire political philosophy," describing nineteenth-century America as a land of "predatory liberty."[66] "Whether engaged in money-lending, 'projecting,' speculating or hog-slaughtering," these ambitious young men "sensed their chances instantly, and each in his way rushed to seize the resources, the key positions of the industrial society being hastily assembled. They would then find themselves, incredibly enough, commanders of strongholds, lords of 'empires' in iron, beef, railroads or oil, to be held naturally for private gain, and once held, defended by them to the last breath of financial life."[67] As Josephson saw matters, economic growth was of no comfort to "the underlying population during the late 1870s and 1880s of workers who found their wages being reduced, of farmers in much greater number who found the value of crops deflated."[68] The implication is clear: Like their medieval predecessors, modern robber barons enriched themselves at the expense of the masses.

Mirroring the account of Britian's Industrial Revolution, the hard evidence contradicts this popular narrative. The evidence shows that

Americans in the Gilded Age experienced unprecedented and broad-based economic growth. Between 1865 and 1900, inflation-adjusted GDP nearly tripled, expanding by an extraordinary 297 percent.[69] Nothing like this had ever happened in American history.[70] And although the US population nearly doubled, real per capita GDP during these years also surged, increasing by 83 percent,[71] with the real value per person of consumer goods produced in the United States for domestic use rising by 119 percent from 1869 to 1900.[72]

These gains were emphatically *not* "captured" exclusively by the rich. Between 1865 and 1900, real annual earnings for all nonfarm workers rose by 62 percent; the next fifteen years would increase these real earnings by another 12.6 percent.[73] The rise in the real hourly wages of manufacturing workers was even greater. In his comprehensive 2009 study of compensation for production workers in America's manufacturing sector, the economist Lawrence Officer found that in 1865 manufacturing workers earned an average hourly pay of $0.71 (in 1982–1984 dollars). A decade later, this pay was 54 percent higher, at $1.09. By 1905 the average wage in manufacturing was $1.83, a real increase over the 1865 wage of 158 percent. By 1915 this wage rose even further, to $2.05, making the average inflation-adjusted manufacturing wage 189 percent higher in 1915 than it was fifty years earlier.[74]

Nor were these gains in real income confined to the manufacturing sector. Despite the agrarian unrest of the era, data reveal that those Americans who remained on farms also experienced significant growth in real incomes. Economists Robert Fogel and Jack Rutner found that over the second half of the nineteenth century, the real per capita income of farmers rose by 65 percent.[75]

Much of the confusion in evaluating the economic performance of the second half of nineteenth-century America arises from the extraordinary decline in general prices that occurred from the end of the Civil War until the beginning of the twentieth century. Industrial and agricultural production soared in the post–Civil War era, far outpacing the growth in the money supply, producing a secular fall in the general level of prices. This fall in prices was also the outcome of the federal government's successful effort to return to the gold standard, which Civil War inflation had previously forced the government to abandon. When the war ended and military outlays fell dramatically, the federal government did not reduce revenues, instead choosing to run large budget surpluses and burn US notes ("Greenbacks") paid into the Treasury in taxes. The Treasury also redeemed government bonds, which backed national banknotes. Both of these actions dramatically reduced the money supply relative to the economy's rising productivity and increasing output. As a result, nominal prices fell sharply, allowing the United States to return to the gold standard in 1879, at the pre–Civil War price of $20.67 an ounce. The price level fell on a secular basis from 1867 until the turn of the century. With general prices falling by almost two-thirds in thirty years, those who look only at nominal wages and prices get a totally distorted picture of the extraordinary growth of *real* incomes during those decades.[76]

The gains in real income greatly improved Americans' quality of life and living standards. Compared to the numbers in 1860, life expectancy at birth in 1900 was 13.7 percent higher, and in 1910 it was 25.2 percent higher.[77] This happy trend occurred largely because of the fall in infant mortality, which declined by 34 percent from 1860 to 1900, and in the next ten years, by another 19.4 percent.[78] The illiteracy rate fell by 47 percent from 1870 to 1900, and within the next ten years it declined by another 28 percent.[79] In 1870 one in five Americans couldn't read or write; forty years later, that number was down to less than one in thirteen. The average daily hours of work in manufacturing facilities fell, and life's staples—food, clothing, and shelter—became far more plentiful, higher in quality, and significantly cheaper.[80] The cost of food, textiles, fuel, and home furnishings fell in inflation-adjusted dollars by 46 percent, on average.[81]

The Gilded Age, in short, was an era of unparalleled improvement in living standards for almost all Americans. Summing up his study of the US post–Civil War era, historian Thomas Schlereth writes,

> Why did American consumer habits gain such momentum from 1876 to 1915? Briefly put, more people (middle class and working class) had more money and more time to purchase more goods, mass produced more

cheaply and advertised more widely. Annual earnings per working person rose in the period and the work week declined—for factory workers, from approximately sixty-six hours in 1850 to sixty by 1890, and then to fifty-five in 1914. Simultaneously, the sheer variety and amount of goods increased.[82]

As American capitalism blossomed, some individuals, of course, earned extraordinary riches. In 1892 there were 4,050 millionaires, with less than 20 percent of these individuals having inherited their wealth.[83] The rest created it and, in the process, reduced poverty, expanded general prosperity, and made it possible for millions of immigrants looking for opportunity and freedom to find both in America. But that mattered little to progressives, who were so obsessed with the 4,050 millionaires that they turned a blind eye to the sixty-six million Americans whose economic well-being improved faster than that of any people who had ever lived. But what progressives refused to see was seen by the millions of immigrants who came to America to share in our bounty and freedom. And as we'll see in chapter 6, these extraordinary improvements in the lives of working Americans continue to this day. America's promise and prosperity are still so appealing today to those who aspire to a better life that we are now building walls to try to keep them out.

Two

PROGRESSIVE ERA REGULATION

The Myth and the History

—————

ROM THE END OF the Civil War through the beginning of the twentieth century, the American economy expanded by almost biblical proportions. In only thirty years, between 1870 and 1900, inflation-adjusted gross national product tripled. Agricultural production more than doubled, and mining and manufacturing grew eightfold and sixfold respectively, rates of economic growth never before experienced in recorded history.[1]

No informed observer disputes that America's economy during this time produced and distributed goods and services on an unprecedented scale. Yet this cornucopia was produced and distributed by economic colossuses, or "trusts," the likes of which had never before been seen. The industrial and financial titans who owned the large firms of the era are said by many to have captured for themselves disproportionate and unfair shares of this amazing bounty by keeping prices artificially high and wages artificially low. America's economy surged, but did it grow by exploiting rather than benefiting ordinary consumers, workers, and their families?

Progressives, who advocated government regulation and, in some cases, the actual breaking up of these economic giants, succeeded in passing antitrust legislation and implementing a broad-based national regulatory system. For seventy years large companies were broken up and regulated in their production, distribution, and price setting. By the

1970s the effects of these regulations on prices, production, and innovations were challenged on a bipartisan basis, and under the leadership of President Jimmy Carter, the Progressive Era regulatory structure was significantly dismantled. Federal price setting and the splintering of large companies was largely abandoned, and a new antitrust standard based on consumer welfare was adopted by law, in court rulings, and in regulatory policy.

Forty years later Progressive Era antitrust views reemerged with the Biden administration's agenda for the Federal Trade Commission (FTC) and other regulatory agencies. So far, the courts have largely checked this new effort, restraining federal efforts to expand legal action against large companies absent hard evidence that their operations harm consumers. Although Congress has shown no interest in passing legislation to reimpose Progressive Era regulations (as of January 2025), the Biden administration's regulatory initiatives and the courts' reaction to them have reignited public debate on antitrust policy.

THE MYTH

If you randomly picked American college students, journalists, and politicians in the early twenty-first century and asked them to describe conditions in the US economy around the turn of the twentieth century, you would likely be given the following account: In the last half of the nineteenth and the beginning of the twentieth century, many industries were dominated by giant trusts. These behemoths grew so big that they gained unassailable monopoly power. If any rivals dared to challenge their market share, these dominant firms quickly bankrupted them with predatory pricing or other unethical business practices. These monopolies then reaped obscene profits by raising prices. Monopoly railroads fixed freight rates to cheat farmers, small businesses, and consumers. They also gave rebates to favored shippers, such as Standard Oil. Such rebates gave these shippers unfair advantages over their rivals.

The account continues, portraying these abuses as the bitter fruits of America's reigning ideology of laissez-faire. With the government on the sidelines, individual consumers and workers had to fend for themselves.

But eventually the economic abuses became so overwhelming that they could no longer be ignored. The government responded positively—at first slowly but then with increased momentum. Starting in 1887 with the creation of the Interstate Commerce Commission, the government finally regulated the railroads. In 1890 monopolies and attempts to monopolize were outlawed by the Sherman Antitrust Act. And after the horrid conditions of the Chicago slaughterhouses were exposed, government inspection of meat at last protected consumers from diseased and dangerous products. When these initial regulatory measures proved inadequate, additional statutes were enacted, allowing the government to set prices and otherwise intervene to protect competitors, workers, and consumers.

Unsurprisingly, this account of the era is found in today's leading collegiate textbooks on American history, such as David Emory Shi's *America: A Narrative History*.[2] Shi tells his readers that among the various tribulations suffered by Americans in the late nineteenth and early twentieth century was the federal government's embrace of laissez-faire.[3] One example of the resulting abuses was the lack of sanitation in the industrial preparation of foods and drugs. These operations, according to Shi, frequently involved "all sorts of unsanitary and dangerous activities."[4] The historical evidence that this author offers in support of his claim is Upton Sinclair's lurid 1906 novel, *The Jungle*. Sinclair described (as quoted by Shi) "piles of meat" coated with "the dried dung of rats"—rats that were then poisoned by the workers and ground up with other meats into final products sold to consumers.[5] Sinclair's and other muckraking journalists' revelations of such horrors prompted Congress to enact, on the same day in 1906, the Pure Food and Drug Act and the Federal Meat Inspection Act.[6]

Yet the problem during this era that, according to Shi, "towered above all" was monopoly: "The threat of corporate monopolies increased during the depression of the 1890s as struggling companies were gobbled up by larger ones."[7] Most infamously, Standard Oil "developed a nearly complete monopoly over the industry."[8] It did so partly because of John D. Rockefeller's remarkable success at pursuing greater operating efficiencies. But other, allegedly less savory means were also used, such as predatory pricing—that is, pricing below cost to bankrupt rivals—and pressuring owners of competing oil refineries to sell their companies on the cheap to Standard. Rockefeller eventually monopolized the oil industry and "forced railroads to pay him secret 'rebates' on the shipments, enabling him to spend less for shipping than his competitors did."[9] And Standard and the oil industry weren't alone: "Many businesses grew to enormous size and power, often ignoring ethics and the law in doing so." Rockefeller, Andrew Carnegie, and other business titans "were extraordinarily skilled at gaining control of particular industries" and "eliminating competition."[10]

These modern-day historians echo the progressive writers of the era. Jack London, a widely read author, in his 1908 novel *The Iron Heel* delivered a scathing indictment of the American society that he believed he then saw around him:

> If modern man's producing power is a thousand times greater than that of the cave-man, why then, in the United States to-day, are there fifteen million people who are not properly sheltered and properly fed? Why then, in the United States to-day, are there three million child laborers? It is a true indictment. The capitalist class has mismanaged. In face of the facts that modern man lives more wretchedly than the cave-man, and that his producing power is a thousand times greater than that of the cave-man, no other conclusion is possible than that the capitalist class has . . . criminally and selfishly mismanaged.[11]

A similar tale was told by Herbert Croly, a leading progressive reformer of the time and a cofounder of the *New Republic*. Croly was outraged that "the fierceness of American competitive methods turned business into a state of dangerous and aggressive warfare."[12] The victors in this war—men such as Rockefeller—won "a species of economic privilege which enable them to wring profits from the increasing American market disproportionate to the value of their economic services."[13] To remedy such ills, "the national government must step in and discriminate, not on behalf of liberty . . . but on behalf of equality and the average man."[14]

In their 1921 *History of the United States*, historians Charles and Mary Beard reinforced this negative view of unregulated capitalism and a positive view of the promise of government intervention.[15] Quoting Theodore Roosevelt, the Beards wrote that "growth of these gigantic aggregations of capital had been the leading feature in American industrial development during the last two decades of the nineteenth century. In the conquest of business by trusts and 'the resulting private fortunes of great magnitude,' the Populists had seen a grievous danger to the republic."[16]

The Beards clearly believed that the Populists' perceptions were real. What the Beards and other contemporary critics failed to do, however, was to look at inflation-adjusted wages, which were rising at unprecedented rates. To his credit, President Roosevelt refused to let the notion that "the fruits of the toil of millions are boldly stolen to build up colossal fortunes for a few" pass without an answer.[17] As described by the Beards, Roosevelt believed that "the average man, wage worker, farmer and small business man . . . was better off than ever before in the history of [the] country."[18] But there is scant evidence that any populist leader, literary critic, historian, or economist of the period took cognizance of the explosion in the production of industrial and agricultural products that was occurring all around them or the fact that these products were more affordable than they had ever been.[19]

THE TRUTH ABOUT THE TRUSTS

The core economic dangers of monopoly power are also the only sure evidence of its existence—namely, restricted output and higher prices. Facing little or no competition, monopolists raise their prices higher than they could if confronted by existing or potential rivals that are ready and able to underprice them. Although monopolists sell less output than they would at lower prices, the monopoly-price premium more than makes up for the lost sales volume. Monopolists thus reap "monopoly profits." And basic economics is clear: The monopolists' gains are swamped by the losses that consumers suffer in the form of higher prices and reduced consumption.[20]

If late nineteenth- and early twentieth-century America was truly dominated by monopoly power, we would expect to find strong evidence of this plague in the form of restricted outputs and higher prices. In a pioneering 1985 study, George Mason University economist Thomas DiLorenzo looked for such evidence. He searched for signs of monopolization during the trust-busting era where it was most likely to be found: in industries accused, during Congressional debates over the Sherman Act, of monopolizing their markets.[21] What he found was surprising. Output in those particular industries actually *increased* by an average of 175 percent between 1880 and 1890, the year the Sherman Antitrust Act was passed—seven times the growth rate of real gross national product. As for prices charged by firms in the purportedly monopolized industries, the prices of their products *fell* three times faster than did the overall consumer-price index.[22]

As explained in chapter 1, this era in US history was one of sustained and significant *deflation*. Prices fell on a secular basis because soaring production far outstripped the growth of the money supply. Notably, most of this productivity growth was driven by the efficiencies of companies like Standard Oil, Swift & Co., Carnegie Steel, American Tobacco, and many of the other firms that allegedly were monopolizing their industries. By virtually every economic measure, including production, real wages, literacy, and mortality, public prosperity and well-being grew faster during these years than in any prior period in American history.

These colossal gains in efficiency arose in no small measure because firms were able to take advantage of much larger economies of scale. Per-unit costs fell as production occurred on a scale never before envisioned as possible. Railways and telegraph lines and, later, trucking companies and telephone lines created a continent-wide market. The profitability of large-scale operations was further enhanced by the swelling of the US population due to what University of Washington economic historian Robert Higgs calls "the greatest volume of immigration in recorded history."[23]

But as indicated by the falling real prices of the outputs of these alleged monopolists and trusts, these firms and industries were, in fact, intensely competitive. What the Wesleyan University economic historian

Stanley Lebergott said about Andrew Carnegie's steel-producing enterprise could be said about nearly every other so-called trust: "Carnegie,
the leading steelmaker of the time, had driven his competitors wild by
improving production processes. Making huge profits, he passed most
of the savings along to customers in price cuts."[24] Monopoly power
was falsely inferred from the sheer size of successful firms (and their
high absolute levels of profits), as well as from the inability of small-
scale competitors to survive in competition against these spectacularly
efficient and robustly competitive larger firms. The evidence, however,
clearly shows that most trusts feared actual and potential competition.
Were that not the case, their pricing and production policies would have
been radically different. Although the term "trust" referred to a formal
legal device allowing trustees to control several different firms as though
these were a single entity, few of the so-called trusts actually adopted this
legal form, and the few that did were largely unsuccessful at behaving
monopolistically. As observed by historian Gabriel Kolko about trusts,
"contemporary usage of the term usually equated it with mere large size
or concentration, without any specific reference to the extent of market
control but with the implicit assumption that large size could be equated
with control."[25]

Kolko himself amply documents the inability of the so-called monopolists or trusts of the era to suppress competition for any length of
time without the government's active assistance. About the steel industry
in the last several years of the nineteenth century, he writes that "there
was continual insecurity within the industry as to what each competitor
might do next. The apprehension was later justified. The dozens of attempts at voluntary pools in various sections of the steel industry took
place after periods of intense price competition, and the pools were in
effect agreements to recuperate before more internecine war."[26] After
examining the history of several industries during that era, Kolko concluded that "in all of these cases we find a fluidity of economic circumstances and radical changes generally slighted by the historian."[27] The
facts that most struck Kolko were "the shifting markets and resources,
the loss of relative power by the dominant companies, [and] the specific
failure of the merger movement in attaining either stability or economic

control."[28] As Kolko observes, "new products, new methods of production, new markets, new sources of supply, and new business combinations always affected the existing distribution of power and shares in older industries. Established firms participated in this growth, but were rarely able to prevent intruders from grabbing their share as well."[29]

Kolko therefore concludes that, while these businesses certainly had monopolistic aspirations, these "aspirations never materialized."[30] Even mighty Standard Oil "treated the consumer with deference. Crude and refined oil prices for consumers declined during the period Standard exercised greatest control of the industry, 1875–1895."[31] Indeed, as Kolko reads the available evidence, "contrary to the consensus of historians, it was not the existence of monopoly that caused the federal government to intervene in the economy, but the lack of it."[32] The legislative and regulatory interventions of the day were thus, Kolko argued, meant to impede competition in order to create and sustain monopoly power for politically influential firms.

Standard Oil

Strong evidence in support of Kolko's conclusion about competition generally—and about Standard Oil specifically—can be found by looking more closely at Standard, which was the canonical monopoly of nineteenth-century America. Despite the legend, the facts refute the belief that Standard ever acted as if it had real monopoly power. Between 1870, the year of Standard's founding, and 1885, the nominal price of Standard's main output, kerosene, dropped by 69 percent, from twenty-six cents per gallon to eight cents. The real price of kerosene over this fifteen-year span fell 60 percent faster than the general level of prices.[33] Five years later, kerosene's real price had fallen by another 8 percent. Even Sen. George Edmunds (R-VT)—the principal coauthor of the Sherman Antitrust Act—admitted in 1890 that "the oil trust certainly has reduced the price of oil immensely."[34] Although Standard's share of the market for kerosene was close to 90 percent for much of the 1880s and 1890s, its incessant and successful pursuit of efficiencies and, even more tellingly, its dramatic cuts in kerosene's price do not support the idea that Standard possessed genuine monopoly power or show that it was acting in ways that harmed consumers. Quite the opposite was the case. Standard's success and large market share resulted from Rockefeller and his lieutenants acting competitively and with great skill and ingenuity. But even with all its efficiencies, Standard could not keep competitors out of the oil industry.

According to its critics, however, Standard's outsized success was built largely on nefarious deeds. Most notable among these misdeeds are predatory pricing and the receipt of secret rebates from railroads. The allegation against Standard regarding predatory pricing was thoroughly debunked in a 1958 study by University of Washington economist John McGee. After detailing several reasons why "predatory pricing" is a fool's strategy, McGee's careful investigation of the historical record led him to conclude that "Standard did not systematically, if ever, use local price cutting in retailing, or anywhere else, to reduce competition."[35] As we've seen, Standard did indeed regularly cut prices, but these cuts reflected Standard's greater efficiencies.[36] The company's nominal cost of refining each gallon fell from 3 cents in 1870 to 0.452 cents in 1885. In real, purchasing-power dollars, Standard's cost of refining fell by an astonishing 80 percent!

Such efficiencies also explain Standard's ability to obtain railroad rebates. No railroad, of course, would have been interested in sacrificing profits to enable a particular shipper, such as Standard, to gain a market advantage. Therefore, because railroads were, in fact, giving rebates to Standard—as they were to firms in other industries—it is reasonable to conclude there must have been some corresponding advantage for the railroads. And there was: Railroads' costs of supplying shipping services to Standard were lower than their costs of supplying shipping services to other refiners. By self-insuring against damage caused by fire, Standard exempted railroads from liability for any such damage. Standard had also built its own facilities for loading and unloading its shipments. In addition, Standard guaranteed railroads a large volume of shipments, enabling railroads to spread their huge fixed costs across a larger volume of shipments. Finally, Standard had invested heavily in access to pipelines and water shipping, which gave it greater bargaining power in negotiating with railroads to keep the rates it paid to ship low.[37]

Standard Oil's large market share resulted from its creative entrepreneurship and superior efficiencies. And significantly, the market "dominance" that it achieved at various times did not protect it from competition. Standard was, in the words of University of Hartford economist Dominick Armentano, "a large, competitive firm in an open, competitive market"[38]—a reality attested to not only by Standard's record of consistently lowering kerosene's price but also by Standard's steady *loss* of market share, which started in the mid-1890s and continued until it was broken up by an antitrust ruling in 1911.[39]

Even though Standard was continuously increasing its output of petroleum products and its consumption of crude oil, its market share decreased steadily throughout this period. Standard consumed and refined increasing volumes of crude oil (39 million barrels in 1892, 52 million barrels in 1902, 65 million barrels in 1906, and 99 million barrels in 1911), yet its share of the market for petroleum products fell from approximately 88 percent in 1890 to 68 percent in 1907, then to 64 percent in 1911. It's obvious that Standard was huge, but it is hard to make the case that it effectively used its market position to raise prices and exert monopoly power. There is little evidence to suggest that Standard was increasingly monopolizing the petroleum industry at the turn of the century or that the antitrust suit against Standard, begun in 1906, was a legitimate response to its actual market behavior. The hard data of the period indicate *no* such increasing monopolization by Standard.[40]

The Rise of the Chicago Meat-Packers

In spite of its historical prominence, Standard Oil was not the principal target of the earliest "trust busters." That distinction belongs to Chicago's centralized slaughtering houses that arose in the 1870s and 1880s. The success of these innovative producers was rapid and huge. According to University of Arizona economic historian Gary Libecap, "slaughtering and meat packing was either the first or second most valuable U.S. industry from 1880 through 1910."[41]

The centralized slaughtering of animals was made economically feasible by the advent of refrigerated railroad cars, which permitted carcasses and fresh meat products to be delivered, for the first time in history, over long distances without becoming tainted with harmful bacteria. Centralized slaughtering, in turn, allowed producers to take advantage of the economies of scale that arose from the slaughtering of many animals in only a handful of locations. Swift & Co. and other Chicago slaughtering houses took advantage of the massive cost savings that came from seizing these economies of scale. The result was a substantial fall in the cost of slaughtering and processing, which, in turn, reduced retail prices, raising American living standards. Additionally, because animals shipped live by rail to hundreds of different locales experienced high rates of weight loss, disease, and death while in transit, the Chicago slaughterhouses achieved extra efficiencies because they shipped carcasses and processed meat products. These cost savings then translated into reductions in the retail price of meat. According to historian Mary Yeager, in a mere six years—from 1883 through 1889—the average real price of beef tenderloins fell by 37 percent.[42] Not surprisingly, as fresh meat became much more affordable, Americans consumed more of it. Rudolf Clemen reports that per capita consumption of beef was 12 percent higher in the 1880s than in the 1870s.[43]

Local butchers naturally complained. So, too, did Midwestern cattle raisers. The rapid rise of centralized slaughtering at first raised the prices of cattle, creating what came to be called "the cattle boom." But many cattlemen overexpanded. After hitting a peak in 1884, the cattle raisers experienced a decline in the real price of cattle, which fell significantly from 1885 through 1891 in what Libecap calls "the longest and most severe fall in cattle prices since the end of the Civil War."[44] Local butchers and cattlemen joined forces in calling on the government—first at the state level and then at the national—to protect them from the Chicago meat-packers, whose products consumers were eagerly (and literally) eating up.

The trustbusters and cattlemen had two distinct complaints. One was that meat from animals slaughtered by the Chicago packers was unsafe; the second was that the business of supplying fresh meat was becoming monopolized. Neither of these complaints stands up to scrutiny based on actual safety and sanitation reports or the economic data concerning consumer prices and production. Nevertheless, the first gave rise to mandated government meat inspection and the second to antitrust legislation.[45]

That the rise of centralized slaughtering made the fresh-meat industry *more*, not less, competitive is attested to by the substantial fall in the real price of fresh meat and the increase in its supply. As for complaints about the meat being tainted or otherwise unsafe, nothing in the historical record backs this claim. As summarized by Libecap, "the record does not indicate that the incidence of diseased cattle or their consumption was very great, and there is no evidence of a major health issue at that time over beef consumption."[46] It is also noteworthy that no record of a rising incidence of tainted-meat sales or food poisoning exists coincident with the rise of Chicago meatpacking. Despite this reality, these complaining producers caught the ears of sympathetic politicians.

A major conference, called by the governor of Kansas, was held in St. Louis in early 1889 to discuss what to do about the *falling* prices of cattle and fresh meat.[47] In attendance were elected officials from several different states. They agreed to push in their respective jurisdictions for the passage of two statutes drafted by the conferees. One statute required that all fresh meat offered for sale be from animals inspected live on the hoof in the county in which that meat is sold—a blatant effort to protect local butchers from the competition of the Chicago packers by fragmenting the market and effectively shutting down Chicago's meat producers. The second was an antitrust statute that declared all trusts to be in violation of the state corporate charter. Significantly, this antitrust statute included in its definition of a trust the ability of "a combination of capital, skill or acts by two or more persons, firms, corporations or association of persons. . . . to limit or reduce the production, or increase *or reduce* the price of merchandise or commodities [emphasis added]."[48]

From 1889 through 1891, four states enacted the inspection statute, and eighteen states enacted some version of the antitrust statute.[49] At the national level, the Sherman Act became law in 1890, and the Meat Inspection Act was signed into law in 1906. US senators at that time were chosen by state legislatures; therefore, policy issues of deep concern to state legislators were also of deep concern to US senators.

A US Senate select committee was created in 1888 to investigate "whether there exists or has existed any combination of any kind by reason of which the price of beef and beef cattle have been so controlled or affected as to diminish prices paid the producer."[50] The Vest Committee (so named after its chairman, Sen. George Vest, Democrat of Missouri) held one of its hearings in St. Louis to correspond with the conference of those state legislators discussing the decline in the prices of cattle and fresh meat.

In May 1890 the Vest Committee submitted its report to Congress, in which four pieces of legislation were recommended.[51] One of these provided for federal inspection of meat. Another was a draft version of what would become the Sherman Antitrust Act in July of that year.[52]

Both state and federal antitrust legislation reflected anger over real prices that were *falling* and, in the process, dramatically benefiting consumers. Although the large and highly visible firms responsible for the quantum leap in efficiency and the fall in consumer prices were called "monopolists" and "trusts," these labels were meant to damn and not to describe.[53] The American economy in the 1880s was almost certainly among the most intensely competitive economies in the history of the world.

There is also no evidence that the Sherman Act further intensified this competition. Steel output grew by 242 percent in the ten years before the Sherman Act (1880–1890), but during the ten years after the Sherman Act, it grew by only 135 percent. Other "monopolized" industries with large differences in growth rates in the decades before and after the Sherman Act include copper (330 percent vs. 133 percent), petroleum (74 percent vs. 39 percent), refined sugar (65 percent vs. 48 percent), and cigars and cigarettes (121 percent vs. 40 percent).[54] Prices tell a similar story. On average, in industries for which data are available, inflation-adjusted prices fell at a faster rate—or rose at a slower rate—in the decade before the Sherman Act than in the decade after it. The real price of steel rails fell by 43 percent from 1880 to 1890 but fell by only 0.7 percent from 1890 to 1900. The wholesale price of sugar fell 22.4 percent from 1880 to 1890 but fell only by 6.1 percent from 1890 to 1900. A similar pattern played out for copper, pig iron, and anthracite coal.[55]

Upton Sinclair

No historical account of Progressive Era regulation can ignore the influence of the avowed socialist author Upton Sinclair and his 1906 novel, *The Jungle*. According to popular reports, this book's bloodcurdling descriptions of the filthy and dangerous conditions that prevailed in the Chicago packinghouses stirred the public to believe that large producers left unregulated by the government were a menace both to consumers and workers. In Sinclair's telling, the packing plants were overrun by vermin that were killed by workers and then tossed into the vats with meat from cows. Indeed, it was alleged that even some workers themselves met the misfortune of being killed, their bodies ground up and mixed with meat products, then sold to unsuspecting consumers.

Alerted by Sinclair to the horrific realities of the meatpacking plants, Congress enacted, with the enthusiastic support of Pres. Theodore Roosevelt, the Meat Inspection Act of 1906. Only then, according to popular legend, was the public protected from the greedy and cruel owners of the slaughterhouses.

However, crucial parts of these accounts overlook significant facts, while other parts are simply false. Absent is the recognition that Sinclair's *The Jungle* was first published in serialization in 1905 in the socialist journal *Appeal to Reason*.[56] He published to agitate for government control of the economy, not to report objectively on slaughterhouse practices. In March 1906, the United States Department of Agriculture's (USDA's) Bureau of Animal Husbandry, a government agency that benefited from the Meat Inspection Act and had expanded its budget and power, investigated the Chicago slaughterhouses. The three investigators "determined that *The Jungle* 'greatly exaggerated' packinghouse sanitation issues and contained 'willful and deliberate misrepresentations.'"[57] In a follow-up report written soon afterward, the USDA accused Sinclair of "willful and deliberate misrepresentations of fact."[58] According to the report, "it is apparent that in his anxiety to be as sensational and 'yellow' as possible the author has . . . throughout the book, selected the worst possible condition which could be found in any establishment as typical . . . and has willfully closed his eyes to establishments where excellent conditions prevail."[59] No evidence of rat dung or rat flesh was found in any of the processed meat products destined for human consumption, and only one instance could be documented of a worker falling into a vat—and that man's body was recovered and buried.[60]

This finding isn't surprising given that, as noted by economic journalist Lawrence Reed, "some 2 million visitors came to tour the stockyards and packinghouses of Chicago every year [and] thousands of people worked in both."[61] As such, it's not credible to suppose that conditions as horrendous as those alleged by Sinclair would have remained unnoticed until exposed by an ideologically motivated novelist. Gary Libecap agrees: "If anything, the theory suggests that the packers had very important reasons for maintaining the quality of their dressed-beef product."[62] Firms with large market shares that sell outputs easily traceable back to the individual firms that sold them (as was the case with the dressed meats from the Chicago slaughterhouses) have a great deal to lose if the public comes to distrust the quality of their products. It is more likely that animal-slaughter horror stories would have been found in the thousands of back rooms and barns in towns and villages, where animals were slaughtered prior to the development of modern processing in Chicago.

Nevertheless, Sinclair was widely believed, and the Meat Inspection Act of 1906 was passed. This legislation, as finally enacted, was actually supported by the Chicago packers. Sinclair had so aroused public fear of processed and refrigerated meat that consumers considered enhanced government inspection as providing needed quality assurance, thus protecting the packers' domestic and foreign markets.[63] And there were two significant bonuses for the big packinghouses. First, taxpayers paid for the inspection that, in the absence of the Act, the meat-packers themselves would have had to fund out of their own pockets. Second, the Act subjected smaller slaughterhouses to disproportionately higher compliance costs per pound of processed meat. Economist Patrick Newman concludes that "despite the cheers of progressives both past and present," in the end the big Chicago packers "ultimately captured the 1906 inspection act: they were able to use it to drive smaller competitors out of business and increase their prices and profits."[64]

AN INTENSELY COMPETITIVE ECONOMY

In reality, the late nineteenth and early twentieth century was an era not of monopolization and exploitation but an era of vigorous industrial competition driven by the implementation of new technologies, new sources of supply, and improved management. Economies of scale produced industrial concentration, but there is little evidence that these so-called trusts were actually able to restrict supply and raise prices. And most of the actual trusts and cartels that subsequently formed in an effort to dampen competition gradually failed—unless government intervention protected them from competition.

The history of the American Sugar Refining trust, "the Sugar Trust," which formed in 1887, illustrates this pattern. The Sugar Trust had only fleeting success at limiting production or raising prices over the ensuing twenty years. US refined-sugar production more than doubled from 1887 to 1907. Despite the trust's efforts to keep them out, competitors built factories and undercut its prices in less time than it took to prosecute a major antitrust lawsuit. In 1893, when Grover Cleveland's administration filed its first Sherman antitrust suit against American Sugar, the margin between the prices of raw and refined sugar was 1.15 cents a pound. By the time the Supreme Court decided the case in 1895, new competitors had driven the margin down to 0.88 cents a pound—a 23 percent decrease.[65]

Unlike the trusts, government tariffs and regulations actually *did* succeed in squelching competition in the Gilded Age. Henry Havemeyer, the first president of American Sugar, stated at a congressional hearing in 1899 that "the mother of all trusts is the customs tariff bill. . . . Without the tariff, I doubt if we should have dared to take the risk of forming the trust."[66]

Genuine competition was reduced also by government regulation of surface transportation. Three years before the enactment of the Sherman Antitrust Act, in 1887, Congress created the Interstate Commerce Commission (ICC). Despite the huge up-front expense of constructing railroads, the decades following the Civil War found more and more locations connected to each other by two or more lines. Competition among railroads was intense, and efforts to cartelize consistently failed, with the granting of secret rebates being a favored means used to cheat cartel agreements.[67] Real rail freight revenues fell 34.7 percent per ton-mile from 1870 to 1890.[68] Economist George Hilton, as well as historian Gabriel Kolko, have found that the railroads' inability to keep rates high incited them to support federal regulation.[69]

Among its many provisions, the Interstate Commerce Act banned rebates as well as differences in rates for long hauls and short hauls. One consequence of the former is aptly described by Stanley Lebergott, who wrote that "the ICC Act created a new harmony of railroads. Working together they created the long-desired parity of long and short haul rates, required by the Act. They did so by raising long haul rates and reducing some short haul rates."[70] But the 1887 act eventually proved too weak to prevent the rebates, secret price cutting, and charging of different rates. In response, in 1903 Congress passed the Elkins Anti-Rebating Act, the first version of which was drafted by an official of the Pennsylvania Railroad.[71] The eminent regulation economist Thomas Gale Moore described the effect of this act: "From the point of view of the railroads, the Elkins Act was a giant step towards stabilizing rates, preventing rebating, and violating understood rate agreements. While the connection cannot be proven, price cutting did become less prevalent and railroad earnings did improve after passage of the act."[72]

Yet both shippers and railroads remained unhappy. Congress's response came in 1906 with the Hepburn Act. According to Moore, this legislation "extended ICC control to express companies, sleeping car companies, and oil pipelines. Bringing these sectors of the industry under control enabled the commission to control rates throughout the railroad industry more effectively."[73] In 2006 Moore offered further assessment, writing, "Railroad regulation was strengthened several times in the early part of the twentieth century. These changes stifled price competition between railroads by prohibiting rebating, discounting, and secret price cutting."[74]

The artificially higher rates (and poorer service) made possible by regulation only further encouraged different modes of shipping to compete with the railroads and pipelines (the latter of which were also subject to ICC control by the 1920s). Most notable among these different modes was trucking. Lobbyists for the railroads—and the ICC itself—urged

Congress to regulate trucking. Truckers put up little resistance. When their losses during the Great Depression mounted, truckers threw their support behind subjecting trucking to ICC regulation. Truckers anticipated that such regulation would protect them, as it had protected the railroads, from competition.

This anticipation proved valid. The Motor Carrier Act of 1935 required each new trucker to obtain a "certificate of public convenience and necessity"—which, in practice, proved very difficult to get.[75] The resulting restriction of the supply of truckers, along with other detailed regulatory requirements, protected incumbent truckers from both new entrants and each other. To protect the prevailing high rates for shipping by rail and by truck, in 1940 Congress expanded the ICC's jurisdiction to cover inland water carriers. Moore aptly summarizes the results: "Thus . . . the ICC controlled all forms of surface freight transportation (air freight was controlled separately)."[76]

Just as the original Interstate Commerce Act was supplemented by follow-up legislation when the earlier statute proved insufficient to satisfy the interest groups, the Sherman Antitrust Act was supplemented with later legislation. In 1914 American consumers and constituents witnessed the enactment of both the Federal Trade Commission (FTC) Act,[77] as well as the Clayton Act.[78] In 1936 the antitrust arsenal was further stocked with the Robinson-Patman Act.[79] The FTC Act both created the Federal Trade Commission and endowed it with, among other powers, the authority to police against unfair competitive tactics. The Clayton Act aimed at remedying what was widely perceived as the Sherman Act's undue vagueness.[80] The Robinson-Patman Act, incited by fears of the success of the A&P Supermarket chain at dramatically *reducing* the retail price of groceries, sought to protect small grocers and other inefficient producers from the competition of more efficient rivals.[81]

THE OVERTURNING OF PROGRESSIVE ERA REGULATION

The 1970s brought two recessions, double-digit inflation, and an end to America's postwar manufacturing dominance, setting off an intense policy debate. As economists, regulators, politicians, business leaders, and policy advocates debated why the US economy seemed to be losing its exceptionalism, there formed a consensus that regulations based on Progressive Era principles were hurting consumers, workers, and the economy. Looking back on the almost ninety-year-long history of anti-trust enforcement in the United States, Robert Bork, perhaps the most eminent antitrust lawyer and scholar of the postwar era, concluded in 1978 that antitrust had been overwhelmingly used to *suppress* competition.[82] Bork decried antitrust's "descent to the status of an internal tariff against domestic competition and free trade."[83]

In the 1960s the focus of academic research shifted from market failure to regulatory failure. After the 1970 bankruptcy of the Penn Central Railroad, when America's largest railroad died from regulatory strangulation, this reevaluation accelerated. Bork and other economically minded scholars, such as Aaron Director, John McGee, Donald Dewey, Richard Posner, and Dominick Armentano, largely succeeded in convincing enforcement agents and courts to turn away from using antitrust legislation to protect competitors—an antitrust standard that had produced higher prices, poorer service, and less innovation. The new goal became protection of consumers.

Ironically, this new consensus in opposing open-ended antitrust had much in common with the skepticism expressed toward Progressive Era regulations by economists nearly a century earlier. During the debate on Progressive Era regulation in the late nineteenth and early twentieth centuries, prominent economists warned that the Sherman Act and other antitrust statutes were unnecessary for keeping markets competitive and would stymie competition, thus harming economic growth and consumers. In 1887 Columbia University economist Franklin Giddings, while recognizing that technological changes were increasing the optimal sizes of firms in many industries, insisted that the conclusion "should not be too hastily accepted" that "competition is to be to a corresponding extent destroyed."[84] Giddings and the most prominent American economist of the era, John Bates Clark, wrote in 1888 that "combinations [trusts] have their roots in the nature of social industry and are normal in their development, and their practical working. They are neither to be deprecated by scientists nor suppressed by legislators."[85] In the same vein, Harvard economist Frank Taussig has explained that "only the test of competition and experience can decide [on the most efficient industrial structures]. Let them fight it out, and let that form of organization survive which does the work most cheaply."[86] By the 1970s the wholesale failure of Progressive Era regulation in promoting the consumers' interests affirmed that the economists at the turn of the twentieth century were right.

On other regulatory fronts, experts charged with protecting consumers, including then–Senate Judiciary Committee staffer Stephen Breyer (a Harvard antitrust law professor who would become a justice of the US Supreme Court) and Civil Aeronautics Board (CAB) Chairman Alfred Kahn, provided the hard evidence that convinced their bosses, Senator Ted Kennedy and President Jimmy Carter, that America needed to reform agency regulation and even to end the regulation of much of the economy. In Senate hearings, America heard that airfares were far cheaper on unregulated intrastate flights within California and Texas than on comparable interstate routes under federal regulation. Any doubt about the consensus that Progressive Era regulation had failed ended when Ralph Nader testified before Kennedy's subcommittee, denouncing regulations that kept prices high, choices few, and competition muted.

The dam broke when Civil Aeronautics Board Chairman Alfred Kahn, an avowed progressive and one of the most consequential economists of the twentieth century, concluded that the most perfect regulatory system could never do as good a job as could imperfect markets and that it was, therefore, in the public interest to deregulate. Proclaiming the CAB a failure, Kahn demanded that he be fired and his agency eliminated.

When airline deregulation passed the Senate in 1978, Senator Kennedy declared, "The success of this legislation is the result of a clear consensus . . . that rigid federal economic regulations of the airlines tends to increase prices, foster inefficiency in operations and perpetuate Government control, bureaucracy and red tape. . . . This consensus has been built brick by brick in recent years by serious and careful nonpartisan examinations of . . . the nature of government and competition in the 1970s."[87]

The Senate passed airline deregulation by a vote of eighty-two to four on October 14, 1978. But airline deregulation was only the beginning. Kennedy noted, "The restrictive price and entry provisions of the Federal Aviation Act . . . were copied directly from the Interstate Commerce Act of the 1880s governing railroads. . . . We need to now look beyond the airlines and the corrective measures we are voting upon today and recognize the fact that . . . heavy regulation, as illustrated by the airline industry, is not the answer."[88] On April 1, 1980, the Senate adopted the Staggers Rail Act to deregulate railroads.[89]

In signing the Motor Carrier Act of 1980, which deregulated trucking, President Carter sounded the death knell on Progressive Era regulation:

> This historic legislation . . . will remove 45 years of excessive and inflationary Government restrictions and red tape. . . . No longer will trucks travel empty because of rules absurdly limiting the kinds of goods a truck may carry. No longer will trucks be forced to travel hundreds of miles out of their way for no reason or prohibited senselessly from stopping to pick up and deliver goods at points along their routes. The Motor Carrier Act of 1980 will bring the trucking industry into the free enterprise system, where it belongs.[90]

Far from hurting consumers, as the progressive myth had alleged, the deregulation of the US transportation system in the 1970s unleashed a wave of invention and innovation that reduced logistical transportation costs—the costs of moving goods as a percentage of GDP—by an astonishing 50 percent over forty years. Airline fares were cut in half on a per-mile basis, while air cargo surged from 5.4 percent of all shipments to 14.5 percent by 2012, making air transit for people and packages a routine part of American life.[91] "Our economy would be much smaller and per capita income significantly lower without these far-sighted changes," explained FedEx CEO Fred Smith.[92]

The Carter administration began oil-price deregulation using its regulatory powers. It then gradually deregulated natural-gas prices with the 1978 Natural Gas Policy Act. The energy deregulation championed by Carter and then Reagan produced abundant oil and gas supplies. And while the deregulation of the communications industry was driven by technological change, court decisions, regulatory action, and, finally, legislation, the Carter regulatory reforms through the Federal Communications Commission made competition the driving force in policy development.

In this Carter- and Kennedy-led reform, the duty of the government was to protect consumers from harm, not to protect producers from competition. Without the productive dynamism released by deregulating airlines, trucking, railroads, energy, and communications, the US economy might not have found its competitive legs as its postwar dominance in manufacturing ended in the late 1970s. The benefits of deregulation continue to this day, clearing the way for many of the powerful innovations now remaking the world. Amazon, Google, FedEx, and Facebook are but a tiny fraction of a long list of progeny produced by lifting the heavy hand of Progressive Era regulation. We reimpose that regulation at our own peril.

THE RETURN OF PROGRESSIVE ERA REGULATION

Proving that no bad idea ever really dies, progressivism has been reborn in the early twenty-first century with public outcries against billionaires and so-called Big Tech. Demands are issued to bust—or at least more heavily regulate—the new allegedly monopolistic "trusts." Robert Reich, who served as President Clinton's labor secretary and token progressive, opined in 2018 that "like the robber barons of the first Gilded Age, those [the tech giants] of the second have amassed fortunes because of their monopolies."[93]

Yet the claim that the twenty-first-century tech industry is monopolistic is even weaker than the allegations of monopoly power leveled against the great industrialists of the Gilded Age. Spewing envy at the Fortune 400 billionaires, whose combined after-tax incomes wouldn't have funded federal, state, and local governments in 2020 for even a week, progressives denounce such people as Bill Gates, who has created hundreds of thousands of jobs and enriched billions of lives. Today, American retirement funds own far more shares of Microsoft than he does.[94]

Tech production and pricing practices provide no evidence that the modern tech industry is monopolized. In fact, many tech products are available to consumers for free, and the inflation-adjusted costs of search-and-text advertising, which supplies much of the revenues of these firms, have fallen by more than 24 percent from the time the government first began to gather these data, in December 2009, to when it stopped gathering these data, in December 2022.[95] For eighty years progressive regulation stifled competition, lowered efficiency, and drove up prices. Is this an experiment America wants to repeat?

The rise of Big Tech is virtually a replay of the rise of scale-driven industrialization that occurred just before and at the turn of the twentieth century. The rapid growth of large firms was fueled by technological innovation and economies of scale, accompanied by declining prices. This time around, extraordinarily, the new "monopolies" are literally giving away many of their products.

There are legitimate policy concerns involving Big Tech, such as collusion with the government to censor expression. But history shows little evidence that breaking up big tech companies or regulating them as monopolies will benefit consumers. Before policymakers repeat the failed experiments of the past, they should determine whether trustbusting is really about protecting consumers or merely about expanding the power of government. If it's the former, the effort is misguided, as no evidence has been presented showing that the scale of the tech industry is harming the consumer. If it's the latter, trustbusters should be forthright about their goal.

The rise of the American high-tech industry has created massive wealth, as evidenced by the fact that the five largest American tech companies now account for 22.6 percent of the value of the Standard and Poor's 500 (S&P 500) and are the cornerstone of virtually every public and private retirement fund in America.[96] Is it in the public interest for Congress to dismember the goose that's laying these golden eggs? Antitrust action against leading US tech companies would shrink American dominance of the world's fastest-growing industry and imperil the enormous buildup of stock equity that secures the retirements of roughly 90 million American workers.[97] Progressives want to use the antitrust laws to break up big tech companies because they believe that bigness in and of itself is bad and leads to a host of other evils, including malign political influence. Conservatives want to use antitrust as a club to get social media companies to curb their political bias.

While there is a long and rich history of using antitrust prosecutorial actions to impose regulatory policies that proponents can't enact into law, both progressives and conservatives would be wise to focus on consumer welfare, as this focus appropriately circumscribes the purpose and reach of antitrust jurisprudence. No one can seriously challenge the hard evidence that big tech companies have delivered enormous consumer benefits. Online shopping, smartphone usage, and social networking are only the beginning of a long list of benefits America has derived from President Clinton's decision not to regulate the internet.[98]

In 1994 Amazon started off by selling books. It then expanded into selling music CDs and DVDs. Later, in 2003, Apple began selling music through iTunes. The Bureau of Labor Statistics (BLS) began calculating consumer price indexes (CPIs) for recreational books, recorded movies, and music in 1997. From December 1997 through December 2023, the nominal price of recreational books fell by 2 percent, movies fell by 2 percent, and recorded music fell by 19 percent. Over the same period, general prices increased by 90 percent.[99]

BLS data show that the price of smartphones fell even more. Research in Motion (RIM) introduced the BlackBerry in 1999, and Apple introduced the iPhone eight years later. The BLS doesn't report a separate CPI category for smartphones, but the cost of cell phones accounts for half of the CPI component for telephone hardware, calculators, and other consumer-information items. Prices for this category of consumer spending have fallen by 77 percent since 2007 and by 92 percent since 1997.[100]

Even these stunning price reductions understate the actual price declines and consumer benefits of new tech products. Since the prices of cell phones didn't enter the CPI until fourteen years after this device was introduced, the index never counted the initial 75 percent drop in cell phone prices that occurred before they were included in the CPI. Nor did the BLS start adjusting the CPI for changes in the quality of smartphones until 2018—missing the extraordinary improvements that occurred in early smartphones. A 2019 National Bureau of Economic Research (NBER) study conducted in the Netherlands estimated the annual value per consumer of one quality improvement, the cell phone camera, at just under €818—about ten times the cost of adding the camera to the phone.[101]

The NBER study also estimated that consumers significantly value social media and apps. If the value of Facebook use to consumers was included in calculations of GDP, the study concludes that annual real GDP growth would have been about 0.1 percentage point greater each year from 2003 through 2017.[102] The study's authors also that found that the value that consumers attach to WhatsApp, Instagram, and map apps, which aren't counted in measures of consumer prices or income, would give a further measurable boost to GDP.

There are striking similarities between today's tech giants and the entrepreneurial businesses accused of being monopolies during the Progressive Era. Before they dismember America's golden goose, legislators and regulators should look not only at the benefits that Big Tech provides to consumers but also at the fact that US tech companies' worldwide leadership depends on policies that encourage innovation and don't punish companies simply for being successful and growing large.[103] The world's five largest tech companies as of April 2024 are Apple, Microsoft, Alphabet (Google's parent company), Amazon, and Meta Platforms (formerly Facebook); their combined market worth is a gargantuan $9.78 trillion. All are founded and based in America. Of the world's twenty largest tech companies, fourteen are currently based in the United States, representing 91 percent of the market capitalization of the world's top twenty tech companies.[104]

If progressives want to destroy America's premier companies, at least they should do it through an open legislative process, one with public debates and votes. Conservatives who believe companies are biased in imposing restrictions on user posts can reconsider the liability protections Congress has granted tech companies regarding content and whether those protections remain beneficial in a time when tech companies shape political debate. But any action the government wishes to take concerning these issues should come in the form of Congressional legislation rather than through antitrust enforcement or agency decisions.

While antitrust enforcement since the 1970s has sought to rise above politics by using economics-based analysis to measure and promote consumer benefits—that is, by being guided exclusively by the consumer-welfare standard—the Biden administration engaged in unraveling this consensus through executive orders, regulatory decrees, and more active antitrust enforcement. Could it possibly be true, as FTC Commissioner Rebecca Slaughter posits, that antitrust is an appropriate tool for fighting racism?[105] Or is Sen. Elizabeth Warren giving us a vision of the nation's future with her proposed Prohibiting Anticompetitive Mergers Act, under which "neither quantitative evidence nor a definition of relevant market or market share" would limit the reach of antitrust action?[106] Senator Warren's standard would require enforcers to evaluate the impact of mergers on the parties' "business ecosystems," including "workers, consumers, customer choice, sellers, small and minority-owned businesses (including farms and ranches), local, rural, and low-income communities, communities of color, privacy, quality, entrepreneurship, and innovation."[107] Warren would undo any mergers that have occurred since 2000 that violate her new standard.

With the consumer-welfare standard uprooted, antitrust regulation would become a license for extensive government control over the American economy, capriciously rewarding favored businesses and punishing disfavored ones. Consumers would be consistent losers. In a sweeping executive order aimed at reimposing Progressive Era regulatory policy across the US economy, President Biden recounted the foundational myths of modern progressivism. The first canon of progressivism holds that breaking up the consolidating industries, or trusts, in the late nineteenth and early twentieth centuries and regulating those industries heavily until the late 1970s benefited the economy and, in President Biden's words, gave "the little guy" a fighting chance.[108] President Biden says, "40 years ago, we chose the wrong path" when the Carter-Kennedy regulatory reforms were adopted.[109] That adoption, it should be noted, is one that then-Senator Biden voted for. To promote this new progressive vision, the president appointed regulators who are openly hostile to those they regulate and to the country's economic system.

CONCLUSION

At its root, progressivism, as well as its regulatory policy, is based on a myth. Whatever the objective of its original proponents, Progressive Era regulation ultimately reduced competition and efficiency and hurt consumers and the country. Based on ninety years of hard evidence that reveals the overwhelming failure of this regulation, a bipartisan consensus was reached in the American government in the 1970s and 1980s to bring that regulatory approach to an end. Under the leadership of President Carter and Senator Kennedy, Progressive Era regulatory policy was either repealed or reformed. Competition within the rule of law, which protects against deception and fraud, along with antitrust intervention confined to policing against business actions that clearly harm consumers, has proven an enlightened policy that has promoted prosperity. It should not be abandoned.

Three

THE MYTH THAT THE
GREAT DEPRESSION WAS
A FAILURE OF CAPITALISM

———

S PEAKING FROM THE US Supreme Court's bench in April 1932, Associate Justice Louis Brandeis declared that "the people of the United States are now confronted with an emergency more se-rious than war."[1] In that month, more than one in five American workers were unemployed, up from three years earlier, when the number hov-ered at much fewer than one in twenty. And unemployment would only worsen, reaching a rate of 25 percent in mid-1933. America's unem-ployment rate remained higher than 20 percent for the next two years and would not fall below 14.3 percent during the rest of the 1930s.[2] As noted by the monetary economist George Selgin, "to put the last figure in perspective, the *peak* unemployment rate during the Great Recession, reached in October 2009, was 10 percent, while the peak for the short-lived 1920–21 recession, which was then the highest rate since the 1890s, was 11.7 percent."[3] Even at its lowest level, the Great Depression's unem-ployment rate was almost 25 percent higher than was the second-highest rate of unemployment during the rest of the twentieth century.[4] The un-employment rate for nonfarm employees—approximately 80 percent of the labor force—was even higher, reaching 37 percent in 1933.[5]

Other measures of US economic performance during the 1930s were equally dismal. Starting in 1930, real GDP fell for four consecutive years. In 1933 it bottomed out at 29 percent below its 1929 level.[6] According to Selgin, "throughout the 1930s U.S. GNP was never less than 20 percent, and was sometimes more than 30 percent, below its potential [full employment] level."[7] Even more telling is the dramatic decline in real income per capita. Milton Friedman and Anna Schwartz note that "per capita real income in 1933 was almost the same as in the depression year of 1908, a quarter of a century earlier. Four years of contraction had temporarily erased the gains of two decades, not, of course, by erasing the advances of technology, but by idling men and machines."[8] It's no surprise, then, that industrial production plummeted. It reached its nadir in July 1932, at half of its pre-Depression peak only three years earlier.[9]

University of Washington economic historian Robert Higgs summarizes the extent and depth of the economic calamity:

> Production of consumer durables fell 50 percent, producer durables 67 percent, new construction 78 percent, and gross private domestic investment almost 90 percent. The real value of U.S. exports and imports dropped nearly 40 percent. . . . Banks failed in waves, and by the end of 1933 nearly ten thousand of them had gone under. In 1931, 1932, and 1933, the after-tax profits of all corporations added up to less than zero. Rental and proprietary income dropped by more than 60 percent. The stock market hit bottom in 1932, having lost more than 80 percent of its value during the preceding three years. Farm-product prices fell by more than 50 percent; net income of farm operators declined by nearly 70 percent; and thousands of farmers surrendered their homes and farms to mortgage lenders and tax collectors. Three states—Arkansas, Louisiana, and South Carolina—and approximately thirteen hundred municipalities defaulted on their debts, and many other states and local governments verged on default. The sky, it seemed, really had fallen.[10]

Making matters worse, this misery lasted far longer than any downturn in American history before or since. By most conventional accounts, the Great Depression spanned a dozen years, ending in earnest, as measured by unemployment, only when America was actively engaged as a combatant in World War II. Living standards returned to their 1929 level only in the postwar expansion, and the stock market's

Dow Jones Industrial Average (DJIA) did not regain its precrash level until November 1954.

THE MYTH

What caused this calamity? And what cured it? Conventional wisdom holds that the cause was greed mixed with fundamental flaws of free-market capitalism. And escape from these deep economic troubles was achieved by the timely correction of these flaws by Pres. Franklin Roosevelt's New Deal policies, which were a profound departure from what was thought to be Herbert Hoover's laissez-faire dogmatism. To complete the recovery, a final assist came from the enormous economic stimulus supplied by wartime spending.

Among laissez-faire capitalism's alleged flaws is its tendency to suffer from underconsumption. A not insignificant number of economists and historians believe this economic illness arises whenever larger and larger proportions of a nation's wealth are accumulated by the rich, who spend smaller shares of their incomes than do the poor. As a result, rising income inequality in the 1920s is said to have caused the amount of goods and services produced to exceed the amount that buyers were willing or able to purchase. Witnessing their warehouses filling with unwanted inventories, producers cut back on production. As they did so, businesses employed fewer workers. The resulting unemployment further reduced workers' ability to spend on consumption goods, which put further pressure on businesses to cut back on production and employment.

Writing in 1951, long-time Federal Reserve Chairman Marriner Eccles gave this explanation of the start of the Depression:

> As mass production has to be accompanied by mass consumption, mass consumption, in turn, implies a distribution of wealth . . . to provide men with buying power. . . . Instead of achieving that kind of distribution, a giant suction pump had by 1929–1930 drawn into a few hands an increasing portion of currently produced wealth. . . . The other fellows could stay in the game only by borrowing. When their credit ran out, the game stopped.[11]

William Leuchtenberg, a University of North Carolina historian, shared this same understanding: "Insofar as one accepts the theory that under-consumption explains the Depression, and I do, then the Presidents of the 1920s are to blame for operating a . . . government responsive mainly to large business corporations. This led, among other unfortunate conse-quences, to the failure to maintain an adequate level of purchasing power on the part of workers and farmers, which left the economy with inade-quate underpinnings."[12]

Arthur Schlesinger Jr., one of the most famous historians of twentieth-century America, also blamed the Depression on underconsumption: "Management's disposition to maintain prices . . . meant that workers and farmers were denied the benefits of increases in their own productivity. The consequence was the relative decline of mass purchasing power."[13] This problem was believed by Schlesinger to have been exacerbated by Treasury Secretary Andrew Mellon's tax policy, which, by "placing its emphasis on relief for millionaires rather than for consumers, made the maldistribution of income and oversaving even worse."[14]

This emphasis on underconsumption as a major cause of the Depression still appears today in leading college-level American history textbooks, such as *America: A Narrative History* by Furman University's David Shi: "In essence, the economy was turning out more products than consumers could buy. . . . At the same time, many business owners had taken large profits while denying wage increases to employees. By plowing profits into business expansion, executive salaries, and stock dividends, employers created an imbalance between production and consumption."[15]

Greed was also blamed for fueling destructive stock market specula-tions. But greed isn't a currency that can be spent. It must be monetized. The alchemy accused of performing this transformation was credit, which was used to finance the purchase of equities by enabling investors to put up only a portion of their prices and then borrow the rest of the money. As margin requirements (the percentage of the purchase price stock buyers had to put up in cash) fell, speculating investors are said to have bought ever-larger quantities of corporate stocks using borrowed funds.[16] The result, according to Robert Heilbroner, one of the most influential popularizers of economics, was "a honeycomb of loans that could bear just so much strain and no more."[17] Heilbroner saw margin buying not only as a major culprit in hoisting share prices far above their true values but also as the cause of the economic downturn when those share prices collapsed, further dragging down the demand for goods and services.

When Wall Street crashed on Black Tuesday, October 29, 1929, some Americans at the time—and even later—accused Pres. Herbert Hoover of initially denying that a problem existed.[18] No less a scholar than Paul Samuelson of the Massachusetts Institute of Technology (MIT)—the first American to win the Nobel Prize in Economics—described Hoover's term as being "quite a number of years" of "inaction."[19] Similarly, John Kenneth Galbraith, while acknowledging that Hoover often met with businesspeople to confer about the economic turmoil, believed that the president did little more than idly talk. Galbraith described these meetings as "no-business meetings," staged events designed to hide the fact that Hoover was "averse to any large-scale government action to counter the developing depression."[20]

Hoover is said to have twiddled his thumbs in the White House, hoping the downturn would miraculously reverse itself, while the nation's economy sank ever more deeply into depression. Unsurprisingly, voters ousted Hoover, replacing him in 1932 with the optimistic and energetic FDR.

Taking office in March 1933, Roosevelt purportedly arrived in Washington with both smart advisors and a plan. The former (the group of advisors) was nicknamed the Brain Trust and was comprised mainly of Ivy League–affiliated scholars committed to using the power of the state to engineer America out of the Depression. The latter (the plan) was the New Deal, a set of policies aimed at recovery of the economy from the Depression, relief of the hardship suffered by millions of Americans, and reform of institutions to ensure that such a catastrophe would never happen again.

Not every part of the plan succeeded, a reality that neither surprised nor discouraged the New Dealers. A crucial aspect of the New Deal was the commitment, in FDR's words, to engage in "bold, persistent experimentation."[21] Historian Shi portrays the New Deal as "a series of trial-and-error actions rather than a comprehensive scheme. None of the well-intentioned but often poorly planned initiatives worked perfectly, and some failed miserably. Yet their combined effect was to restore hope and energy to a nation eager for dynamic leadership."[22]

In the popular mind, the New Deal met with much success. As described by historian Joseph Conlin, "the greatest positive accomplishment of the New Deal was to ease the economic hardship suffered by millions of Americans."[23] Harvard historian Samuel Eliot Morison agreed: "The New Deal was just what the term implied—a new deal of old cards, no longer stacked against the common man."[24]

This success, however, was obviously incomplete given that unemployment remained in double digits throughout the 1930s. Why? We're told that although Roosevelt moved far in the necessary direction, political constraints prevented him from going full bore to completely escape the Depression. As Heilbroner wrote, "the government program of investment was never carried out to the full extent that would have been necessary to bring the economy up to full employment."[25] Such investment had to await America's involvement in the Second World War.[26] Nevertheless, it is generally believed today that without FDR's interventions, America's economy in the 1930s would have remained in much worse shape. According to historian Eric Rauchway of the University of California, Davis, "the Depression was really bad, but the New Deal really helped."[27] Actress Jane Fonda summed up ninety years of public opinion when she praised Roosevelt and his New Deal for having "lifted this country out of Depression."[28]

This account is widely told and believed. It is also a myth. The Great Depression was not caused by human character flaws—greed and myopia—recklessly left unbridled by a laissez-faire government. Nor does the Depression serve as evidence that free-market capitalism suffers a natural tendency to chronic, economy-wide overproduction. Further, the New Deal almost certainly extended the Depression, as is evidenced by the fact that America's recovery lagged behind that of most other developed nations. Genuine recovery likely didn't arrive until *after* the war ended.

GETTING THE FACTS STRAIGHT ON THE GREAT DEPRESSION

Before the 1930s the country had repeatedly experienced economic downturns, all of which were milder and far shorter than what would become the Great Depression. These repeated recessions and financial panics were the result of the combination of a fractional-reserve banking system, prohibitions on branch banking, and an agricultural economy with seasonal variations in the demand for money.[29] Financial pressures occurred in the spring and fall, as currency was drawn out of banks to fund planting in the spring and to fund the harvest in the fall. Periodically, the banking system gave way under the financial strain, producing financial panics and economic downturns. The most historically significant of the pre–Great Depression downturns was the Banking Panic of 1907.

In May 1907, economic activity began to slow. However, as reported by Milton Friedman and Anna Schwartz in their 1963 book, *A Monetary History of the United States, 1867–1960*—a book that was instrumental in Friedman winning the Nobel Prize—through September of that year, "the contraction showed no obvious signs of severity."[30] The downturn sharply worsened only when, following the failure of the Knickerbocker Trust Company in October 1907, a full-blown banking panic erupted. Depositors rushed to get their money out of the banks from October 1907 through February 1908, and a banking collapse ensued, causing the money supply to fall by 5 percent.[31] GDP during this downturn shrunk by 12 percent and industrial output by 17 percent.[32] The stock market shed 15.9 percent of its value.[33] Yet unemployment topped out at only 8 percent.[34] The contraction lasted just over one year.[35] The chief significance of this downturn, however, is the banking panic that accompanied it, along with the successful efforts that brought the panic to a close. These efforts induced Congress to establish a commission to study the panic and recommend changes in the nation's banking system.

With no formal lender of last resort in place in 1907, bank clearinghouse associations in large banking centers acted as nongovernmental "quasi-central banking" institutions, as they had done in past panics.[36] In addition to ensuring that the public had access to important information about banks that had suspended conversion of deposits into currency, clearinghouses also helped reduce runs on solvent but illiquid banks by issuing currency substitutes, or "scrip." The effect was positive, as explained by St. Lawrence University economist Steven Horwitz: "The actions taken to issue the loan certificates and other currency substitutes to meet the rise in relative demand for currency were both necessary and effective. In fact, total losses from all issues of clearinghouse currencies were virtually nil. Despite the illegality of the currency substitutes, they circulated widely and easily."[37]

Also helping to calm the panic was J. P. Morgan, who had organized a pool of funds—$25 million in total—to be deposited in New York banks. John D. Rockefeller chipped in by depositing $10 million of his own into New York financial institutions, and the US Treasury deposited another $25 million.[38] New York banks were especially important for two reasons. First, New York banks held disproportionately large amounts of the reserves of America's regional banks, so runs on New York banks would cascade throughout the country. Second, they were a major source of loans for stock purchases on the New York Stock Exchange; a significant withdrawal of this source of credit would risk crashing the stock market.

The efforts of bank clearinghouse associations, Morgan, and the US Treasury ensured that the worst of the 1907 banking panic would pass in less than a month. It was completely over by February 1908. Still, the specter of the banking crisis and the success of the private response sparked a call in Congress for significant monetary reform. A leading voice for this reform was a powerful Republican senator from Rhode Island, Nelson Aldrich, who demanded, "Something has got to be done. We may not always have Pierpont Morgan with us to meet a banking crisis."[39]

To investigate possibilities for such reform, in 1908, Congress created the National Monetary Commission, which was chaired by Senator Aldrich. The commission submitted its report to Congress in 1912, warning that the country has "no provision for the concentration of the cash reserves of the banks and for their mobilization and use whenever needed in times of trouble. . . . Experience has shown that the scattered cash reserves of [the country's] banks are inadequate for purposes of assistance or defense at such times."[40] An institution to serve as lender of last resort was recommended. The National Monetary Commission provided the framework and impetus for the Federal Reserve Act of 1913.[41]

Twelve years after the end of the panic of 1907, the Federal Reserve system was put to the test by the depression of 1920–1921, which was the last major economic slump before the Great Depression. And in its depth, if not its duration, this early 1920s downturn was indisputably major. Friedman and Schwartz describe it as "characterized by an unprecedented collapse in prices" and "one of the most rapid declines on record."[42] From its peak in January 1920, real industrial output was 33 percent lower when it hit its trough fourteen months later, in March 1921.[43] This decline was significantly steeper than the fall in industrial output during the same time span at the start of the Great Depression when, after hitting its peak in July 1929, real industrial output fell over the next fourteen months by 24 percent.[44] Unemployment in the 1920–1921 depression reached, on the most conservative estimate, 8.7 percent and possibly rose to as high as 11.7 percent.[45] The stock market lost nearly half—46.6 percent—of its value.[46] Real GNP fell by as much as 9 percent.[47] Yet a vigorous and sustained recovery began less than a year and a half after this downturn began.[48] This recovery was so quick and complete that the financial writer James Grant nicknamed it "the Forgotten Depression."[49] The economy not only recovered but boomed for seven years. Wesleyan University economist Stanley Lebergott describes that decade by saying that "the gain in the standard of living during the 1920s . . . was without precedent in U.S. experience."[50]

Two factors stand out in assessing the performance of the new Federal Reserve—and the government generally—during the depression of 1920–1921. First, the Board of the Governors of the Federal Reserve refused to perform the duty given it by the Federal Reserve Act to act as lender of last resort. Fortunately, the independent regional Federal Reserve branches used their collective powers to provide liquidity to regional and rural banks and, in the process, prevented a financial panic.

It's important to emphasize that supporting solvent but illiquid banks was not a policy endorsed by, much less implemented by, the Federal Reserve Board in Washington or by the uniquely powerful Federal

Reserve Bank of New York. As economists Ellis Tallman and Eugene Nelson White put it, "the individual Federal Reserve banks in the districts most exposed to agricultural price shocks caused a reallocation of liquidity to those regions, even as total liquidity shrank. The result was to mitigate the effects of the shocks to the weakest districts, reducing the likelihood of a panic."[51]

The second factor—perhaps the most remarkable feature of the Forgotten Depression—is what the president and Congress did in terms of fiscal policy in response to the downturn: *nothing*. Describing the 1920–1921 downturn as "America's last governmentally unmedicated depression," James Grant writes that "the successive administrations of Woodrow Wilson and Warren G. Harding met the downturn by seeming to ignore it—or by implementing policies that an average 21st century economist would judge disastrous."[52]

In stark contrast, when the economy next fell seriously ill, in 1929, the distressed patient was immediately set upon by hordes of modern economic healers experimenting with the latest economic remedies. Following the independent action of the regional Federal Reserve branches during the 1920–1921 depression, in 1923 Federal Reserve reforms concentrated the power to conduct monetary policy in Washington. When the Great Depression came, the Federal Reserve stood by, allowing one-third of all the banks in the country to go out of business and the money supply to fall faster than prices.

CLEARING DECKS

Before zeroing in on what actually caused the Great Depression's unprecedented depth and duration, we must first clear the decks of some popular fallacies. Chief among these is the notion that the Depression was caused by the October 1929 stock market crash. American industrial production had begun to decline two months earlier, in August 1929, which is the official start (as reckoned by the National Bureau of Economic Research) of the formally defined initial recession, which lasted from August 1929 to March 1933.[53] As noted by Marquette University economist Gene Smiley, "there is now widespread agreement that the 1929 stock market crash did not cause the Great Depression. Instead, the initial downturn in economic activity was a primary determinant of the ending of the 1928–29 stock market bubble."[54] Smiley adds, however, that "the stock market crash did make the downturn become more severe beginning in November 1929. It reduced discretionary consumption spending and created greater income uncertainty," which promoted further economic contraction.[55]

Another invalid explanation of the Great Depression and of the stock market crash is the assertion that financial speculation had run amok because the public could purchase corporate shares on unusually small margins—that is, members of the general public were said to be purchasing shares with dangerously large proportions of borrowed funds. The reality, as Smiley found, is that "margin requirements through most of the twenties were essentially the same as in previous decades. Brokers, recognizing the problems with margin lending in the rapidly changing market, began raising margin requirements in late 1928, and by the fall of 1929, margin requirements were the highest in the history of the New York Stock Exchange."[56]

Yet another fallacy is that the share of national income going to workers in the 1920s fell, thus leading to underconsumption. In fact, the share of income going to workers *rose*. In the decade of 1919 to 1929, the real earnings of nonfarm workers rose in eight of those ten years. By 1929 these earnings were 26 percent higher than in 1919.[57] Not surprisingly, Nobel laureate economist Simon Kuznets found that the proportion of total income paid as wages and salaries in the United States increased from 57.8 percent in 1919 to 59.8 percent in 1929.[58]

Nor is it true that in the 1920s expenditures on consumption outputs became inadequate to maintain full employment. As noted by Stanley Lebergott, "per capita total consumption did not in fact decline during the late 1920s. It continued to rise along its 1900–1920 growth path."[59] Lebergott's data show that inflation-adjusted per capita personal-consumption spending rose in every year of the 1920s except the depression year of 1921. By 1929 such spending was 25 percent *higher* than in 1920.[60] Lebergott drives this point home by observing that during the 1920s, American households greatly increased their purchases of consumer durables, such as automobiles and then-newfangled electrical household appliances.[61] According to Hillsdale College historian Burton Folsom, "the percentage of GNP that went to consumption expenses did not fall, but actually rose from 68 percent in 1920 to 75 percent in 1927, 1928, and 1929."[62]

Blaming the Depression on underconsumption and then attributing that to the "maldistribution" of wealth served to justify the desired policy response: increased government spending along with higher and more progressive taxation. If it were widely realized that the Depression had instead resulted from the collapse of investment and business confidence, few of the policy goals of the Roosevelt administration could have been justified.

THE GREAT CONTRACTION

To understand what actually caused the Great Depression, it's helpful to distinguish the initial downturn from the Depression's unprecedented length. As reported by Alan Greenspan and Adrian Wooldridge, "the Fed fueled the speculative frenzy of 1926–28 by keeping interest rates too low in order to sustain the value of the pound sterling by encouraging a flow of capital into Britain. It then overcompensated by raising interest rates four times in 1928 and 1929, from 3.5 percent to 6 percent, making it harder for business people to borrow and invest."[63] The Fed blundered further by allowing the money supply to continue to shrink. From August 1929 (the month the downturn began) to October 1930, Milton Friedman and Anna Schwartz report that "the money stock declined 2.6 per cent."[64] This was "a larger decline than during the whole of all but four preceding reference cycle contractions [i.e., the pre-Great Depression economic downturns studied by Friedman and Schwartz]—1873–79, 1893–94, 1907–08, and 1920–21."[65] It's not surprising, therefore, that a banking panic erupted in late 1930. What *is* surprising is the Fed's catastrophic failure to act as a lender of last resort, the primary function Congress had created the Fed to perform. Starting in late 1930, the Fed's mismanagement of the money supply went from being bad to being cataclysmic.

Unlike in 1907, when private clearinghouse associations, J. P. Morgan, other private financiers, and the Treasury Department mobilized liquidity to stop the panic—and unlike in the early 1920s, when regional Federal Reserve banks used their then-significant autonomy to effectively serve as lenders of last resort—by the late 1920s, the only available lender of last resort was the Federal Reserve Board in Washington, DC. (As mentioned, earlier that decade, starting in 1923, the Fed had taken steps to centralize monetary powers in Washington.)[66] But as documented by Friedman and Schwartz, it neglected to perform this most central duty. In Friedman and Schwartz's telling, as a worried public sought to hold more cash by withdrawing money from banks, the Fed should have increased the supply of dollars to prevent the money supply from collapsing. Instead, the Fed did nothing. Spending and bank lending (and, hence, investment) fell precipitously as the public clung to cash. All told, from August 1929 through March 1933, the real supply of dollars fell by over a third.[67] Dubbed by Friedman and Schwartz as "the Great Contraction," the inevitable result of this massive shrinkage of the money supply was a massive contraction of production and employment.[68] Celebrated Carnegie Mellon monetary economist Allan Meltzer agrees. Writing about 1929–1933, Meltzer argues that "the critical flaw was . . . domestic decisions at critical times to not interfere with the contraction of money and credit and the resulting deflation." He goes on to note that "if the Federal Reserve had prevented the decline in money, falling prices would have raised real balances [i.e., raised households' and businesses' purchasing power], created an excess supply of money, stimulated spending, and limited or ended the decline when the economy began to recover in spring 1930."[69] But instead, the Fed did nothing, and the money supply actually fell faster than prices in three of the first four years of the Depression.[70]

As summarized by Friedman's biographer Jennifer Burns, "the Fed stood by as money drained from the banking system and the economy collapsed. What appeared to be a failure of markets was in fact a failure of men."[71] And the particular men who failed were those who ran the Federal Reserve system—those men whose main job it was to prevent banking panics and a collapse in the money supply.

Why this grotesque error? Friedman and Schwartz blame incompetent leadership at the Fed. A complementary explanation was offered by University of Georgia economist Richard Timberlake, who argues that Fed leadership was then enthralled by a false monetary notion called the "real bills doctrine."[72] The real bills doctrine holds that if banks loan only to finance the "legitimate" needs of trade—as opposed to issuing loans used to finance speculation—the loans can be paid back, and the banking system can be self-sustaining and in need of no lender of last resort. Whatever the reason, the Fed unquestionably allowed the money supply to collapse—a collapse that had devastating consequences for America and the world.

In an extraordinary speech made at Milton Friedman's ninetieth birthday party, Ben Bernanke, then Chairman of the Federal Reserve Board and subsequent 2022 winner of the Nobel Prize in economics, accepted Milton Friedman and Anna Schwartz's conclusion that the Great Depression was triggered by the failed policies of the Federal Reserve. "Let me end my talk by abusing slightly my status as an official representative of the Federal Reserve. I would like to say to Milton and Anna: regarding the Great Depression, *you're right, we [The Fed] did it. We are very sorry. But thanks to you, we won't do it again.*"[73]

HOOVER, THE FATHER OF THE NEW DEAL

Contrary to popular myth, Pres. Herbert Hoover was emphatically *not* a devotee of laissez-faire capitalism. He himself boasted, upon accepting the GOP nomination for reelection in August 1932, "We might have done nothing. That would have been utter ruin. Instead, we met the situation with proposals to private business and to the Congress of the most gigantic program of economic defense and counterattack ever evolved in the history of the Republic."[74] This boast was truthful. The historical record confirms that Hoover intervened in a manner that no previous president during any downturn had ever done.[75] George Selgin says, "There are few more successful examples in history of the propaganda technique known as the 'big lie' than the charge that Herbert Hoover was a 'do nothing' president."[76]

In real, price-adjusted dollars, the US government's expenditures rose every year during Hoover's term. By the beginning of 1933, the federal government was spending nearly twice as much as it had spent four years earlier. On public works alone, Hoover's spending was enormous. Selgin finds that on public-works projects, "the Hoover administration spent more than the previous *nine* administrations combined, notwithstanding that their undertakings included the Panama Canal."[77] When it came to spending taxpayers' money, Hoover was no skinflint. The Revenue Act of 1932 *raised* all personal income-tax rates, with the highest rate ballooning from 25 percent to 63 percent. Ordinary income earners saw their income-tax rates rise from a range of 1.5 to 5 percent and from 4 to 8 percent. Also hiked was the tax rate on corporate income, rising from 12 percent to 13.75 percent, as well as several excise taxes. The federal estate-tax rate more than doubled, from 20 percent to 45 percent.[78]

Despite Hoover's tax increases, the budget deficit in 1931 was more than half of all federal expenditures, and that of 1932 more than 43 percent of such expenditures.[79] A substantial budget deficit was run also in 1933.[80] Hoover's deficits in peacetime were so large and unprecedented that a major theme of Franklin Roosevelt's 1932 presidential campaign was his promise to balance the budget and put an end to Hoover's fiscal irresponsibility.[81]

Perhaps an even worse blunder by Hoover was his attempt to keep prices and wage rates from falling. He used the Federal Farm Board, created during the first few months of his presidency, to establish "stabilization corporations" designed to artificially buoy farm prices. When this cartelization scheme failed, Hoover proposed paying farmers to not grow crops.[82] No less harmful to a functioning economy was Hoover's successful jawboning of Henry Ford and other corporate leaders to extract promises not to cut wage rates, a policy that exacerbated unemployment.[83] On the topic, in 1933, prominent University of Chicago economist Jacob Viner noted that

> In past depressions wage reductions have contributed to recovery by making possible restoration of profit margins for industry in spite of the fall in commodity prices. During the New Era, the Hoover Administration

became apostles of the . . . doctrine that high wages are a guarantee and an essential of prosperity. At the beginning of the depression, Hoover pledged industry not to cut wages, and for a long time large-scale industry as a rule adhered to this pledge.[84]

Hoover believed that prosperity resulted from high wage rates—a belief that no doubt also encouraged him in 1931 to sign the Davis-Bacon Act, which required that union wage rates be paid to all workers on construction projects receiving federal funds.[85] But Hoover had matters backward. High wage rates don't cause prosperity. As Steve Horwitz puts it, "prosperity, thanks to the accumulation of capital that increases the productivity of labor, leads to higher wages."[86] A consequence of Hoover's wage policies was that one of the keys to reducing unemployment (especially when the money supply is contracting)—namely, allowing wage rates to fall to levels that make workers profitable to employ—was impeded.

The most notorious of Hoover's responses to the downturn was the Smoot-Hawley Tariff, which he signed into law in June 1930. With this act, average US tariff rates on dutiable imports were raised by nearly 50 percent. Dartmouth economist Douglas Irwin found that Smoot-Hawley "significantly reduced imports but failed to create jobs overall because exports fell almost one-for-one with imports."[87] This outcome surprised no competent economist, and it certainly didn't surprise any of the 1,028 economists who signed a letter urging Hoover to veto the Smoot-Hawley bill.[88] Although this infamous restriction on international trade didn't *cause* the Great Depression, it did worsen it, not least because other governments predictably retaliated by raising tariffs on their countries' imports of American goods.

ROOSEVELT'S POLICIES WORSENED AND EXTENDED THE DEPRESSION

Unlike the myth about Hoover refusing to intervene to reverse the downturn, no one doubts that Pres. Franklin Roosevelt actively used the power of the state to combat the Depression. His New Deal famously extended US government power into unprecedented territories. Yet despite the reverence with which many historians and the general public continue to regard the New Deal, those policies simply cannot be credited with having "cured" the Great Depression. Indeed, all available evidence suggests that the New Deal worsened and extended Americans' economic misery.

The most obvious justification for this negative assessment of the New Deal's success at promoting economic recovery is, of course, the fact that the unemployment rate never fell below 14.3 percent at any time in the 1930s while FDR was in the White House. It was still north of 10 percent as late as January 1941.[89] While the Depression was a worldwide phenomenon, the recovery of employment and industrial production in the United States lagged significantly behind most of the world's developed nations. League of Nations data on employment in developed countries from 1929 through 1938 show that nearly a decade after the stock market crash, total employment in the United States was still almost 20 percent below the pre-Depression level. In contrast, total employment in the United Kingdom and in Sweden was *up* by 10 percent; in Italy, up by 12 percent; in Australia, up by more than 20 percent; and in Denmark, up by almost 40 percent. Employment in Germany was up 12 percent, and employment in Japan had risen 45 percent. The only surveyed country with a labor market as bad in 1938 as that of the United States was France.[90] It is perhaps no coincidence that, more so than in any other Western nation, the French government's response to the Great Depression most resembled that of the United States (see figure 3.1). As George Selgin observes, "France was one of the few countries, and the only major one, that took longer to recover from the Great Depression than the United States. It was also the only country that resorted to policies closely resembling, and inspired by, the New Deal."[91]

Industrial production tells a story similar to that told by employment. By the end of 1938, in the other five most developed countries, industrial production was, on average, almost 16 percent above its 1929 level. In the United States, however, industrial production was still down by 20 percent.[92] Astonishingly, these League of Nations' data on employment and industrial production have been, for all practical purposes,

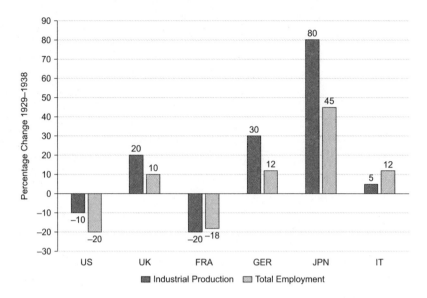

Figure 3.1. League of Nations Data on Industrial Production and Employment 1929–1938. *Source:* J. E. Meade, ed. *World Economic Survey, Eighth Year, 1938–1939* (League of Nations, 1939), 11, 12, and 13.

almost totally neglected by contemporary and subsequent historians and economists in assessing the New Deal and the United States' recovery.[93]

A significant recovery began in 1934 as real GDP started to rise at an accelerating rate.[94] This improvement was reflected in the stock market. By February 1937 the Dow Jones Industrial Average had recovered 43 percent of the value it had shed between August 1929 and its low point of June 1932.[95] And while unemployment remained high, by 1937, its rate, at 14.3 percent, was more than 10 percentage points lower than in 1933. Roosevelt even spoke in January 1937 as if it were an established fact that the Depression was ending.[96]

Why this recovery? Gold inflows from Europe surely played a big role. Between March 1933 and May 1937, the US stock of monetary gold tripled.[97] As these reserves increased, so, too, did the money supply, thus providing much-needed fuel for increased economic activity.

Another important factor promoting recovery was the demise of the National Industrial Recovery Act (NIRA). Following the act's June 1933 passage, National Recovery Administration (NRA) codes began being formed. As documented by UCLA economists Harold Cole and Lee Ohanian, using the powers granted by the NIRA the government orchestrated NRA cartelization of American industry with the objective of preventing prices and wages from falling. This cartelization, combined with the government-aided strengthening of labor unions, impeded a decline in prices and wages and, in the process, reduced consumption and employment, thus *stifling* economic recovery.[98] But by the spring of 1934, a full year before the Supreme Court formally neutered the NIRA in May 1935, the NRA was plagued with what Central Michigan University economist Jason Taylor calls a "compliance crisis."[99] This increasing disregard of NRA rules, even with the NIRA still on the books, likely added fuel to this recovery. As Selgin reports, "by the time the Supreme Court rendered its decision, most of the NRA's codes of fair competition had been as many dead letters for months. With forced monopolization of the economy waning and gold pouring into the country and increasing the money supply, the economy began to stir."[100] The short-lived recovery was muted in December 1936, when the Treasury started to "sterilize" gold inflows by offsetting the impact gold inflows had in expanding the money supply and easing credit.[101]

The economy then kicked hard into reverse. The Roosevelt Recession of 1937–1938 had commenced. It would become, in the words of Douglas Irwin, "the third-worst US recession in the 20th century (after 1929–32 and 1920–21)."[102] From its "recovery" high in April 1937, by May 1938 the Fed's monthly index of industrial production was down by nearly a third.[103] Real GNP fell by 11 percent.[104] The DJIA lost 47 percent of its value.[105] The unemployment rate almost doubled.[106]

Friedman and Schwartz pin much of the blame for this steep downturn on a series of Fed decisions in the second half of 1937 to increase—and, eventually, to double—banks' reserve requirements.[107] The Fed took this step because it worried that the large amount of excess reserves that were built up in the banking system would soon be loaned out, sparking an inflationary increase in the money supply. But according to Friedman and Schwartz, banks—still recalling the panic and Fed inaction of four years earlier—viewed these reserves as a necessary cushion; from the banks' perspective, these reserves weren't excessive at all. Selgin nicely summarizes Friedman's and Schwartz's thesis:

So, when the Fed increased banks' required reserves . . . the banks proceeded to rebuild their excess reserve cushions. With only so many reserves in the system, this meant limiting their required reserves by reducing their loans, investments, and deposits. The resulting decline in bank credit and the money stock helped bring about the 1937–8 recession, just as the Great Monetary Contraction of 1929–33 led (once again, according to Friedman and Schwartz) to the first Great Depression downturn.[108]

SPENDING, TAXING, AND REGIME UNCERTAINTY

Although he campaigned in 1932 against Herbert Hoover's deficit spending, once in office, FDR continued this loose budgetary policy, even slightly deepening the annual budget deficit during his first year in office. The budget remained in deficit during each year of FDR's long presidency. These deficits were not caused by a decrease in receipts, which increased in real-dollar terms every year of Roosevelt's tenure except 1939 (when they fell slightly). As for federal outlays, despite dipping in 1935 and declining somewhat more steeply in 1937 and 1938, throughout the 1930s, real expenditures kept ahead of real receipts. By 1939, real federal government expenditures were more than double their level a decade earlier, and were roughly 80 percent higher than in the year FDR first took office, 1933.[109] For the 1930s as a whole, the US government spent, in real terms, almost twice as much—93 percent more—per person than it had spent per person during the 1920s.[110] A decade of deficit financing and generally rising government expenditures failed to restore the US economy to health.

Matters weren't helped by Roosevelt's tax policies. After skyrocketing from 25 percent to 63 percent in 1932, in 1936 the top marginal personal income tax rate was raised further, from 63 percent to 79 percent, where it remained for the rest of the decade.[111] Also in 1936, the top corporate-income tax rate rose from 13.5 percent to 15 percent. In 1938 it was hiked again to 19 percent, and in 1940 it was more than doubled, to 38.3 percent.[112] Because taxing income necessarily dampens productive activity, these tax increases only added to the burdens that investors, entrepreneurs, and property owners bore in their efforts to revitalize the industrial and commercial activities essential to a market economy.

An especially controversial and harmful New Deal tax was the levy on undistributed profits introduced in 1936. Initially intended to replace the tax on corporate income, when implemented it acted as a surtax on retained earnings rather than serving as a substitute for the corporate income tax, which was not abolished.[113] The tax burden on corporations only got heavier.

FDR marketed the undistributed-profits tax to the public as a means of protecting small businesses from being, in FDR's words, "gobbled up or wiped out" by "concentrated wealth and economic power."[114] But the president was warned even by officials in his own Treasury department that the measure would likely backfire: Small or young firms rely especially heavily on retained earnings. These firms are less able than larger and more established ones to tap into credit markets for funding to endure downtimes or to expand. Taxing retained earnings would therefore hit smaller and younger firms relatively harder than larger and older firms. The extraordinarily negative impact on large and small firms, the economy, and the recovery has been confirmed by Columbia University's Charles Calomiris and Glenn Hubbard.[115] Unpopular from the start, the surtax on undistributed profits was soon watered down and then, in 1939, repealed.

By the late 1930s, the New Deal's failure to bring economic recovery was so obvious that even Treasury Secretary Henry Morgenthau commented upon it. In May 1939, he said the following to the House Ways and Means Committee:

> We have tried spending money. We are spending more money than we have ever spent before and it does not work. And I have just one interest, and if I am wrong . . . somebody else can have my job. I want to see this country prosperous. I want to see people get a job, I want to see people get enough to eat. We have never made good on our promises. . . . I say after eight years of this Administration we have just as much unemployment as when we started . . . . And an enormous debt to boot! We are just sitting here and fiddling and I am just wearing myself out and getting sick. Because why? I can't see any daylight.[116]

America's economy remained mired in the Depression, with workers idled not only because of the heavier tax and regulatory burdens but also—and perhaps even more so—because of the political uncertainty and fear created by Roosevelt and the New Deal. Hoover began but FDR greatly accelerated the government's unprecedented and unpredictable intrusions into economic affairs that had long been the preserve of private, competitive markets. Assessing these fundamental changes in America's economic system, Amity Shlaes wrote in 2023 that "Roosevelt told Americans that 'the only thing we have to fear is fear itself.' Yet it was the New Deal that fostered fear, prolonging the trouble. The very arbitrariness of the New Dealers' moves caused markets and employers to freeze in their tracks."[117]

The arbitrary policy shifts—such as initially promoting monopolization of industry before reversing course to ramp up antitrust actions against many successful firms—were accompanied by increasingly hostile populist tirades against private business. FDR thundered publicly against "economic royalists."[118] As University of Texas historian H. W. Brands notes, "Roosevelt did not identify these evil men by name . . . but he painted their actions in lurid detail."[119] Calling the growing group of businesspeople and investors who objected to his administration's infringements on traditional property and contract rights "an economic autocracy," Roosevelt warned that "they will take the course of every autocracy of the past—power for themselves, enslavement for the public."[120] Brands writes that with this "incendiary" performance, "Roosevelt came disturbingly close to the demagoguery not only of Father Coughlin and the late Huey Long but also of the fascists of Europe."[121]

Roosevelt was only warming up. Five days later, he spoke of the country's economy with guests at the Democrats' 1936 annual Jefferson-Jackson Day Dinner, saying, "We are at peace with the world; but the fight goes on. Our frontiers of today are economic, not geographic. Our enemies of today are the forces of privilege and greed within our own borders."[122] Those forces revealed themselves by their opposition to the New Deal, and against these evil forces, Roosevelt promised to "save" the good people of America "from being plowed under by the small minority of business men and financiers, against whom you and I will continue to wage war."[123] Brands describes Roosevelt as having launched "a scorched-earth campaign against wealth and conservatism."[124] It was a campaign that was too much even for Roosevelt's onetime friend and fellow Democrat Al Smith. He accused FDR of being a demagogue "who would incite one class of our people against the other."[125]

Roosevelt obviously relished his new populist role. On Halloween, just days before the 1936 election, he boasted to an enthusiastic crowd in Madison Square Garden of his administration's "struggle with the old enemies of peace—business and financial monopoly, speculation, reckless banking, class antagonism, sectionalism, war profiteering."[126] He then hit his crescendo, a moment that could only frighten anyone who dared oppose New Deal methods for economic salvation: "Never before in all our history have these forces been so united against one candidate as they stand today. They are unanimous in their hate for me—and I welcome their hatred. I should like to have it said of my first Administration that in it the forces of selfishness and of lust for power met their match. I should like to have it said of my second Administration that in it these forces met their master."[127]

Roosevelt's war on business and wealth was so traumatic that the League of Nations attributed a portion of the United States' poor economic performance to it: "The relations between the leaders of business and the Administration were uneasy, and this uneasiness accentuated the unwillingness of private enterprise to embark on further projects of capital expenditure which might have helped to sustain the economy."[128]

This same conclusion was reached by an astute onlooker from across the Atlantic. Despite his strategic reserve in criticizing FDR, Winston Churchill, in 1934, wrote that one of the dangers "to President Roosevelt's valiant and heroic experiments seems to arise from the disposition to hunt down rich men as if they were noxious beasts. . . . The question arises whether the general well-being of the masses of the community will be advanced by an excessive indulgence in this amusement."[129] He further observed that in America, "confidence is shaken and enterprise chilled, and the unemployed queue up at the soup kitchens or march out to the public works with ever growing expense to the taxpayer and nothing more appetizing to take home to their families than the leg or wing of what was once a millionaire. . . . It is indispensable to the wealth of nations and to the wage and life standards of labour, that capital and credit should be honoured and cherished partners in the economic system."[130] Churchill warned, "There can never be good wages or good employment for any length of time without good profits, and the sooner this is recognized, the sooner the corner will be turned."[131]

Common sense and the raw facts of 1930s America confirm that when government is openly hostile to the market's profit-and-loss system, as well as to the sanctity of private property on which that system depends, economic performance will wane. Writing in 1949, the UCLA economist Benjamin Anderson observed that "the New Deal policy . . . had made capital timid in the extreme" and that "the failure to get out of the depression in the years 1933 to 1939 [was] due to the great multiplicity of New Deal 'remedies,' all tending to impair the freedom and efficiency of the markets, to frighten venture capital, and to create frictions and uncertainties, and impediments to individual and corporate initiative."[132]

But it wasn't until sixty years after the New Deal that this thesis about it was put to an empirical test. In a series of papers written in the 1990s, the economic historian Robert Higgs formalized and tested this thesis. What Amity Shlaes calls "arbitrariness," Higgs calls "regime uncertainty." Such uncertainty, he argues, was rampant in New Deal America, especially in the last half of the 1930s. It prevented recovery. Higgs found that "the insufficiency of private investment from 1935 through 1940 reflected a pervasive uncertainty among investors about the security of their property rights in their capital and its prospective returns. This uncertainty arose, especially though not exclusively, from the character of federal government actions and the nature of the Roosevelt administration during the so-called Second New Deal from 1935 to 1940."[133]

Specifically, as the New Deal progressed, investors increasingly feared that their "property rights in their capital and the income it yields [would] be attenuated by further government action. . . . The possibility that the United States might undergo an extreme regime shift seemed to many investors in the late 1930s and early 1940s not only possible, but likely."[134] Allan Meltzer concurred, writing that, in the New Deal era, "policy changes, reinforced by changing rhetoric, maintained a state of flux in which long-term planning was difficult."[135]

This fear and uncertainty were understandable. As documented above, Roosevelt's rhetoric grew increasingly belligerent toward businesspeople. And although the US Supreme Court did not immediately rubber-stamp all New Deal programs—it famously ruled in 1935 that key provisions of the NIRA were unconstitutional—with FDR's threat to pack the Supreme Court, followed by that tribunal's famous "switch in time that saved nine" in 1937, the courts could no longer be counted on to stand as a bulwark to protect property rights from government overreach.[136] This was especially true in a global political environment that seemed ever more favorable toward government control of the economy.

In support of his regime-uncertainty thesis, Higgs musters evidence from public opinion polls taken during the 1930s, as well as from observations about the era from historians. But he seals his case with support from a third source: financial markets. Of course, the poor performance of the stock market throughout the 1930s testifies to investor pessimism. Higgs, though, dives more deeply into the details of financial-market performance by first looking at data on gross private domestic investment.

We can divide gross private domestic investment into three components that correspond to differing lengths of the newly created capital's expected economic life: gross private new construction (the longest lived); gross private producers durables (intermediate); and additions to business inventories (the shortest lived). During the last five years of the 1920s, on average, these components constituted the following proportions of private investment: 0.62, 0.32, and 0.06, respectively. During the business recovery in progress during the first three years of the Second New Deal (1935–37), however, the proportions were 0.38, 0.44, and 0.18, respectively, showing a marked shift away from the longest-term investments. The proportions remained much the same during the second business recovery of the Second New Deal (1939–41), when they were 0.45, 0.40, and 0.15, respectively. Clearly the real investments made during the first and second Roosevelt administrations remained far more concentrated in short-term assets than the investments made during the latter half of the 1920s.[137]

Further, as the New Deal gained momentum and FDR's rhetoric against businesspeople grew more hostile, yields on long-term bonds relative to yields on short-term bonds rose to "extraordinarily high levels."[138] This spread likely indicated an acute fear of the future and a diminishing confidence that investors' property and contract rights would be respected. The abnormally high rates creditors were demanding for long-run investments persisted until early 1942, when Roosevelt sharply muted his attacks on business, as private industry had become essential to the war effort.[139]

Eight stagnant years after the 1929 downturn, the great American manufacturer Lammot du Pont II needed no empirical study to recognize the following:

> Uncertainty rules the tax situation, the labor situation, the monetary situation, and practically every legal condition under which industry must operate. Are taxes to go higher, lower or stay where they are? We don't know. Is labor to be union or nonunion? . . . Are we to have inflation or deflation, more government spending or less? . . . Are new restrictions to be placed on capital, new limits on profits? . . . It is impossible to even guess at the answers.[140]

Economic uncertainty and prosperity are sworn enemies. When uncertainty reigns, prosperity fades. Uncertainty undermines prosperity by sapping investor and consumer confidence, choking off entrepreneurship and private investment, and suppressing consumer spending.

CONCLUSION: THE DEPRESSION WAS A FAILURE OF GOVERNMENT AND NOT CAPITALISM

The Great Depression remains the deepest and longest economic downturn in America's history. And although it started in the summer of 1929 as an ordinary downturn, the Depression was transformed into an unprecedented economic calamity not by the failure of markets but by the failure of government. The Fed failed to perform its primary mission, which was to be a lender of last resort to prevent banking crises and a collapse of the money supply. The Fed compounded its original error not only by raising reserve requirements three times between August 1936 and May 1937, fearing that what it believed to be excess reserves held by the commercial banking system would lead to inflation, but also by sterilizing incoming gold flows, thus preventing a helpful expansion of the money supply. The Fed failed to understand that the commercial banks had lost their confidence because, although the reserves appeared excessive to the Fed, the bankers viewed these reserves as necessary protection for banks in the absence of the Fed's reliable support. This policy error only deepened and prolonged the Depression.

In addition, the White House and Congress blocked the operation of the price system, raised tax rates, obstructed trade, and threatened the sanctity of private property. And the courts would eventually rubber-stamp this unprecedented assault on America's market economy. Far from revealing any weaknesses, contradictions, or evils of the free-market system, the Great Depression instead revealed the peril posed by government domination of markets. Like all human institutions, American capitalism has its failings, but what failed in the 1930s wasn't capitalism. What failed was the American government. In its conduct of monetary, fiscal, and regulatory policy, it turned what would have been an ordinary recession into a depression that became the most traumatic economic experience in American history.

POSTSCRIPT: WHEN AND WHY THE DEPRESSION ENDED

Conventional wisdom holds that the Great Depression was finally ended by the onset of World War II. The dramatic increase in the government's wartime expenditures—much of which was funded through borrowing—is commonly credited with raising economy-wide spending by enough to fully awaken the nation from its long-running nightmare. Representative of this conventional wisdom is University of Florida economist J. R. Vernon, who writes that as late as 1940, "the recovery was less than half-complete" but that over the next two years, "World War II fiscal policies were, then, instrumental in the overall restoration of full-employment performance."[141] Popular accounts from both then and now concur: "What ultimately ended the depression," long-time *Washington Post* columnist Robert Samuelson writes, "was World War II."[142]

It's true that by 1942 unemployment had disappeared. But while wartime spending and mobilization eliminated unemployment, they didn't restore pre-Depression living standards. Real per capita personal consumption was lower from 1942 through 1945 than it had been before the war.[143] But there is, however, a more important reason to be skeptical of the claim that the Depression was ended by wartime spending. When the war ended, government spending declined precipitously while, simultaneously, millions of workers were released into a private economy that was largely freed of wartime controls and no longer producing huge quantities of war materials.[144] If high government spending had been the key to ending the Depression and keeping the economy at full employment, the rapid and drastic cut in spending when the war ended, along with demobilization, would have sent the economy back into a depression. Indeed, many economists at the time predicted that if the government cut spending and removed wartime controls, a new depression would ensue. In 1943 the future Nobel laureate Paul Samuelson warned that

> the final conclusion to be drawn from our experience at the end of the last war is inescapable—*were the war to end suddenly, . . . were we again planning to wind up our war effort in the greatest haste, to demobilize our armed forces, to liquidate price controls, to shift from astronomical deficits to even the large deficits of the thirties—then there would be ushered in the greatest period of unemployment and industrial dislocation which any economy has ever faced.*[145]

To avoid this fate, Samuelson insisted that the government must continue to run the "astronomical deficits" in peacetime that it ran during wartime. In 1942 the budget deficit was 12.4 percent of GDP. The deficit rose in 1943 to 26.9 percent of GDP.[146] The size of these deficits would remain little changed throughout the war.[147] To put these wartime deficit figures in perspective, the US government budget deficit for 2024 will be about 6.6 percent of GDP.

Paul Samuelson wasn't alone in his dread. In 1944 Gunner Myrdal, another future Nobel laureate, feared that as "the Federal demand for war materials diminishes and gradually disappears, and . . . the central control is replaced by free enterprise," there would be "a high degree of unrest" or perhaps even an "epidemic of violence."[148] Also pessimistic were economists associated with the Bureau of the Budget. They predicted that, absent huge peacetime budget deficits, demobilization would have "strong deflationary tendencies," leaving between eight to twelve million workers unemployed.[149]

As it turns out, the advice of these economists was ignored—and fortunately so. From its wartime high in 1944, US government spending fell over the next four years by 75 percent.[150] According to Naval Postgraduate School economist David Henderson, this colossal spending reduction "brought federal spending down from a peak of 44 percent of gross national product (GNP) in 1944 to only 8.9 percent in 1948."[151] As for the budget deficit, it was cut by more than 50 percent in 1946, and in 1947, it disappeared altogether, even becoming a small surplus. In 1948 the budget surplus ballooned to nearly a quarter of total federal expenditures.[152]

Yet even in the face of rapid demobilization, the speedy removal of wartime economic controls, and massive cuts in government spending and the budget deficit, the economy boomed. During the four-year period from 1945 to 1948, the unemployment rate was never higher than 3.9 percent.[153] Additionally, real personal consumption per capita rose significantly starting in 1946. By 1949 Americans were consuming 22 percent more than they had consumed only four years earlier, and the prewar economy was restored.[154]

This postwar boom cannot plausibly be attributed—as one popular myth would have it—to Americans going on a spending spree to satisfy "pent-up demands" for goods.[155] If this theory were correct, once these pent-up demands were satisfied, the chronic underconsumption that was allegedly the Depression's root cause would have again reared its head and plunged the economy back into a severe recession.[156] But in spite of a mild and short downturn near the very end of the 1940s, industrial production continued to rise more or less steadily for decades.[157] In short, this great postwar boom testifies *against* theories of underconsumption. From 1947 to 2007, the US economy grew at an average annual real rate of 3.4 percent.[158]

The chief causes of America's postwar success were the restoration of a largely free market and an end to the extreme uncertainty regarding the sanctity of property and contract rights fomented by FDR's New Deal policies. Polling conducted in the immediate postwar era found that "business and professional people felt much less threatened by Truman than they had by Roosevelt."[159] Also, after surveying the immediate postwar opinions of business leaders, Herman Krooss discovered that "for most business leaders, the mood during the first couple of years after V-J Day was one of cautious confidence and optimism"—a finding that Higgs describes as reflecting "a far different mood from that of business leaders between 1935 and 1941."[160] In November 1954, two years into the Eisenhower administration, the stock market finally reached its pre-Depression high. It would continue to grow impressively. With confidence restored, the power of government constrained, and the rule of law reaffirmed, America had recovered from the Great Depression.

Four

THE MYTH OF TRADE HOLLOWING OUT AMERICAN MANUFACTURING

W HEN THE GUNS FELL silent in 1945, Europe and Asia lay in ruins, and half of the world's GDP was produced in the United States—a stark change from just seven years earlier. In 1938, the year before the start of the Second World War, the United Kingdom was exporting more manufactured products than the United States, while Germany, France, Italy, and Japan combined were exporting more than twice as much as the United States.[1] But only fifteen years later, in 1953, US manufacturing exports were nearly twice as many as the United Kingdom's and a third more than those of Germany, France, Italy, and Japan combined.[2] Despite the Marshall Plan, the formation of the European Coal and Steel Community, the Treaty of Rome establishing the European Community, and a surge in world trade, even as late as 1960, four of every ten dollars of global output was made in America.[3] The war changed the face of the global economy and ushered in what is commonly regarded as the golden age of American manufacturing—an age spanning roughly the first three decades following World War II. By 1975, when the postwar period and the golden age of American manufacturing ended, industrial output in America was 232 percent greater than when the postwar era had begun.[4]

American industry dominated postwar global manufacturing, and manufacturing formed the cornerstone of American prosperity. As a share of US GDP, manufacturing output rose from 25 percent in 1947 to its postwar peak of 28.1 percent in 1953. As war-torn Europe and Asia began to rise from the ashes of World War II, global competition in manufacturing intensified. Nevertheless, in 1975 manufacturing still accounted for more than 20 percent of the United States' total output.[5] As for manufacturing employment, 39 percent of America's nonfarm workers, an all-time high, were employed in manufacturing at the peak of the war effort in 1943. Although this figure dropped rapidly when peace was restored, it was still at 22 percent when the postwar period ended in 1975.[6]

Unemployment during this era was consistently low, and wage growth was consistently high. The Bureau of Labor Statistics described unemployment as being "relatively stable during the 1950s and 1960s, usually between 3 and 4.5 percent."[7] From January 1948 through December 1975, the average monthly unemployment rate was 4.9 percent.[8] As for wages, during that same twenty-eight-year span inflation-adjusted hourly compensation for all nonfarm workers rose by 93 percent.[9] Real manufacturing wages in the 1950s rose even faster as these wages shot upward by 50 percent in only a decade.[10] No other period since World War II has witnessed a comparable growth in manufacturing wages. And inflation-adjusted per capita GDP rose by a postwar record of 73 percent between 1950 and 1975.[11]

Also notable is the fact that in most years from the end of the war through 1975, America ran a trade surplus—that is, it exported more goods and services than it imported.[12] Throughout the postwar period, US private investment abroad was a major factor in the redevelopment of Europe and Japan, as well as in the rise of Korea and Taiwan. Those investments still enrich Americans today, with S&P 500 companies earning approximately 40 percent of their revenues on production and sales outside of the United States.[13] By any definition, the postwar period in America was the very definition of a golden age of manufacturing.

THE MYTH

By most historic and contemporary accounts, the golden age of American manufacturing ended in the mid-1970s, and with it went opportunity and prosperity for ordinary Americans.[14] Taking for granted that

Americans in the early twenty-first century are less fortunate than their parents, in 2013 President Barack Obama looked back with nostalgia on the past, professing that "during the post–World War II years, the economic ground felt stable and secure for most Americans, and the future looked brighter."[15] President Biden was no less nostalgic for an economy driven by manufacturing. Just days after being sworn into office in 2021, while signing an executive order titled "Strengthening American Manufacturing," he promised to "rebuild America" by making manufacturing "the engine of American prosperity now."[16] *New York Times* writer Jim Tankersley expressed the sentiment of many in pining for "the Golden Era of the middle class that boomed after World War II."[17]

These—and countless similar—wistful recollections of the postwar era convey the presumption that the economy has failed ordinary Americans during the fifty years since the end of this golden age of American manufacturing. Much of the blame for this perceived stagnation is attributed to what is viewed as America's worsening fortunes on the global economic stage. In contrast to postwar America's thriving as a net exporter and the world's dominant manufacturing nation, in the half-century since—and especially after China joined the World Trade Organization (WTO) in 2001—good jobs are said to have been destroyed and wages kept flat by lopsided trade agreements, unfair trading practices abroad, and imprudent tariff reductions at home.

Writing in 1993, just before the installation of the North American Free Trade Agreement (NAFTA) and amid discussions of transforming the General Agreement on Tariffs and Trade (GATT) into the more comprehensive WTO, consumer advocate Ralph Nader predicted that "the Fortune 200's GATT and NAFTA agenda . . . would cost jobs [and] depress wages levels."[18] In 2016 two-time Republican presidential aspirant Pat Buchanan agreed with Nader, flatly stating that "these trade deals have de-industrialized America."[19] Campaigning for the presidency in 2016, Donald Trump concurred:

> We allowed foreign countries to subsidize their goods, devalue their currencies, violate their agreements and cheat in every way imaginable, and our politicians did nothing about it. Trillions of our dollars and millions

of our jobs flowed overseas as a result. I have visited cities and towns across this country where one-third or even half of manufacturing jobs have been wiped out in the last 20 years. Today, we import nearly $800 billion more in goods than we export. We can't continue to do that. . . . America has lost nearly 1/3 of its manufacturing jobs since 1997. . . . At the center of this catastrophe are two trade deals pushed by Bill and Hillary Clinton.[20]

In his 2017 inaugural address, Trump portrayed the United States as having suffered an "American carnage," in no small part because of America's increased trade with the rest of the world:

We've enriched foreign industry at the expense of American industry. . . . We've made other countries rich while the wealth, strength, and confidence of our country has disappeared over the horizon. One by one, the factories shuttered and left our shores, with not even a thought about the millions upon millions of American workers left behind. The wealth of our middle class has been ripped from their homes and then redistributed across the entire world. . . . We must protect our borders from the ravages of other countries making our products, stealing our companies, and destroying our jobs. Protection will lead to great prosperity and strength.[21]

Although on the opposite side of the political spectrum from Donald Trump, Sen. Elizabeth Warren (D-Massachusetts) echoes Trump's claims about trade. Seeking her party's 2020 nomination for the presidency, in 2019 Senator Warren declared, "We have had a lot of problems with losing jobs, but the principal reason has been bad trade policy."[22] Senator Warren isn't alone in the ranks of those on the political left who share Trump's skepticism of trade. Other prominent Democrats who vigorously oppose free trade include, but are hardly limited to, Rep. Marcy Kaptur (D-Ohio), former three-term US Senator Sherrod Brown (D-Ohio), and Sen. Bernie Sanders (I-Vermont).[23]

While many people expected that President Biden would resume the practice of Presidents Reagan, Bush (I and II), Clinton, and Obama—of negotiating for lower tariffs through trade-expansion agreements—he instead kept most of Trump's protectionist measures in place—even expanding some of them—and thus proving that skepticism of free trade remains prevalent across the political divide.[24] This skepticism shows no signs of waning. Just as the 2024 presidential campaign was kicking into high gear, Trump's former US trade representative, Robert Lighthizer, took to the pages of *The Economist* to claim that "evidence of the failure of free-trade policy can be seen in the effect it has had on America's middle class. The economy lost millions of high-paying jobs, and the earnings of American workers have been stagnant for decades."[25]

Trump, Biden, Lighthizer, and other prominent public officials, such as Senate Democratic Leader Charles Schumer (D–New York), believe that foreign trade has been devastating for America's economy and point with great anxiety to the long string of annual US trade deficits.[26] Starting in 1976, the value of American imports has annually exceeded the value of American exports. Over the entire forty-eight years—1976 through 2023—Americans imported, in 2023 dollars, $22.2 trillion more in goods and services than they've exported.[27] It appears that Americans have been consuming more than they've produced for nearly half a century, a fact that is said to explain why the absolute number of workers in American manufacturing peaked in 1979, soon after the run of chronic trade deficits began. As of October 2024, the absolute number of Americans employed in manufacturing was down by 34 percent from its peak in June 1979.[28]

Warnings about US trade deficits aren't issued exclusively by public officials. In 1998 Economic Policy Institute economist Robert E. Scott spoke on the topic to the Senate Finance Committee, asserting that "the steady growth in our trade deficits over the past two decades has eliminated millions of U.S. manufacturing jobs. . . . For the past two decades, our living standards have stagnated, and the level of income inequality in our society has increased dramatically."[29] In 2015 the economist John Komlos of the University of Munich wrote that "by outsourcing jobs, it [the United States] has relegated millions of U.S. workers—especially the low-skilled ones—to the underemployment rolls. As the country imports products it could have produced at home, the trade deficit relegates many more to poverty . . . and to food stamps . . . and to near poverty."[30]

Rochester Institute of Technology economist Amitrajeet Batabyal—in a paper whose title declares that "International Trade Has Cost Americans Millions of Jobs"—insists that "the trade deficit has had different impacts on regions within the United States. Some regions are devastated by lay-offs and factory closings, while others are surviving but not growing the way they might if new factories were opening and existing plants were hiring more workers."[31] American Compass founder Oren Cass has also sounded the alarm against US trade deficits, claiming that "large, per-sistent trade deficits are bad for America."[32]

The popular wisdom on trade is clear. It holds that America's economy has been severely damaged over the past half-century by excessive expo-sure to the global economy. As Lighthizer writes, "America has come as close as almost any major country in history to eliminating significant tariffs. It was a bold experiment, and it has failed."[33] In his opinion, pro-tective tariffs "are the vital part of any serious reindustrialization" and are necessary "to reduce America's trade deficit."[34] When campaigning in early 2024, President Trump promised to implement those tariffs, starting with a levy on all imports of at least 10 percent.[35]

The notion remains prevalent that America's manufacturing sector has been, in President Biden's words, "hollowed out."[36] This belief in the decline of US manufacturing since the end of the postwar era is at the root of today's prevalent belief that trade has hurt ordinary American workers. Protectionists argue that since the end of the postwar era, each expansion of trade has harmed America. Fortunately for America and the world, their arguments are verifiably wrong.

DEBUNKING THE MYTH THAT TRADE HOLLOWED OUT AMERICAN MANUFACTURING

After World War II, there emerged a strong consensus in the United States and the Western world in favor of free and open trade. Scarred by the economic destruction wrought during the Great Depression by the Smoot-Hawley Tariff of 1930, as well as sobered by the challenges of rebuilding Europe and Japan and stopping the spread of communism,

Americans saw economic isolationism as untenable.[37] According to Dartmouth College economist Douglas Irwin, "to officials at the time, the lesson of the 1930s was absolutely clear: Like appeasement in the realm of diplomacy, protectionism was a serious economic policy mistake that helped make the decade [of the 1930s] a disaster."[38] From Truman to Reagan to Obama, on a bipartisan basis, protectionism was not viewed as a viable national policy.

This openness to trade was only strengthened by the United States' emergence from the war with its productive capacity intact, with a modern capital base, and with a trained labor force—the legacies of having served, in FDR's words, as "the great arsenal of democracy."[39] Much of the developed world was in rubble, and fifty million people, including a significant percentage of the skilled labor force in Europe and Asia, were dead. As a result, America enjoyed a virtual monopoly in heavy manufacturing for the next quarter century.

Led by the United States and Great Britain, the General Agreement on Tariffs and Trade was launched in 1947 with the express goal of lowering tariff rates worldwide.[40] But because of the wartime ruin, global trade increased only slowly at first, with the United States dominating the world market. As the Marshall Plan helped promote the rebuilding of Europe and other aid went to Japan, and as US private firms invested heavily abroad, the demand for US goods soared, generating large trade surpluses.[41] Under these unique immediate postwar conditions—the result of a cataclysmic event hopefully never to recur—US industries could easily accede to demands for higher wages from industry-wide labor unions, which had been strengthened by New Deal legislation. The granting of higher wages across major industrial sectors did not disadvantage individual companies relative to their US competitors, because the wage increases were largely granted by all their domestic competitors, and foreign competition was still negligible. As noted by University of Connecticut economist Richard Langlois, "the hobbling of the country's foreign competitors in the war had endowed American firms with a decided, if arguably artificial, comparative advantage in mass production, one that continued to generate rents for the manufacturing sector through the 1960s. This created a weak selection environment in which ineffective structures and practices, including those driven by antirust policy and industry-wide unionism, could endure unchallenged."[42]

But challenges did eventually come as Europe and Asia rebuilt. This extraordinary global dominance of American industry could, of course, not last. And it didn't. By the mid-1970s, Europe and Japan had rebuilt, and Korea and Taiwan had become industrialized. A system of wealth creation based on trade and market-driven economies was beginning to crush the Soviet Union and transform China, and it would eventually win the Cold War. Combined with major advances in technology, especially the advent of containerized shipping in the 1960s, these developments brought economic opportunity and greater prosperity to billions.[43] With this resurgence of economic activity in Europe and Asia, America's share of global manufacturing output started to fall and, along with it, America's share of global manufactured exports. By 1977 the global share of American manufactured exports had returned to its prewar level, although, in absolute terms, US industrial output had grown by more than 611 percent since 1938.[44] Yet the memory of America's immediate postwar economic experience fuels the myth that the postwar period was the norm and that the growing prosperity and economic successes of other nations, along with our growing trade deficits, have "hollowed out" America's manufacturing sector and, thus, caused the incomes of ordinary Americans to stagnate for decades.

In fact, there has been no stagnation in the income of working Americans. In real purchasing-power dollars, 66.3 percent of all American households currently have incomes that would have put them in the top 20 percent of income recipients in 1967.[45] Nor has the labor market been stagnant. In America in 2025, total employment is more than twice as high as it was in 1975. Additionally, the average monthly unemployment rate over the most recent five non-pandemic years was, at 4 percent, more than two percentage points lower than the average monthly unemployment rate (6.1 percent) for the last five years (1971–1975) of America's golden age of manufacturing.[46]

Most important for debunking the myth is that there has also been no hollowing out of US manufacturing. While America's *share* of global manufacturing output and manufactured exports has declined, this fact alone says nothing about what has happened to the absolute size of American manufacturing output, industrial capacity, or manufactured exports. In reality, each of these has risen. America's global share has fallen only because other countries have recovered from the destruction of the war or developed economically and, in the process, increased their manufacturing outputs and exports. Mistaking the enrichment of other countries relative to America for American economic stagnation or even decline violates both logic and the lessons of history. It is based on the false notion that if one party gains from trade, the other party must lose. The reality is that when people in one country engage in free exchange with the people of another country, while some industries decline, more productive industries rise, wages go up, and the people of both countries benefit.

Manufacturing Output and Capacity

Far from declining over the past half century, American manufacturing output has risen and thrives to this day. Except during recessions, manufacturing output continued to grow after the postwar period ended. US manufacturing output in October 2024 was 12.3 percent *higher* than when China joined the WTO, 55.6 percent *higher* than when NAFTA began, and 173 percent *above* its level when America last ran an annual trade surplus.[47] These facts plainly contradict President Trump's 2016 campaign line: "We don't make things anymore."[48]

The state of American manufacturing looks even better when we track manufacturing firms' *value added*, which is the market value of manufacturing output in excess of the value of the inputs used in its production.[49] In inflation-adjusted dollars, manufacturing value added reached its all-time high in the second quarter of 2024—at a level more than 34 percent higher than when China joined the WTO.[50] Not only do we Americans continue to make plenty of things, but the economic value that we currently add when we make these things is far and away the highest in the world.[51]

Given the consistently strong growth of manufacturing output and value added, it's no surprise that investments in American manufacturing have also grown. In inflation-adjusted dollars, the total amount of investment made in American manufacturing in 2019 (just before the pandemic) was 25 percent more than it was in 2001 when China joined the WTO, and 215 percent more than in 1975.[52] Interestingly, the growth in the total annual amount of investment in American manufacturing over the twenty-four-year period from 1952 (the first year for which the data are available) through 1975—all golden age of manufacturing years—was 127 percent in inflation-adjusted dollars. Yet in the next twenty-four-year period, from 1975 through 1998—after the golden age—the growth in inflation-adjusted annual manufacturing investment was *higher*, at 158 percent.[53] This investment was made not only by US-headquartered companies but also by foreign investors. Cato Institute trade scholar Scott Lincicome has shown that "among Organisation for Economic Co-operation and Development nations . . . the United States is the top recipient of manufacturing foreign direct investment (FDI)—more than doubling the second-place nation."[54] Because no one invests in an enterprise or economy believed to be uncompetitive or the hapless victim of bad trade policy, this robust investment in America reveals that investors with skin in the game do not regard the golden age of American manufacturing as having ended in the 1970s.

And these investments further expand America's industrial capacity—that is, Americans' ability to make things. Industrial capacity in the United States has increased dramatically since the end of the war. As shown in figure 4.1, after growing steadily from 1967 until 1994 (the year NAFTA took effect), growth in US industrial capacity *accelerated* until the 2001 recession. Although this growth then slowed, it did not stop, and it certainly didn't turn negative. As of October 2024, America's capacity to produce industrial outputs was at an all-time high and 11 percent greater than when China joined the WTO, 63 percent greater than when NAFTA took effect, and 145 percent greater than in 1975.[55]

The slowing of the growth of industrial capacity at the turn of the millennium, as shown in figure 4.1, is a worldwide phenomenon. It coincided with the rise of the tech industry. Relatively few major tech companies have employees who are classified by the Bureau of Labor Statistics as

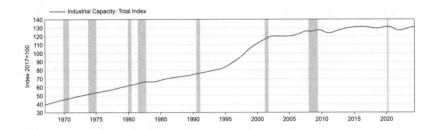

Figure 4.1. Industrial Capacity: Total Index. *Source:* Federal Reserve Bank of St. Louis, "Industrial Capacity: Total Index (CAPB50001S)," FRED Economic Data, accessed December 2, 2024, https://fred.stlouisfed.org/series/CAPB50001S.

working in manufacturing. As the famous economist and public servant George Schultz predicted, the decision by the BLS not to classify programming as manufacturing, although software now accounts for half the value of a new car, distorts the measure of manufacturing output and employment. The design of tech products and computer chips is dominated by American tech giants. This design is a major component in the value of those products and chips, yet very little of the US tech industry's production is counted in the official statistics as manufacturing output.[56]

The explosion in the tech industry since 2000, along with the fact that almost all of the US tech industry's output is counted in official government statistics as services, has been a major cause of the 7.6 percent rise in the percentage of GDP produced by the service industry.[57] The flattening out of industrial capacity shown in figure 4.1 coincides with the rise of the tech industry and, at least in part, reflects the fact that little of the production of US tech companies is counted as manufacturing.

Manufacturing Employment

Many of the claims about America's allegedly hollowed-out manufacturing sector are rooted in the failure to distinguish manufacturing *output* from manufacturing *employment*. Manufacturing employment, as a share of total employment, has been in secular decline in every developed country in the world since at least the start of the twenty-first century.[58] By all outward and visible signs, mechanization and computerization in the twenty-first century are reducing the number of workers employed to produce a fixed value of manufactured output in the same way that mechanization and hybrid crops in the twentieth century reduced the number of workers employed to produce a fixed value of agricultural output. Unlike manufacturing output, therefore, manufacturing employment in the United States has indeed declined, and it continues to decline on a secular basis.

The absolute number of manufacturing jobs in America reached its zenith in June 1979, just as the world's production capacity had fully recovered from World War II. This number has since fallen significantly.[59] A more meaningful measure—manufacturing employment as a share of total nonfarm employment in the United States—has also fallen. As noted earlier, this figure peaked at 39 percent in November 1943 and has declined steadily in the eighty years since. Even in the first three decades following the end of World War II, the percentage of America's nonfarm workers employed in manufacturing fell by ten percentage points, from 32 percent to 22 percent. While the share of manufacturing employment in the United States did, in fact, decline after world manufacturing recovered, this decline was a continuation, without any significant acceleration, of a downward trend that began decades earlier. As of October 2024, only 8.1 percent of America's nonfarm workers held jobs classified by the BLS as "manufacturing."[60]

The simultaneous rise in US manufacturing output and fall in manufacturing employment indicates that manufacturing workers have become much more productive over the postwar years. This conclusion is confirmed by figure 4.2, originally constructed by University of Michigan–Flint economist Mark Perry in 2012 and recently updated by him to 2023, as it shows the remarkable improvement in manufacturing workers' productivity from the end of the war through the end of the Great Recession. Perry finds that "factory workers [in 2011] produced more output in an hour than workers in 1946 produced in a day."[61] This massive increase in per-worker output was produced not by longer worker hours but instead by successful investments in both physical and human capital.[62]

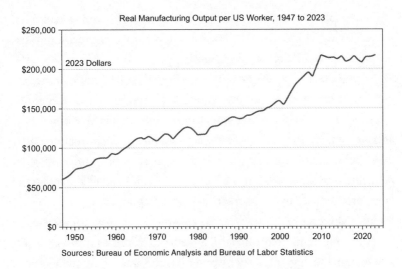

Figure 4.2. Real Manufacturing Output per Worker, 1947 to 2023

Although the rate of growth in the productivity of workers in the non-farm-business sector slowed very slightly after the Great Recession ended, it nevertheless continued to rise.[63] But the productivity of manufacturing-sector labor, as shown in figure 4.2, peaked at the end of the Great Recession and has since stagnated.[64] There is no consensus on why productivity across the economy slowed after 2010 and stagnated in manufacturing. Some of this decline in labor productivity might be attributable to the surge of the regulatory burden imposed on businesses during the tepid Obama recovery. In addition, protectionist policies by the Trump and Biden administrations and the retaliation they generated drove up the costs of component parts and made US manufacturing less efficient. The Bureau of Labor Statistics attributes at least part of the decline in productivity to manufacturers hiring lower-productivity workers.[65]

When technological improvements simply produce more of the same product, productivity is easy to measure. But when productivity creates totally new or dramatically improved products, productivity is extremely difficult to measure, and the reliability of productivity measures becomes increasingly questionable.[66] With the rapid development and implementation of new technology that is occurring today throughout the economy, the decline in both manufacturing and economy-wide productivity is difficult to understand.

As manufacturing-worker productivity started to stagnate in 2011, more workers were required to produce greater amounts of manufactured products. While employment in manufacturing continued to fall as a percentage of the workforce, total employment in manufacturing rose slightly, showing that one way to increase employment in manufacturing is to make labor less productive.[67] Unfortunately, stagnation in labor productivity makes workers and society poorer.

Since the end of World War II, as Americans have increased their spending on items that official US statistics count as services, and as real manufacturing output per worker has exploded, employment in US manufacturing has declined. If the decline in American manufacturing employment were mainly caused, as protectionists assert, by manufacturing activities leaving America and setting up shop on foreign soil, American manufacturing output and industrial capacity would also have declined. Yet both rose, implying that the fall in manufacturing employment was primarily the result not of a decline in American manufacturing but, instead, of a rise in American manufacturing productivity.

The fact that the loss of American manufacturing jobs was caused overwhelmingly by improved technology rather than by trade was documented in 2017 by Ball State University economists Michael Hicks and Srikant Devaraj. They found that "almost 88 percent of job losses in manufacturing in recent years can be attributable to productivity growth, and the long-term changes to manufacturing employment are mostly linked to the productivity of American factories" rather than to imports. The study found that automation had an effect on manufacturing jobs that was 7.3 times bigger than was the effect of imports.[68] Other studies assign a somewhat smaller role to automation at reducing manufacturing employment than do Hicks and Devaraj, with these studies finding that some of this decline is due also to the increase in consumer demand for services relative to manufactured goods.[69] But no one doubts that the single largest cause of the decline in manufacturing employment is increased manufacturing-worker productivity.

The fall in manufacturing employment is not confined to the United States; it is occurring across the globe. Harvard economist Robert Z. Lawrence found that the share of manufacturing employment as a percentage of total employment has fallen steadily—and at rates comparable to those in the United States—since the early 1970s in Australia, Canada, France, Italy, Japan, the Netherlands, and the United Kingdom.[70] This downward trend has taken hold even in China, although at a slower rate.[71] The share of the workforce employed in manufacturing has continued to fall in the twenty-first century not only in the United States but in all developed and developing countries. The only places where manufacturing employment is growing today is in the least-developed countries, which are only now beginning to significantly engage in manufacturing.[72] The bottom line is that American manufacturing workers have increasingly specialized in producing higher-valued outputs, while many of the lower-value jobs have been replaced by machines both in the United States and in developing countries.

Since the Reagan economic boom began in 1983, automation has been increasingly driven by competition for American workers, who have become better educated and benefit from growing employment opportunities. Service-sector employment and wages exploded after World War II.[73] In 1967, 46 percent of Americans twenty-five and older had not completed high school, and only about 9 percent had graduated from a four-year college. By 2021 the number of Americans in this age group without a high school diploma had plunged to 8.9 percent, while those with at least a four-year college degree had more than quadrupled to 37.9 percent.[74] Very few of these highly educated Americans were looking for jobs as laborers in factories, mills, and shipyards. Unable to profit while paying wages to attract many of these workers away from employment in high-paying service sectors such as medicine, research, law, finance, higher education, and information technology, manufacturers responded by investing heavily in automation.

The resulting decades-long decline in manufacturing employment mimics what happened a century earlier in agriculture. In the late nineteenth century and the twentieth century, increasing opportunities for workers in cities and towns drove up wages, thus inciting farmers to implement labor-saving agricultural technologies. Farm jobs plummeted, yet agricultural output rose because agricultural technology improved. Farm jobs weren't stolen; they were abandoned for better opportunities off the farm. From 75 percent in 1800, the percentage of Americans working on the farm fell to 33 percent by 1900, then to 1.6 percent by 2000, while the value of farm production soared.[75] Is it any surprise that the same process is at work in the twentieth and twenty-first centuries in manufacturing? Had we, the authors of this book, followed in our own family's footsteps, we would have spent our working lives as laborers in manufacturing plants—Gramm in a textile mill and Boudreaux in a shipyard. Instead, prodded by our mothers through college and graduate school, each of us spent our working lives in the service sector (education, government, and finance). The jobs we chose to hold pay more and offer better working conditions than the ones we would have performed in the mill and shipyard. We weren't denied those manufacturing jobs to our detriment; it was more that those manufacturing jobs were destroyed by our seizing better opportunities for our benefit and that of our families. This same process was at work for millions of other American families.

An analysis of manufacturing employment is not complete without some note of the rise of the new economic colossus in the American economy: the tech industry. The explosion of the value of high-tech goods produced in America and the number of high-paying jobs in the tech industry has become an increasingly important factor in the labor and equity markets in the twenty-first century. The decision of the Bureau of Labor Statistics to exclude programming from the definition of manufacturing has had a significant impact on measured manufacturing production and employment. This has become especially important as the technical components in the value of manufactured goods have increased dramatically. The people who produce, for instance, new SUVs—the workers who make the tires, the axles, the frame, the body, and the seats—are counted as manufacturing employees, but those who did the programming and the design work behind all of the technical gadgets that make the modern automobile are generally not counted as manufacturing employees. With the development of artificial intelligence and the value it is likely to add to American productivity, this statistical distortion is destined to get even larger. It is important, therefore, when noting the decline in manufacturing jobs, that we take into account the rapid growth in tech jobs, which are classified as being in the service sector and, on average, pay more than twice as much as jobs in the manufacturing sector.[76]

Trade Agreements

Despite the relentless thriving of the American economy in general and of American manufacturing in particular, trade critics like Donald Trump and Robert Lighthizer on the political right and Bernie Sanders and Hillary Clinton on the left assert that postwar agreements to expand trade were "self-destructive" and led to a "disaster."[77] An examination of postwar trade agreements shows that the agreements signed by the United States have required US trading partners to lower their tariffs, on average, more than Americans were required to lower theirs. For example, after China joined the WTO, Beijing cut the average tariff rate it imposed on foreign-produced goods from 14.6 percent in 2000 to 4.7 percent in 2014. But the United States didn't change its tariffs on Chinese-produced goods.[78] Moreover, China's December 2001 admission to the World Trade Organization did not, contrary to some claims, accelerate the loss of manufacturing jobs.[79] From January 1976, when America's still-unbroken stream of annual trade deficits began, through December 2001—when China joined the WTO—manufacturing jobs, as a share of all nonfarm jobs, fell at an average monthly rate of 0.193 percent. Since then (through October 2024), that rate of decline *slowed* to 0.143 percent.[80]

Under NAFTA, Mexico reduced its tariffs on imports from the United States from roughly 12.5 percent to zero, while Canadian tariffs on US goods dropped from roughly 4.2 percent to zero. In return, US tariffs on Mexican and Canadian imports fell from 2.7 percent to zero.[81] Contrary to Ross Perot's dire prediction that NAFTA would cause "a giant sucking sound" of US jobs being drawn into Mexico, in the seven years between the time NAFTA took effect (January 1994) and the end of the century (December 2000), US nonfarm employment grew by 20 percent and US manufacturing output by 45 percent. As of October 2024, total nonfarm employment was 41 percent higher than in January 1994, and manufacturing output was higher by 56 percent.[82] Interestingly, in the seven years from January 1994 through December 2000, the total number of US manufacturing jobs rose by 2 percent, after having fallen by 3.5 percent in the seven years immediately before NAFTA took effect.[83] Many of the imports from Mexico were component parts used in US manufacturing. Cheaper component parts undoubtedly made US-manufactured goods more competitive in the United States and around the world.

More generally, trade agreements have lowered trade barriers worldwide and established a rules-based system of global commerce. Since the creation of GATT in 1947, the average tariff rates of member countries have fallen significantly, from about 40 percent on dutiable imports to around 5 percent.[84] Although offset somewhat by rising nontariff barriers to trade, the overall result of GATT/WTO and other trade agreements has been to expand global trade enormously. Today the volume of world trade is forty-five times greater than it was in 1947.[85]

Countries, including the United States, sometimes cheat on their trade-agreement commitments. We have every right and obligation to enforce trade agreements. When disputes under the agreements arise, the first step should be to attempt to settle these questions according to the provisions found in the agreements, which, for the WTO, includes submitting disputes to that agency's appellate body. Unfortunately, starting with the Obama administration but accelerating under Trump, the US government has effectively killed the WTO's appellate body by blocking the appointment of new judges as openings have emerged and, in the process, denying the enforcement agency the ability to operate.[86] The Biden administration has continued to block the WTO's enforcement process.[87]

It is the height of hypocrisy to complain, on the one hand, that trade partners are cheating and the WTO is powerless to do anything about it while, on the other hand, actively refusing to enable the WTO to operate the enforcement mechanisms that are central to the trade agreements we have signed. Protectionist policies under Presidents Trump and Biden violate the very trade agreements we have signed, and it has been the policy of both administrations to deny the enforcement agency a quorum so that it will not bring action against the United States.

It is important to understand that small groups can exert tremendous political influence in America. For a century the US government funded an expensive farm program in the name of saving the family farm, but all the while the bulk of the money was going to large farms and corporate entities as the number of family farms plummeted. Political support for these farm programs, in addition to the vested interests of farm-state members of Congress, was due to the fact that the farm vote was, in national elections, a swing vote that the farm program could move. When President Trump imposed tariffs on steel and aluminum in the name of national defense and then applied those tariffs in violation of NAFTA against Mexico and Canada, only a tiny number of workers were affected positively. But because these workers are swing voters in the very states that determine the outcomes of presidential elections, when Biden took office the steel and aluminum tariffs were among the few Trump policies that he did not overturn. The fact that there are many more workers in industries that use steel and aluminum as inputs than there are in mills that produce steel and aluminum is beside the point. As long as unionized industrial workers are swing voters, protectionist policies advertised as boosting manufacturing are likely to continue. The benefits of these tariffs are concentrated, while their higher costs are dispersed.

TRADE DEFICITS AND ECONOMIC GROWTH

A constant theme among protectionists is that trade deficits, which occur when Americans purchase more foreign goods and services than US producers sell to foreigners, and capital surpluses, which occur when foreigners invest more in the United States than Americans invest abroad, make the United States an economic loser in the process. According to President Trump, "since 2000 the U.S. has racked up $17 trillion in cumulative trade deficits with the world. Only a fool or fanatic would dismiss these facts as irrelevant."[88] He further asserts that when foreigners are net investors in the United States, there is a "hemorrhaging of America's lifeblood."[89] But this is a myth.

A good start in debunking this myth is to look at our national experience with trade deficits and surpluses and, hence, with positive and negative net foreign investment. When the United States operated under the gold standard, if imports exceeded exports and that difference was not offset by gold coming into the country in the form of net foreign investments, the country lost gold, the money supply declined, and nominal prices and wages fell. The fall in prices and wages reduced imports by making domestic goods cheaper relative to foreign goods. At lower prices, the demand for American exports rose and investing in the United States became more attractive to both foreign and domestic investors. Prices and wages declined until the fall in imports, rise in exports, and increases in net foreign investment combined to stop the outflow of gold. If exports exceeded imports and the excess of exports over imports was not offset by Americans investing more abroad than foreigners invested in the United States, the quantity of gold coming into the country would rise, and the process would work in reverse. Under the gold standard, prices and wages adjust until the trade balance offsets the capital account balance.

With today's market-determined ("flexible") exchange rates, when net exports don't equal net capital flows, the supply and demand for dollars are unequal, and the value of the dollar rises or falls to bring the two into balance. In either case, the value of the dollar changes or gold flows into and out of the country until the nation's deficit or surplus in its trade balance is offset by surpluses or deficits in its capital account balance.

From 1607, when the first English settler stepped ashore at Jamestown, to 1896, America ran chronic trade deficits.[90] As a beacon of economic freedom and opportunity, America attracted foreign labor and capital and generated economic growth on a scale unprecedented in human history.[91] From the end of the Civil War to the turn of the twentieth century, fourteen million immigrants arrived in search of freedom and opportunity and found both. In America, capital coming principally from Holland and Britain met labor from all over the world; they then fell in love with each other and transformed America into an economic colossus.

The United States ran trade deficits and capital surpluses as foreign capital continued to seek the higher returns generated by American industrialization in the post–Civil War period. Far from a "hemorrhaging of America's lifeblood," these investments enriched both America and the foreigners who invested in it. By 1900 industrialization in America had reached par with the developed countries of the world, and Americans were beginning to make significant investments abroad. By 1915 US earnings on foreign investments exceeded foreign earnings on US investments.[92] World trade reached a peak in 1910 that would not be equaled again until 1975.

US exports soared in the aftermath of the destruction in Europe from World War I. With the Great Depression and the global spread of protectionist policies, US exports and imports spiraled downward. The United States ran trade surpluses in 102 of the 120 months of the 1930s, a decade that began with the Smoot-Hawley Tariff and during which Americans remained mired in a deep depression.[93] The result of that protectionist regime was a collapse in the world's trading system, which further deepened the Great Depression.[94]

From the end of World War II through 1975, the United States ran trade surpluses in most years and prospered. With much of the developed world in ruins, America's intact productive capacity ensured that American industry dominated world manufacturing. US exports generally outpaced imports for three decades. The Marshall Plan and other aid packages, as well as a surge in private US investment abroad, provided the initial impetus for rebuilding the economies of Europe and Japan. Massive postwar exports drove up the demand for US labor, producing growth in wages and benefits that far outstripped any comparable period since. These extraordinary gains were a product of postwar trade. Protectionists pretend that, starting in the late 1970s, increased trade ended the postwar golden age of American manufacturing, but they leave out the fact that the destruction of the war and the explosion of trade in the immediate postwar period produced this "golden age" in the first place.

By the mid-1970s, Europe and Japan had risen from the ashes of World War II, and Korea and Taiwan had become major industrial powers. But, in the process, US trade surpluses vanished. Starting in 1976, America has run annual trade deficits for forty-eight consecutive years, and there is no end to these deficits in sight.

During the Reagan revitalization, which began in the first quarter of 1983, strong economic growth attracted large inflows of foreign investment. As a result, the real value of the US trade deficit in goods and services in Reagan's final year in the White House, 1988, was more than triple its 1980 value. The Clinton boom that began four years later had an even bigger impact on the trade deficit. By the end of Bill Clinton's eight-year tenure, the real value of America's annual trade deficit was nearly ten times larger than in the year he was first elected (1992). By contrast, during the weakest period of postwar recovery, 2009–2016, the trade deficit *fell*. In the last year of President Obama's second term (2016), the trade deficit was 38 percent lower than in 2008. With President Trump's tax cuts and regulatory relief, economic growth expanded, and even after the implementation of his tariffs in 2018, by the start of the pandemic, America's trade deficit was 23 percent higher than when Trump took office at the beginning of 2017.[95]

These experiences show that the more dynamic and open is America's economy, the more attractive it is to global investors. It appears to be a given that when the American economy is performing near its potential, it becomes an irresistible magnet for the world's talent and capital. How does a BMW plant in South Carolina or a Kia plant in Georgia make the United States poorer?

While it is difficult to make the argument that America loses when foreign companies build new facilities in America, what about when foreigners buy existing American companies, as when Nippon Steel attempted to purchase US Steel? Do such purchases mean that the United States is getting poorer? No. Those who best know the value of US Steel are its shareholders, and they obviously think the sale will make them richer and allow them to invest in areas that will yield them higher rates of return on their capital. If their assessment is correct—and they have powerful incentives not to err—the sale will raise the value of their capital and the wealth of the nation.

Nor is it true that when American businesses or the US government borrow from foreigners that Americans' net wealth necessarily declines. Debt can lead to riches or poverty depending on how productively the borrowed funds are used. When *government* borrows either domestically or from foreigners, we should be concerned as to how efficiently the money is used, as it is seldom used in ways that generate income to allow the government to repay the debt plus interest. The problem, however, is with the government and not with those who lend the money.

In the nearly fifty years since the United States last ran a trade surplus, what has happened to the inflation-adjusted value of America's capital stock? Has our country been "plundered," and has there been a "hemorrhaging of America's lifeblood," as President Trump claims? Again, no. Since 1975, when America last ran an annual trade surplus, the inflation-adjusted value of America's capital stock has risen 178 percent, with a 36 percent increase since China joined the WTO.[96] Furthermore, the real net worth of the average American household just prior to the pandemic in 2019 was 106 percent higher than it was when China joined the WTO.[97]

America's trade deficits and capital-account surpluses, which result from the free choices of consumers and investors attempting to maximize their individual well-being in a highly competitive economy, are more like blood *infusions* that strengthen America's economy. The inflation-adjusted aggregate level of foreign direct investment in the United States was, in 2019, 114 times greater than in 1975, when America ran its last annual trade surplus.[98] Trade economist Daniel Ikenson estimates that foreign investments in US manufacturing are now responsible for 8.4 percent of US manufacturing output.[99] Postwar America has been a magnet for talent and capital, both of which provided fuel to keep America the strongest economy in the world. What Pericles said about Athens 2,500 years ago can accurately be said about America today: "Where the prize is highest, there, too, will you find the best and the bravest."[100]

Perhaps most importantly, there is no correlation between trade deficits and job creation. Figure 4.3 plots US civilian employment (shown by the light line) against the US goods and services trade balance (shown by the dark line). There is no evidence that the trend of employment growth in America changed when the United States started running annual trade deficits in 1976. The reason is straightforward: Investments in America fuel job creation no less than does demand for American exports.

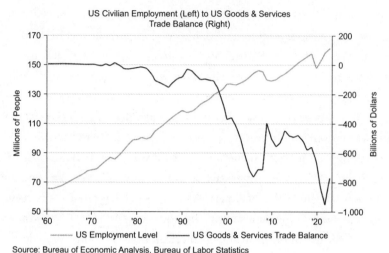

US Civilian Employment (Left) to US Goods & Services Trade Balance (Right)

Source: Bureau of Economic Analysis, Bureau of Labor Statistics

Figure 4.3. US Civilian Employment and the US Goods and Services Trade Balance. *Source:* Assembled for the authors by Nicholls State University economist Jonathan Murphy from data from the US Bureau of Economic Analysis and the US Bureau of Labor Statistics.

If it seems counterintuitive that trade deficits do not hamper America's historical economic success, consider that by focusing only on the balance of trade in goods and services, we engage in single-entry bookkeeping. This focus misses half the picture. As alluded to above, in every year when the United States ran a trade deficit it also ran a capital *surplus*, which provided capital to expand productivity, employment, and economic growth. It is a simple truth that when people trade freely with buyers and sellers abroad, the total value of the trade balance and the capital balance must equal out. Only governments and criminals can take more than they give.

PROTECTIONISM AND TRADE DEFICITS

The value of the dollar is set on the world's largest and most nearly perfect market. Its value reflects economic decisions made by billions of foreigners who seek dollars to buy American goods and services and invest in the United States, as well as by hundreds of millions of Americans who demand foreign currencies to buy foreign goods and services and invest abroad. Government transfers, such as foreign aid, are a mere rounding error in a world dollar market that averages $6.6 trillion of transactions every day.[101] If, for a nanosecond, the supply and demand for dollars were unequal and our trade and capital accounts did not exactly offset each other, the value of the dollar would rise or fall to make it so.

When viewed in the context of the world market for US dollars, it becomes clear that protectionist policies, absent any other changes, don't deliver the promised reduction in trade deficits. Nothing proves this fact better than the evidence of the impact of Trump's first tariffs, which were implemented in early 2018. Goods subject to these tariffs became more expensive, and Americans instead bought more domestic substitutes; however, the United States produced these substitutes less efficiently and sold them at higher prices than were available on the world market. By reducing demand for foreign goods, tariffs reduced the dollars Americans were trying to convert into foreign currencies and thus decreased the supply of US dollars in the world currency market, raising the value of the dollar and making American exports less attractive. The result was lower employment in the industries in which the United States is more efficient and most competitive, and higher employment in industries in which the United States is less efficient. Protectionism didn't create jobs on net, and the nation was made poorer as the economy became less efficient. Jobs were simply transferred from efficient and competitive industries to inefficient and uncompetitive ones. As a result, the effect of the Trump tariffs reduced the level of real GDP as the Congressional Budget Office (CBO) had predicted: the annual rate of economic growth fell from 3 percent in 2018 to 2.3 percent in 2019.[102]

When President Trump imposed tariffs on steel and aluminum, one result was that American producers who use steel and aluminum as inputs paid higher prices for those metals. But the numbers of additional jobs created in steel and aluminum production were a trifling 1,000 and 1,300, respectively. For every American employed in making steel or aluminum in 2018, thirty-six were employed by firms that use steel or aluminum as inputs.[103] While total employment grew due to more favorable tax and regulatory policy, implementation of the tariffs in early 2018 caused the number of manufacturing jobs to fall by an estimated seventy-five thousand, as Dartmouth's Douglas Irwin reported.[104] Not surprisingly, the percentage of jobs in manufacturing at the onset of the pandemic was slightly lower than when Trump took office.[105] From the time Trump's first tariffs were announced up until the arrival of the pandemic, manufacturing output fell by 2.2 percent, and the rise in real wages for manufacturing workers lagged behind the rise in real wages for all private sector nonsupervisory production workers as a whole.[106]

This failure of the tariffs to revive manufacturing output continued during President Biden's term in office. Of course, manufacturing output recovered from its pandemic low, which occurred in April 2020. However, after reaching its post-pandemic high in October 2022, American manufacturing output was slightly *lower* in October 2024 than it was immediately prior to the implementation of Trump's first tariffs.[107]

TARIFFS AND THE NINETEENTH-CENTURY AMERICAN ECONOMY

Proponents of protective tariffs often cite the nineteenth century as an example of how tariffs can spur industrialization and economic growth by protecting US producers from foreign competition. Robert Lighthizer insists that "when America grew in the 19th century from a modest agricultural country into the world's largest economy, tariffs were critical to its success."[108] He's not alone. Patrick Buchanan, University of London economist Ha-Joon Chang, the American conservative intellectuals Oren Cass and Michael Lind, and many other protectionists frequently cite America's impressive nineteenth-century economic expansion as evidence that tariffs promote economic growth.[109] But the facts don't bear out this claim.

In the first half of the nineteenth century, a political movement led by Henry Clay, often referred to as the "American System," sought to fund roads, canals, and bridges using money from the sale of public lands and the imposition of higher tariffs.[110] The chief nineteenth-century American intellectual proponent of protectionism as an industrial policy was the publisher Henry Carey, who championed the Morrill Tariff of 1863 as a major funding source for the Civil War. He also fought unsuccessfully against the resumption of the gold standard and postwar tariff reductions.[111] Carey's case for protectionism and public investment was bolstered both by Alexander Hamilton's earlier calls for subsidies to promote upstart American industries from established foreign rivals, as well as by the influential work of the German and American economist Friedrich List, the era's most notable academic proponent of industrial protectionism.[112] But Alexander Hamilton, who supported the industrial subsidies that Congress rejected, was skeptical of high tariffs, as no tax revenue is collected on goods that tariffs keep out of the country, and tariffs funded 90 percent of the government. He also was concerned, as Irwin notes in analyzing Hamilton's *Report on Manufactures*, that high tariffs "sheltered inefficient and efficient producers alike, led to higher prices for consumers and gave rise to smuggling which cut into government revenue."[113]

America's remarkable economic dynamism and growth during the nineteenth century is undeniable, as is the fact that the US government used tariffs throughout that century as its principal source of revenue. Congress did not have the constitutional authority to tax income until 1913, and early efforts to tax whiskey caused a rebellion. Taxing imports was administratively easy, and because these taxes were passed along to consumers in the form of higher prices, tariffs (at least at moderate levels) were politically expedient, as many of the ultimate payers of these taxes didn't realize they were being taxed. But as the government increased tariffs to fund infrastructure projects, they became a major political issue. Political opposition and market forces worked overtime to reduce average tariffs on imports.

The earliest US tariffs were meant to raise revenues, not to protect industries. While the Tariff Act of 1816 was clearly aimed in part at paying off debts from the War of 1812, those supporting the tariff also touted its impact in protecting domestic producers. Douglas Irwin describes this tariff as the first one in American history with any serious protectionist intent.[114] The protectionist argument would be used again in the 1820s, when tariffs were raised not only to fund extensive public works but also to protect manufacturers. By 1830, as a result of the 1828 "Tariff of Abominations," the average tariff rate on all merchandise imports hit an all-time high of 57.3 percent.[115] From 1816 through 1830, US industrial output grew at an average annual rate of 4 percent.[116]

The election of Andrew Jackson marked the rise of the Democratic Party, which emerged as a political backlash to the 1828 tariff. With the Democratic sweeps in the elections of 1828 and 1830, tariffs were reduced. Starting in 1831, average tariff rates on all merchandise imports began to fall. This decline wasn't steady, but it was dramatic. By 1860 the average tariff on all imports was down to only 15.7 percent, one of the lowest tariff rates in the world, having fallen 72 percent over this thirty-year period. During these three decades, when the average tariff on merchandise imports fell on a secular basis, the average annual growth rate in industrial output was 6.7 percent—more than 40 percent higher than it was during the earlier years when average tariff rates were rising.[117] By 1860 industrial output was 563 percent greater than in 1830. This increase in output far outpaced the 144 percent growth of the US population.[118] Irwin describes the few decades immediately preceding the Civil War—decades of falling average tariff rates—as a period of "rapid industrialization," adding that "between 1839 and 1859, the manufacturing sector expanded from about 15 percent of GDP to 21 percent of GDP."[119]

During the Civil War, the government hiked tariff rates to fund the war effort. By 1870 the average tariff stood at 44.9 percent. From 1870 to 1890, average tariff rates on all imports again fell, this time to an average rate of 29.6 percent, a 34 percent decline.[120] As average tariff rates fell, industrial output grew during these two decades at an average annual rate of 6 percent—one-third faster than was experienced during the era of rising tariff rates from 1816 through 1830.[121] In 1890 the McKinley Tariff sought to raise industrial tariffs, but in the 1890 and 1892 elections the free-trade Democrats were swept into power and reduced industrial tariffs.[122] Despite the severe panic of 1893, economic growth and industrialization continued to expand for the rest of the century.[123] In short, the most rapid periods of industrial expansion in nineteenth-century America occurred when average tariffs on all merchandise imports were falling.

While proponents of more government spending used the politically expedient argument that their tariffs also helped infant industries by protecting them from foreign competition, the nation's longest-serving secretary of the treasury, Albert Gallatin, writing in 1831, rejected the conclusion that high tariffs promoted economic growth:

> Free of restrictions, which, permitting every man to pursue those occupations for which he was best fitted, had in less than two centuries converted the wilderness into an earthly paradise; and out of a few persecuted emigrants, had created a prosperous, happy, and powerful nation. Under the auspices of that system of freedom, the American people, amidst all the fluctuations and vicissitudes incident to human affairs, had never ceased to make the most rapid progress in agriculture, arts, and commerce. To ascribe that unexampled and uninterrupted prosperity, which even legislative errors cannot arrest, to a tariff is one of the most strange delusions by which intelligent men have ever suffered themselves to be deceived.[124]

Nearly half a century later, in 1875, the great British economist Alfred Marshall visited America to investigate firsthand whether or not protective tariffs fuel economic growth. Before coming to America, Marshall, impressed especially by the theories of Henry Carey, believed that the theory of "infant-industry" protection had some merit in practice. But what he witnessed in the United States changed his mind. In 1903, reflecting on his trip to America, Marshall said,

> I found that, however simple the plan on which a protective policy started, it was drawn on irresistibly to become intricate; and to lend its chief aid to those industries which were already strong enough to do without it. In becoming intricate it became corrupt, and tended to corrupt general politics. On the whole, I thought that this moral harm far outweighed any small net benefit which it might be capable of conferring on American industry in the stage in which it was then.
>
> Subsequent observation of the course of politics in America and elsewhere has strengthened this conviction. It seems to me that the policy adopted in England sixty years ago remains the best, and may probably remain the best, in spite of increasingly rapid economic change, because it is not a device, but the absence of any device. A device contrived to

deal with any set of conditions must become obsolete when they change. The simplicity and naturalness of Free Trade—that is, the absence of any device—may continue to outweigh the series of different small gains which could be obtained by any manipulation of tariffs, however scientific and astute.[125]

The nineteenth century was a period of rapid growth in American industrial output, and that growth was strongest in periods when average tariffs were falling, not rising. Nevertheless, it seems clear that tariffs were largely incidental to the extraordinary economic expansion of America in the nineteenth century. That period of stupendous growth occurred in a country with more economic freedom than any people who had ever walked the face of the earth had experienced. That freedom unleashed productive effort and spawned entrepreneurship that, combined with the huge natural resources of the country and unrestricted foreign investment and immigration, produced the American economic miracle. To attribute this economic growth to the government's tax policy or any other single cause would be foolish, but there is no basis on which to argue that the industrialization of America was promoted by the fact that tariffs were the nation's chief revenue source in the nineteenth century or, more generally, that America's economic growth was fueled by protectionism.

PROTECTING JOBS RATHER THAN CONSUMERS

In an effort to avoid the overwhelming economic logic and evidence showing that freedom to trade fuels economic growth and high living standards for working people, contemporary protectionists are now trying to reorient the trade debate by claiming post-Enlightenment policies have mistakenly emphasized consumption rather than jobs and production. Asserting, as former Sen. Marco Rubio (R-Florida) has done, that "what the market determines is most efficient may not be best for America," these protectionists insist that the objective of trade policy should be to promote good, well-paying jobs rather than the well-being of consumers.[126] Oren Cass contends that an economy should emphasize "a healthy labor market, rather than merely rising consumption."[127]

Robert Lighthizer puts the point even more starkly: "Americans are producers first, consumers second."[128] On its surface, this argument has some appeal. Aren't jobs at least as important as consumption? But at its root, prioritizing jobs over consumption is a siren song, and like all sirens' songs, it leads to a trap.

Production is the means that enables consumption. Productive activities—including, of course, human work—are therefore necessary for consumption. And because that which isn't yet produced cannot be consumed, production must occur chronologically before consumption. No serious person discounts the importance of production or doubts that consumption is possible only to the extent that we produce. But contrary to the claims of people such as Rubio and Lighthizer, it doesn't follow that production is undervalued or suppressed in an economy in which consumers are free to spend their incomes as they choose.

In a free society, consumers determine what is produced by exercising their right to spend the incomes they have earned, through their work and thrift, to promote their well-being. The prices that emerge from free consumer choices direct labor and other resources to produce the mix of goods and services that consumers most want to acquire. Businesses that can most efficiently produce what consumers want and sell it at the lowest prices get to produce these outputs. Those businesses that are not competitive are either forced out of business or directed into other lines of production.[129] In a market-driven system, consumers decide what is produced, how it is produced, and which jobs are created; however, those who are calling to shift the focus from consumption to jobs are really proposing that we allow them to tell society which jobs are created, where labor is employed, and how capital is invested. The proposal to focus the economy on "good jobs" and not the free decisions of those who earned the income in the first place is industrial policy under which self-appointed guardians, using subsidies and tariffs, tell the plebs what is best for them to produce and consume. This debate is as old as man. The idea of allowing the "best and brightest" to choose has been tried and rejected for eons. Letting those who earn their income by the sweat of their brow decide how they spend their income is a new and revolutionary idea.

In light of the nation's ample experience with what government decision-making promotes, who can possibly believe that politicians and bureaucrats have unique insights both into what is in the people's best interest to produce, and unique information about how best to produce it? And even if government officials did possess such insight—which all the lessons of history deny—experience teaches that these officials would, over time, promote their own interests at the expense of the interests of workers and consumers.

In reality, the push for tariffs and industrial subsidies is mostly the result of transactional politics. Would Republicans and Democrats in the election year of 2024 have tried to outbid each other to have American taxpayers and consumers pay $900,000 per job created or saved in manufacturing when those jobs pay, on average, roughly $92,000 annually if those unionized industrial employees weren't the swing voters in the states that decided the 2024 presidential election?[130] And when the bills for that policy arrive, who pays? When foreigners retaliated in response to the recent industrial tariffs, the cost to American farmers was $27 billion in lost sales. The Trump administration responded by increasing the amounts taxpayers paid as farm subsidies.[131]

And when the government tries to conceal the negative effects of tariffs and subsidies, the costs grow. In 2023 Morris Chang, founding chairman of Taiwan Semiconductor Manufacturing Corporation, which accepted billions of dollars in subsidies to build computer-chip manufacturing facilities in Arizona, mused that "if you give up the competitive advantage in Taiwan and move to the United States—which has already happened—costs would be 50% higher than in Taiwan."[132] If US-subsidized computer chips cost 50 percent more than the world market price, how long will it be before Washington imposes tariffs on foreign-made chips? As chips play a significant role in modern manufactured goods, will domestic producers be able to compete in selling products made with more expensive inputs?

When firms in a free market produce outputs that consumers won't buy, the money they lose is their own. They are compelled by their personal interests to correct their errors as quickly as possible or to find other lines of business. But when government industrial-policy planners and tariff advocates make mistakes, they have strong incentives to try to cover up their mistakes with more subsidies and tariffs. When Americans didn't buy the Edsel, Ford lost money and stopped selling the model. In contrast, when Americans didn't buy heavily subsidized electric vehicles (EV), the government imposed tariffs on EV imports—taxes that consumers pay. These mistakes multiply, and the costs to society grows.

NATIONAL DEFENSE

Trade skeptics frequently toss national defense considerations into their arguments for higher tariffs. The reason is obvious: As even Adam Smith acknowledged, "when some particular sort of industry is necessary for the defence of the country," there is a practical case "to lay some burden upon foreign, for the encouragement of domestick industry."[133] Allowing free trade to jeopardize the government's ability to conduct war—and the country's ability to endure it—is obviously unwise. But the national defense exception must be handled with extreme care. As University of Virginia economist Leland Yeager observed, "against any supposed gain in strategic self-sufficiency must be balanced the loss in productivity and in real national income that barriers to specialization and trade impose. Such a loss means that fewer goods and services are available for consumption, investment, and defense."[134] While recognizing that in particular instances protection can be justified to promote national defense, it is important also to recognize the cost of this protection and the potential for its abuse.

We must expect that domestic producers will attempt to exploit this exception for their own gain, even when free trade poses no real risk to national defense—for example, when, during the first Trump presidency, it was argued that America's military might was compromised by steel imported from Mexico and Canada, two geographically adjacent American allies. Today virtually all who plead for protection reflexively insist that failure to heed their pleas will weaken America's ability to defend itself from Chinese diplomatic intrigue and military aggression. Furthermore, because trade restrictions imposed in the name of national defense aren't costless, care must be taken to ensure that protection of, say, the steel industry for national defense purposes doesn't inadvertently undermine national defense by shrinking other domestic industries using steel as an input (e.g., the machine-tool industry, the aircraft industry) that are equally, or perhaps even more, vital to national defense.[135] Because the very purpose of protection is to shield domestic producers from formidable competitors, and because competition is the best spur to efficiency and innovation, the risk is real that protected firms will become less efficient and less innovative over time. The protection that today might enhance a nation's security could tomorrow undermine that security by weakening protected firms' incentives to produce efficiently and develop new and better outputs.

This possibility is not merely theoretical. Consider the costly national experience with the Merchant Marine Act of 1920, better known as the Jones Act, which has raised costs and impeded economic production for over one hundred years. The Jones Act requires that any ship used to transport cargo between US ports must be American flagged, American built, and American owned, as well as crewed by Americans.[136] The promise of these requirements was that they would ensure a larger and better merchant marine fleet that could be tapped and used in wartime.[137]

The Jones Act has failed in virtually every respect. It has failed to build and preserve a strong US merchant marine fleet and a merchant ship-building industry. The cost of shipping among US ports is so costly under the Jones Act that foreign products are delivered in foreign vessels when US goods would have been produced, transported, and sold more cheaply if not for the inflated cost of shipping these goods domestically under the Jones Act. The Jones Act fleet is almost three times older than international merchant ships and much more expensive to operate. Former Clinton Treasury Secretary Lawrence Summers evaluated the Jones Act, concluding, "This should be cautionary with respect to the possible long run adverse effects of current industrial policy measures."[138]

CONCLUSION

Trade wars, like all wars, empower the government as plowshares are beaten into swords. And the first casualty in trade wars is economic freedom, with the second being prosperity. Ultimately, at the heart of to-day's trade debate, the question is not whether trade deficits and capital surpluses are better than trade surpluses and capital deficits. The core question is who should decide which is better. America has prospered under trade deficits and trade surpluses. Why, then, should the government try to override the collective wisdom of hundreds of millions of Americans acting voluntarily in their best interest as they judge it, spending and investing their own money, and incited by the prospect of gain and disciplined by the risk of loss? Only a genuine and narrowly defined national defense interest can justify protectionism to override the collective economic decisions of a free people.

The redeeming value of democratic governments is that they re-spect rather than override the decisions of their people about how to exchange the fruits of their labor in the pursuit of their happiness. While most Americans never stop to think about it, few nations in history have ever gained more from trade than modern America. Fred Smith, the founder and executive chairman of FedEx Corporation (the world's largest airfreight carrier), estimates that "by early this century, trade represented over 25% of United States economic activity, providing millions of high-paying jobs and significantly lowering the cost of living for every American family by over $10,000 dollars per year."[139] In 2015 the President's Council of Economic Advisers estimated that "middle-class Americans gain more than a quarter of their purchasing power from trade. Trade allows U.S. consumers to buy a wider variety of goods at lower prices, raising real wages and helping families purchase more with their current income."[140] The Peterson Institute estimated in 2022 that the average American household's total gains from international trade included $19,500 in lower prices, higher wages, and increased returns on their investments.[141]

Economic freedom and openness to trade have been the catalyst for breathtaking human advancements throughout history. Openness to trade was central to the cultural and material advances in ancient Athens—not coincidentally, the birthplace of democracy. In 431 BC Pericles expressed his pride in such developments, saying, "The fruits of the whole earth flow in upon us; so that we enjoy the goods of other countries as freely as our own."[142] His pride was justified, for as the historian Will Durant summarizes, "it is this trade that makes [ancient] Athens rich, and provides, with the imperial tribute, the sinews of her cultural development. The merchants who accompany their goods to all quarters of the Mediterranean come back with changed perspective, and alert and open minds; they bring new ideas and ways, break down ancient taboos and sloth, and replace the familial conservatism of a rural aristocracy with the individualistic and progressive spirit of a mercantile civilization."[143]

The same openness and freedom that worked in ancient Greece produced similar miracles everywhere. William Bourke Cockran, a Democratic congressman from New York and one of the nation's great advocates of free trade, drove home this point to the citizens of London in the early 1900s:

> Your Free Trade system makes the whole industrial life of the World one vast scheme of cooperation for your benefit. At this moment, in every quarter of the globe, forces are at work to supply your necessities and improve your condition. As I speak, men are tending flocks on Australian fields, and shearing wool which will clothe you during the coming winter.
>
> On Western fields men are reaping grain to supply your daily bread. In mines, deep underground, men are swinging pick-axes and shovels to wrest from the bosom of the earth the ores essential to the efficiency of your industry. Under tropical skies dusky hands are gathering from bending boughs luscious fruit which, in a few days, will be offered for your consumption in the streets of London. Over shining rails locomotives are drawing trains; on heaving surges sailors are piloting barks; through the arid desert Arabs are guiding caravans all charged with the fruits of industry to be placed here freely at your feet.
>
> You alone, among all the inhabitants of the earth, encourage this gracious tribute and enjoy its full benefit, for here alone it is received freely, without imposition, restriction, or tax, while everywhere else barriers are raised against it by stupidity and folly.[144]

The modern era of globalization began taking shape three hundred years ago. Although occasionally interrupted by war and spasms of economic nationalism and mercantilism, the spirit of commerce and innovation has prevailed. When billions of complete strangers are left free to trade and share the innovations, efficiencies, and prosperity that their genius produces, humanity flourishes. Freedom to trade spreads prosperity and ideas in ways that not only inspire the economic innovations that bring forth the cornucopia of a near-miraculous quantity and quality of goods, but also promote greater mutual interdependence, understanding, and toleration.

John Locke

Voltaire

Adam Smith

Thomas Jefferson

The Enlightenment freed and empowered people to think their own thoughts and ultimately to have a voice in their government. Men and women secured the right to worship as they choose and to own the fruits of their labor, thrift, risk-taking, and entrepreneurial capacity. These revolutionary ideas unleashed a creative force the world had never known and in a short three hundred years produced material abundance of biblical proportions.

Karl Marx

Friedrich Engels

Nineteenth-century mill

The profits from Engels's father's mills allowed him to spend his life as an opponent of capitalism and to fund the work of Karl Marx, capitalism's greatest critic. The fruits of capitalism thus funded the rise of its intellectual opposition.

"The downbeat narrative of working-class life during the Industrial Revolution may be cathartic to some. But it is not good history. . . . It is time to think the unthinkable: these writers viewed themselves not as downtrodden losers, but as men and women in control of their own destiny; that the Industrial Revolution periled the advent not of a yet 'darker period,' but the dawn of liberty." *Statement by Emma Griffin, former president of the Royal Historical Society and professor of modern British history at Queen Mary, University of London.*

J. P. Morgan

John D. Rockefeller

Andrew Carnegie

Gustavus Swift

Senator John Sherman, champion
of the Sherman Antitrust Act

President Jimmy Carter

"This historic legislation . . . will remove 45 years of excessive and inflationary government restrictions and red tape. . . . No longer will trucks travel empty because of rules absurdly limiting the kinds of goods a truck may carry. No longer will trucks be forced to travel hundreds of miles out of their way for no reason or prohibited senselessly from stopping to pick up and deliver goods at points along their routes. The Motor Carrier Act of 1980 will bring the trucking industry into the Free Enterprise System, where it belongs." *Statement by President Carter in signing the Motor Carrier Act of 1980.*

"The success of this legislation is the result of a clear consensus . . . that rigid federal economic regulations of the airlines tends to increase prices, foster inefficiency in operations and perpetuate government control, bureaucracy and red tape. . . .This consensus has been built brick by brick in recent years by serious and careful non-partisan examinations of . . . the nature of government and competition in the 1970s." *Statement by Senator Edward Kennedy on the passage of airline deregulation.*

Alfred Kahn, chairman of the Civic Aeronautics Board

The dam broke on overturning Progressive Era regulations when Civil Aeronautics Board chairman Alfred Kahn, an avowed progressive and one of the most consequential economists of the twentieth century, concluded that the most perfect regulatory system could never do as good a job as could imperfect markets, and therefore it was in the public interest to deregulate. Proclaiming the CAB a failure, Kahn demanded that he be fired and his agency eliminated.

Rep. Willis Hawley and Sen. Reed Smoot

The Smoot–Hawley Tariff of 1930 deepened the Depression and spread it worldwide. No single trade action in American history has had a greater negative effect on the well-being of Americans and people all over the world than the passage of the Smoot–Hawley Tariff. Its failure was a major factor in the decision of the United States to expand trade to promote the postwar recovery.

President Franklin Roosevelt with Treasury Secretary Henry Morgenthau

"We have tried spending money. We are spending more money than we have ever spent before and it does not work. And I have just one interest, and if I am wrong . . . somebody else can have my job. I want to see this country prosperous. I want to see people get a job, I want to see people get enough to eat. We have never made good on our promises. . . . I say after eight years of this Administration we have just as much unemployment as when we started. . . . And an enormous debt to boot! We are just sitting here and fiddling and I am just wearing myself out and getting sick. Because why? I can't see any daylight." *Statement by Secretary of the Treasury Henry Morgenthau before the House Ways and Means Committee in May 1939.*

Winston Churchill

In assessing America's economic policy under FDR, Winston Churchill in 1934 wrote: "Confidence is shaken and enterprise chilled, and the unemployed queue up at the soup kitchens or march out to the public works with ever growing expense to the taxpayer and nothing more appetizing to take home to their families than the leg or wing of what was once a millionaire. . . . It is indispensable to the wealth of nations and to the wage and life standards of labour, that capital and credit should be honoured and cherished partners in the economic system. . . . There can never be good wages or good employment for any length of time without good profits, and the sooner this is recognized, the sooner the corner will be turned."

President Harry Truman

President John F. Kennedy

President Dwight D. Eisenhower

President Ronald Reagan

From 1933 to 2018 under thirteen presidents the fundamental trade policy of America was to expand international trade. The Marshall Plan helped economic recovery in Germany, and other aid was targeted to Japan. But the opening of trade triggered the postwar expansion that rebuilt Europe and Japan, that won the Cold War, and reduced the number of people living in abject poverty by an extraordinary 84 percent. Today, per capita income in America is nearly 350 percent higher in real purchasing power dollars than it was in 1947.

Closed mill in the 1970s

Trade Representative Robert Lighthizer and President Donald Trump

While various protectionist measures were implemented to deal with economic and political pressures between 1933 and 2018, the first significant reversal of America's trade policy occurred when President Trump imposed his first tariffs. Those tariffs were continued and expanded by President Joe Biden and are being further expanded during Trump's second term.

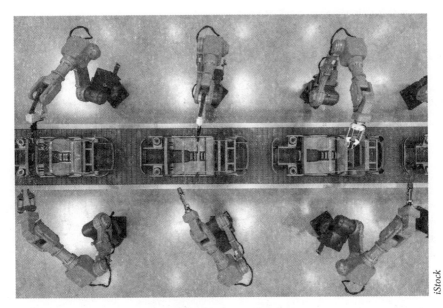

Auto assembly line with robots

America dominates the world in high-tech

Modern technological prowess today allows American industry to produce 2.5 times the level of manufacturing output we produced 50 years ago with only 8.1 percent of the labor force employed in what the Bureau of Labor Statistics defines as manufacturing.

Chairman Alan Greenspan

President Barack Obama

President Bill Clinton

The financial crisis, often referred to as the subprime crisis, occurred when the federal government encouraged and guaranteed loans to people who were unable to pay them back. President Obama blamed the financial crisis on private greed and specifically on deregulation of the financial markets, especially under the Gramm-Leach-Bliley Act, which was signed into law by President Clinton. President Obama demanded a massive expansion in government regulation of the financial sector. The *New York Times* identified Alan Greenspan as the person most responsible for the subprime crisis. Paradoxically, Chairman Greenspan was one of the few public figures who warned of the growing liability of the federal government through guaranteed subprime loans held by Fannie Mae and Freddie Mac. President Clinton and his former Secretary of the Treasury, Larry Summers, have consistently argued that Gramm-Leach-Bliley had nothing to do with the subprime crisis.

The Federal National Mortgage Association headquarters in Washington, DC

A common sight in America during the subprime crisis

By 2007, roughly half of all mortgages being made in America were high-risk loans. When housing prices stopped rising and these mortgages began to default, they caused the collapse of the worldwide market for mortgage-backed securities, which triggered the insolvency of financial institutions that caused the financial crisis. As the housing crisis mounted, financial regulators had more power, larger budgets, and more personnel than ever. But facing the choice of implementing the existing safety and soundness regulations or fulfilling the new affordable-housing goals, financial regulators did not sound the alarm. There is no evidence suggesting that if financial regulators had even more resources or authority to intervene that anything would have been different.

Ebenezer Scrooge

Warren Buffett

Though sweeter and more generous than Ebenezer Scrooge, Mr. Buffett resembles the Victorian-era financier in his restrained consumption. Money was of no use to Scrooge because he didn't spend it, but accumulators like Scrooge financed the investments in railroads and factories that gave nineteenth-century England the highest living standards in the world at that time and, not incidentally, also helped to enrich Americans when their funds were invested across the Atlantic. Would the public really be better off if government diverted Mr. Buffett's billions from promoting general prosperity? When he dies he will either give his wealth away or government will take 40 percent of it in death taxes. But he has benefited mankind more in making the money than he will by giving it away or than government will ever achieve by spending it.

Bill Gates

In earning their vast
fortunes, did their success
make you richer or poorer?

Elon Musk

Newly arrived immigrants passing the Statue of Liberty

They came by the millions in search of opportunity and freedom and in America they found both.

One of many books in the nineteenth century by Horatio Alger

While there are few records of books checked out of libraries in the nineteenth century, if the library in Muncie, Indiana, is a good indicator, then books by the rags-to-riches author Horatio Alger were the most read books in the last half of the nineteenth century.

President Lyndon B. Johnson signing the Declaration of the War on Poverty, 1965

Poverty in America: Lexington, Kentucky, 1936

"The War on Poverty is not a struggle simply to support people, to make them dependent on the generosity of others. It is a struggle to give people a chance. It is an effort to allow them to develop and use their capacities as we have been allowed to develop and use ours, so that they can share, as other share, in the promise of this nation." *Lyndon B. Johnson, "Special Message to Congress Proposing a Nationwide War on the Sources of Poverty."*

"The lessons of history show conclusively that continued dependency upon relief induces a spiritual and moral disintegration fundamentally destructive to the national fiber. To dole out relief in this way is to administer a narcotic, a subtle destroyer of the human spirit. It is inimical to the dictates of a sound policy. It is in violation of the traditions of America." *Franklin D. Roosevelt, "Annual Message to Congress," January 4, 1935.*

President Franklin D. Roosevelt

By most historical accounts Washington's grandmother came to America as an indentured worker. George Washington became one of the richest men in North America, the nation's hero in leading the Continental Army to victory in the Revolutionary War, and the first president of the United States. According to King George III, George Washington was "the greatest man in the world." Opportunity in America was alive and well then and by all evidence is alive and well now.

President George Washington

Five

THE FINANCIAL CRISIS MYTH

Deregulation Caused the Financial Crisis

INTRODUCTION

According to the National Bureau of Economic Research, the recession that sparked the financial crisis of 2008—often called the Great Recession or the Subprime Crisis—started in December 2007 and ended in June 2009.[1] Over this span, inflation-adjusted GDP fell by 4.3 percent.[2] This decline was the largest of any postwar recession. Unemployment peaked at 10 percent in October 2009, a few months after the recession formally ended. That wasn't the highest postwar unemployment rate to that date, a distinction that belongs to the peak unemployment rate of 10.8 percent during the 1981–1982 downturn; however, the Great Recession's high unemployment rate lasted much longer.[3]

The sharp fall in housing prices and the accompanying spike in mortgage defaults, especially on subprime loans, fractured the foundations of the world's financial markets and sent the global economy into a recession. The Federal Reserve Bank expanded the money supply, thus injecting liquidity into the financial system, and the Treasury proposed that Congress adopt a financial bailout, which it did by providing aid in the form of loans to both troubled financial institutions and some nonfinancial businesses. Federal Home Loan Mortgage Corporation (Freddie Mac) and Federal National Mortgage Association (Fannie Mae) failed and were taken into government receivership.

The financial crisis is now often called the Great Recession not because of the depth of the recession in terms of unemployment but because the recovery following the recession was the weakest in the postwar period as well as the rest of American history, excepting the recovery following the Great Depression of the 1930s. The economic and political fallout of the recession, which occurred during the 2008 elections, triggered a major debate on the causes of the recession and the policy responses that were required to bring about recovery. Proponents of expanded government regulation of the financial system argued that the financial crisis was caused by deregulation and greed. Opponents of expanded regulation, in contrast, argued that the financial crisis was caused by a government housing policy that filled the economy with subprime loans that defaulted in the face of declining housing prices, and they called for a major reform of government housing policy. Those who blamed deregulation and "greed" won the 2008 elections, wrote the history of that recession, and adopted the economic and regulatory policies that defined the ensuing recovery.

THE MYTH

Conventional wisdom today holds that the rise and collapse of housing prices, as well as the resulting economy-wide negative repercussions, were caused by a toxic mix of ideology-driven deregulation and ruthless greed. Released from government oversight, mortgage bankers engaged in predatory lending. These bankers concocted complex mortgage loans designed to fool unsuspecting homebuyers into borrowing large sums of money on terms that eventually proved impossible for many of these borrowers to meet. Making matters worse, clever financiers recklessly securitized these high-risk mortgages and sold the securities to investors who negligently treated them as less risky than they really were. When home values began to fall in 2007 and mortgage defaults rose, the house of cards soon collapsed, thus causing the Great Recession.

Not surprisingly, Sen. Barack Obama offered this account of a noxious brew of deregulation, myopia, and greed when he was campaigning for the presidency in 2008, following eight years of Republican stewardship of the White House. He asserted that "the biggest problem in this whole process was the deregulation of the financial system."[4] Two years later, when signing into law the Dodd-Frank Act—the signature piece of legislation enacted in response to the Great Recession—President Obama said that "unscrupulous lenders locked consumers into complex loans with hidden costs . . . while the rules left abuse and excess unchecked."[5] Campaigning for reelection in 2012, President Obama repeated the same charge. In July of that year, speaking about Republicans, he said the following to an audience in Roanoke, Virginia: "But I just want to point out that we tried their theory for almost 10 years . . . and it culminated in a crisis because there weren't enough regulations on Wall Street and they could make reckless bets with other people's money that resulted in this financial crisis, and you had to foot the bill."[6]

Similar sentiments were expressed in 2009 by *Time* magazine, which placed part of the blame on, among many others, Pres. George W. Bush for having "embraced a governing philosophy of deregulation."[7] Most of the blame, however, was placed on Federal Reserve chairman Alan Greenspan, as well as on one of the authors of this book (Gramm), who was accused of writing legislation described as having repealed the Glass-Steagall Act and, thus, allegedly permitting banks once again to recklessly gamble depositors' funds in securities markets.[8] Judge Richard Posner, whose long-standing skepticism of regulation is well-credentialed, published a book in 2009, *A Failure of Capitalism*, that identified deregulation as the chief cause of the mess.[9] According to Posner, "as regulatory and customary restrictions on risky lending by banks eroded, banks became willing to make 'subprime' mortgage loans—a euphemism for mortgage loans at high risk of defaulting."[10]

A majority of the ten members of the Financial Crisis Inquiry Commission created in 2009 by Congress "to examine the causes, domestic and global, of the current financial and economic crisis in the United States," voted along party lines (all six Democrats voted for the findings of the commission, and all four Republicans voted not to concur in those findings) to place unscrupulous mortgage lenders and deregulation at the center of the crisis:

There was an explosion in risky subprime lending and securitization, an unsustainable rise in housing prices, widespread reports of egregious and predatory lending practices, dramatic increases in household mortgage debt, and exponential growth in financial firms' trading activities, unregulated derivatives, and short-term "repo" lending markets, among many other red flags. Yet there was pervasive permissiveness. . . .

The sentries were not at their posts, in no small part due to the widely accepted faith in the self-correcting nature of the markets and the ability of financial institutions to effectively police themselves. More than 30 years of deregulation and reliance on self-regulation by financial institutions, championed by former Federal Reserve chairman Alan Greenspan and others, supported by successive administrations and Congresses, and actively pushed by the powerful financial industry at every turn, had stripped away key safeguards, which could have helped avoid catastrophe.[11]

Despite the passage of time, perceptions about the crisis have changed little. Interviewed in 2018, retired Rep. Barney Frank, chairman of the House Banking Committee in 2008, continued to argue that the root cause of the Great Recession "wasn't so much deregulation as non-regulation."[12] And in a 2023 piece in Forbes Advisor, financial journalists Wayne Duggan and Michael Adams describe the crisis as having "started as a classic tale of greed and deregulation."[13] One result, in the eyes of these writers, was that "banks and mortgage lenders became increasingly predatory with their lending practices in the years leading up to the Great Recession. Mortgages became easier to get, with fewer standards in place to ensure borrowers could repay them."[14]

This tale of a mix of cupidity and blind ideological opposition to regulation—a tale in which venal villains were set free to prey upon the innocent and weak in a manner that imperiled the entire economy—is widely believed. The problems with this explanation come into view only when you examine the facts.

GETTING THE FACTS STRAIGHT

Simply said, the financial crisis of 2008 was caused by a lot of banks making a lot of loans to a lot of people who either could not or would not pay the money back. As Columbia University's Charles Calomiris and Stanford University's Stephen Haber put it, "what everyone agrees on . . . is that the systemwide crash of 2007–09 was led by a crisis in housing finance, particularly in the market for 'subprime' loans."[15] But this explanation raises three key questions. First, why did private lenders, whose job was to assess credit risks and who would suffer economically by making bad loans, decide to make so many bad loans? Second, why did the federal government, through Fannie Mae and Freddie Mac, guarantee these loans? And third, why did the army of financial regulators, with massive enforcement powers, allow twenty-eight million high-risk loans to be made, securitized, and held by regulated financial institutions? Calomiris and Haber summarize the matter nicely: "Any coherent account of the subprime crisis must . . . explain how it was that so many lenders ended up making so many risky loans while maintaining very little capital to protect themselves against insolvency."[16]

The principal origin of massive subprime lending and the crisis can be traced back to September 12, 1992. On that day, presidential candidate Bill Clinton proposed, in his campaign book *Putting People First*, using private "pension fund contributions" for "investments" in government priorities, as well as "passing a more progressive Community Reinvestment Act" to "ease the credit crunch in our inner cities."[17] Seldom has such a radical proposal been so ignored during a campaign and then only later produced such devastating consequences.

After his election, President Clinton tapped Secretary of Labor Robert Reich to lead efforts to employ private pension funds to promote public objectives. In 1994 Mr. Reich, in congressional testimony, called on private pension funds to join the administration's Economically Targeted Investment efforts, which included the promotion of so-called affordable housing. Reich assured skeptics that these "economically targeted investments" would be just as safe as the conventional investments that pension funds would make absent this plan.[18] Later in the same hearing, Henry Cisneros, Clinton's secretary for the Department of Housing and Urban Development, insisted to Congress that "pension investments in affordable housing would be as safe as pension investments in stocks and bonds."[19]

Because only six pension funds ultimately agreed to invest in the government's program to promote affordable housing, even though the investments were backed by $100 million in federal grants and guarantees, the program never took off. In the end, even labor unions that strongly supported President Clinton rejected the effort to direct any part of their members' retirement savings toward someone else's welfare.

The Clinton administration lost that battle to use American workers' retirement savings to fund low-income housing, but they ultimately won the war by drafting the US Department of Housing and Urban Development (HUD), Fannie Mae, Freddie Mac, and the commercial banking system into the "affordable housing" effort. It did so by exploiting a minor provision in a 1977 housing statute, the Community Reinvestment Act (CRA), the original purpose of which was simply to require banks to meet local credit needs in their service areas.

Using newly expanded CRA requirements, bank regulators began to pressure banks to make subprime loans. Guidelines turned into mandates as each bank was assigned a letter grade on its making of CRA loans. Banks could not even open ATMs or branches, much less acquire another bank, without a passing grade—and getting a passing grade was no longer about meeting local credit needs. Increasingly, passing grades were gotten by making subprime home loans.[20] As then-Federal Reserve Chairman Alan Greenspan testified to Congress in 2008, "the early stages of the subprime [mortgage] market . . . essentially emerged out of the CRA."[21]

In 1993 Fannie and Freddie were required to make 30 percent of their mortgage purchases "affordable housing loans." But then political pressure intensified on Fannie and Freddie to buy ever-greater amounts of mortgage loans made to riskier borrowers. Calomiris and Haber explain:

> Under pressure from activist groups, Congress began to place regulatory mandates on the government-sponsored enterprises (GSEs) that purchased and securitized mortgages, which included the Federal National Mortgage Association (FNMA, commonly known as Fannie Mae), and the Federal Home Loan Mortgage Corporation (FHLMC, commonly known as Freddie Mac), and the federal home loan banks (FHLBs). Fannie Mae

and Freddie Mac, in particular, were required to repurchase mortgage loans made to targeted groups (i.e., individuals who had low incomes or lived in urban locations that were defined as underserved). . . . In order to meet these targets, Fannie and Freddie had to weaken their underwriting standards. By the mid-1990s, Fannie and Freddie were agreeing to purchase mortgages with down payments of 3 percent (instead of the 20 percent that had been the industry standard). Soon afterward, they were buying mortgages with weak credit scores. By 2004, they were agreeing to purchase vast amounts of risky mortgage loans, including so-called Alt-A loans with little or no documentation of income (which are also known as liar loans or low-doc loans).[22]

Fannie's and Freddie's minimum quota for "affordable housing" loans was raised to 40 percent in 1996 and to 42 percent in 1997; then, in 2000, HUD ordered the quota raised even further, to 50–55 percent. Freddie and Fannie dutifully met those goals each and every year until the subprime crisis erupted. By 2008, when both government-sponsored enterprises collapsed, the quota had reached 56 percent.[23] An internal Fannie document made public after the financial crisis ("HUD Housing Goals," March 2003) clearly shows that by 2002 Fannie officials knew perfectly well that these quotas were promoting irresponsible practices: "The challenge freaked out the business side of the house [Fannie] . . . The tenseness around meeting the goals meant that we . . . did deals at risks and prices we would not have otherwise done."[24]

The mortgage market shows the dramatic results of this shift in policy. According to the nonprofit National Community Reinvestment Coalition, total CRA lending from 1977 through 1991 totaled $8.8 billion. But from 1992 through the first half of 2007, the enormous sum of $4.5 *trillion* was committed—an increase of more than 51,000 percent![25] Peter Wallison, the general counsel at the US Treasury under President Reagan, found that from 1988 to 1992, 78 percent of the residential mortgage loans acquired by Fannie and Freddie were solid prime loans with healthy down payments and a well-documented capacity of borrowers to make mortgage payments. But by 1999, only 45 percent of their acquisitions met this prudent standard.[26] According to Edward Pinto, former executive vice president and chief credit officer at Fannie Mae, in 1991, GSEs did not purchase loans with down payments of 3 percent or less. By 2007, they were purchasing $140 billion of loans with down payments of 3 percent or less, and half had *no* down payments.[27]

By 2008 roughly half of all outstanding mortgages in America were high-risk loans. In 1990 very few subprime loans were securitized. By 2007 most of them were. Pinto summed up his report to the Financial Crisis Inquiry Commission (FCIC) as follows: "The financial crisis had a single major cause: the accumulation of an unprecedented number of weak mortgages in the US financial system. When these mortgages began to default, they caused the collapse of the worldwide market for mortgage-backed securities, which in turn caused the instability and insolvency of financial institutions that we called the financial crisis."[28]

The vast majority of subprime loans were securitized by government-created entities, Freddie and Fannie, as a direct result of congressional mandates. Banks made subprime loans in response to government regulations flowing from the CRA. Additionally, banks held large quantities of mortgage-backed securities because government regulators had encouraged these holdings by rating mortgage-backed securities as being as creditworthy as US government debt.[29] There was plenty of greed and negligence, but it was concentrated in the government.

Everything appeared to work fine as long as accommodative monetary policy and capital inflows from abroad kept interest rates low and fueled the upward float of housing prices. The rate of homeownership grew from 64 percent in 1993 to 69 percent in 2006. But when monetary policy tightened, the housing bubble burst and the mortgage-default rate soared.

It is stunning that, to this day, no one has explained how twenty-eight million high-risk loans (the number calculated by the American Enterprise Institute's Peter Wallison) got around the safety and soundness rules that dominate federal and state banking laws. What happened to the enforcement army, with its laws and regulations, its power to investigate and mandate corrective action, and its ability to fine and imprison violators?

Whatever went on inside the various agencies, financial regulators—whose job was to enforce safety and soundness regulations—ultimately

deferred to the government's goal of "affordable housing." Conflicted legislation created conflicted regulations and regulators. Safety and soundness considerations required that regulators slam on the brake, while
affordable housing goals required them to step on the gas. Government
policy tried to make private wealth serve both government and private
purposes. But wealth cannot serve two masters, and in the end, the dominant master was the government.

When the subprime crisis broke in the presidential-election year of
2008, there was little chance for a serious discussion of its root causes.
Candidate Barack Obama weaponized the crisis by blaming greedy
bankers, who allegedly had been unleashed when financial regulations were "simply dismantled."[30] He would go on to blame them for taking
"huge, reckless risks in pursuit of quick profits and massive bonuses."[31]

In fact, the answer is to the contrary: When the crisis struck, all
available records show that banks were *better* capitalized and *less* lev-
eraged than they had been in the previous thirty years—that is, compared to the past, banks had more assets on hand to meet economic
challenges. The Federal Deposit Insurance Corporation's (FDIC's) reported capital-to-asset ratio for insured commercial banks in 2007 was
10.37 percent—51 percent higher than in 1978.[32] Federal Reserve data
on all insured financial institutions show that the capital-to-asset ratio
in 2007 was 10.3 percent, almost double its 1984 level, with the biggest
banks having doubled their capitalization ratios.[33] The FDIC found that
in September 2007, 98 percent of all FDIC institutions, which held 99
percent of all bank assets, were "well capitalized," and only forty-three
smaller institutions were undercapitalized.[34]

Furthermore, US banks were by far the best-capitalized banks in the
world.[35] While the collapse of thirty-one million subprime mortgages
fractured the base of the world's financial system, the US banking system
would have fared even worse under such massive stress at any time in the
thirty years prior to 2007.

In reality, virtually all of the undercapitalization, overleveraging,
and "reckless risks" resulted from ill-considered government policies
and poorly designed regulations. Federal regulators followed international banking standards that treated most subprime-mortgage-backed

securities as very low risk, with lower capital requirements that gave banks the incentive to hold them. Government quotas forced Fannie Mae and Freddie Mac to hold ever-larger volumes of subprime mortgages, and politicians "rolled the dice" (the words of then-Chairman of the House Banking Committee Barney Frank) by letting Fannie and Freddie operate with a leverage ratio of 75 to 1—compared with Lehman's leverage ratio of 29 to 1.[36]

THE DEREGULATION MYTH

Similarly, it's a myth that banks had been deregulated before the crisis. From 1980 to 2007, four major banking statutes—the Competitive Equality Banking Act (1987); the Financial Institutions, Reform, Recovery, and Enforcement Act (1989); the Federal Deposit Insurance Corporation Improvement Act (1991); and Sarbanes-Oxley (2002)—undeniably *increased* bank regulations and reporting requirements. The charge that financial regulation had been dismantled rests almost solely on the disputed effects of the 1999 Gramm-Leach-Bliley Act (GLB).

Before GLB, the decades-old Glass-Steagall Act prohibited deposit-taking commercial banks from engaging in securities trading. GLB, which was signed into law by President Bill Clinton, allowed newly created financial-services holding companies to compete in banking, insurance, and the securities business through subsidiaries of the holding companies. The newly created financial-services holding companies were subject to new regulation by the Federal Reserve Bank and required to meet new higher capital standards. But each activity was still required to operate separately, and each remained subject to all the regulations and capital requirements that had existed before GLB. The Congressional Research Service states that "primary supervision of all components, be they banking, insurance, or securities firms, remain with their federal or state line supervisor."[37] In fact, the summary of GLB provided to Congress by the Congressional Research Service contained no reference to any deregulatory provision in the bill. As explained in the analysis of the bill at the Federal Reserve History website, GLB "kept in place the existing regulators for financial subsidiaries of financial services holding companies but gave the Fed the role of 'umbrella supervisor.'"[38] In recognition of the costs of the additional regulation that GLB would impose, the CBO increased its estimate of regulatory costs in projecting expected federal outlays in 2000–2004.[39]

A bank operating within a highly capitalized financial-services holding company was still subject to Glass-Steagall, which, contrary to repeated assertions, was *not* repealed by GLB. Furthermore, Glass-Steagall had never banned banks from holding mortgages or mortgage-backed securities in the first place. Critics have never been able to show how GLB triggered the financial crisis, because the crisis sprang from financial institutions holding mortgages and mortgage-backed securities, which banks were allowed to hold even before GLB, and it did *not* stem from their securities or insurance activities, which is what GLB allowed them to provide through subsidiaries of financial-services holding companies. Significantly, GLB holding companies, with their diverse asset base, held up *better* during the financial crisis than those institutions not operating as part of financial-services holding companies.

When he signed the law, President Clinton noted, "[The] removal of barriers to competition will enhance the stability of our financial services system. Financial services firms will be able to diversify their product offerings and thus their sources of revenue. They will also be better equipped to compete in global financial markets."[40] The financial crisis proved his point. Financial institutions that used GLB provisions to diversify fared better than Lehman Brothers and the other firms that didn't. Of the eleven major financial firms that failed in the run-up to the September 2008 crisis, not a single one—not Lehman, Bear Stearns, Fannie, Freddie, AIG, Merrill Lynch, IndyMac, Washington Mutual, New Century Financial, Ameriquest, or Countrywide—was a GLB financial holding company. It also seems clear that if GLB were the problem, the crisis would have originated in Europe, where Glass-Steagall requirements had never been adopted and banks were always free to sell securities and insurance.

Regarding GLB, President Clinton has always insisted that "there's not a single, solitary example that it had anything to do with the financial crash."[41] This conclusion has never been refuted. When asked about it by the *New York Times* in 2012, Elizabeth Warren, then a law professor at Harvard, agreed that the financial crisis would not have been avoided had GLB never been adopted.[42] Even President Obama effectively exonerated GLB from any real culpability in the financial crisis when, with massive majorities in both houses of Congress, he chose not to repeal GLB. In fact, Dodd-Frank *expanded* GLB by using its financial-services holding company structure to impose new regulations on systemically important financial institutions.

When no evidence was ever presented to link GLB to the financial crisis, some people who blamed the crisis on deregulation turned their attention to the Commodities Futures Modernization Act (CFMA), specifically to credit default swaps. They charged that CFMA deregulated swaps and that credit default swaps were the real culprit in causing the crisis.

But because swaps had never been under the regulatory jurisdiction of the Commodities Futures Trading Commission (CFTC), the CFMA could not and did not deregulate them. When, in 1998, the CFTC chairman suggested that she was considering an attempt to regulate swaps as futures, there was a major market reaction because of the uncertainty this created regarding the enforceability of swap contracts. The Clinton administration repudiated the proposal, and the president, secretary of the Treasury, chairman of the Federal Reserve, and SEC chairman all asked Congress to reaffirm the then-existing law under which swaps were not futures and did not fall under the jurisdiction of the CFTC. In the words of Sen. Tom Harkin (D-Iowa), the ranking member of the Agriculture Committee (the committee with jurisdiction over the CFTC), "the language of the bill clarifies what is already the current state of the law."[43]

It is amazing how well the swap market for credit default swaps functioned during the financial crisis, given the generally weakened condition of the underlying assets. That market never lost liquidity, and the default rate on swaps remained low. The problem was the poor quality of the underlying mortgages that credit default swaps were based on.

TRIGGERING THE FINANCIAL CRISIS

The financial crisis grew from a confluence of two factors. The first was the unintended consequence of using a monetary policy developed in the last half of the twentieth century to combat inventory-cycle recessions to deal with a speculative-bubble recession in 2001. The second was the politicization of mortgage lending.

In the inventory-cycle recessions of the last half of the twentieth century, when involuntary buildups of inventories occurred, there was a retrenchment in the production chain. Workers were laid off, and investment and consumption slumped, including activity in the housing sector. In contrast, the 2001 recession was brought on when investment collapsed due to the bursting of a speculative bubble in the equity market focused on tech stocks. Unlike in the previous postwar downturns, in the 2001 recession consumption and home building remained strong despite the collapse in investment. But in 2001, the Fed acted as if it were in 1981. Its sharp, prolonged monetary easing only further stimulated a housing market that was already booming, thus triggering six years of double-digit increases in housing loans.[44] This process was reinforced by the inflow of foreign capital that further depressed interest rates.

Buyers then bought houses they couldn't afford, believing they could refinance in the future and benefit from the ongoing appreciation. As housing prices rose, many people took out second mortgages to convert some of their home appreciation into income. Lenders assumed that even if everything else went wrong, houses could still be sold for more than the lenders were owed and the loans could be fully repaid. This mentality permeated the market, from the originators to the holders of securitized mortgages, and from the rating agencies to the financial regulators—a mentality reinforced by the resilience of the postwar housing market.[45]

Meanwhile, mortgage lending was becoming increasingly politicized. The Community Reinvestment Act's requirements led regulators to foster looser underwriting and encouraged the making of more and more marginal loans. Looser underwriting standards spread beyond subprime loans to the entire housing market.

CRA and federal housing policy not only pressured lenders to make risky loans, they also gave lenders the excuse *and* regulatory cover to make those loans. Countrywide Financial Corporation cloaked itself in righteousness and silenced any troubled regulator by being the first mortgage lender to sign a HUD "Declaration of Fair Lending Principles and Practices." Given privileged status by Fannie Mae as a reward for having "the most flexible underwriting criteria,"[46] Countrywide became the world's largest mortgage lender—until it became the first major casualty of the financial crisis.

By the time the housing market collapsed, Fannie and Freddie faced three quotas. The first was for mortgages to individuals with below-average income, set at 56 percent of their overall mortgage holdings. The second targeted families with incomes at or below 60 percent of the area median income, set at 27 percent of Fannie's and Freddie's holdings. The third targeted geographic areas deemed to be underserved, with the goal set at 35 percent of their holdings.

Blinded by the experience of the postwar period, when average housing prices had been remarkably stable, rating agencies and regulators viewed securitized mortgages, even subprime and undocumented Alt-A mortgages, as embodying little risk. The problem was not that regulators weren't empowered; it was that they weren't alarmed.

Rated as low-risk by regulators worldwide, subprime securities were injected into the arteries of the global financial system. When the housing bubble burst, the financial system lost the indispensable ingredients of confidence and trust. We all know the rest of the story.

In reality, the financial "deregulation" in the two decades before the financial crisis is a myth. As the housing crisis mounted, financial regulators had more power, larger budgets, and more personnel than ever. And yet, with the notable exception of Federal Reserve Chairman Greenspan's warning about the risk posed by the massive subprime mortgage holdings of Fannie and Freddie, regulators, who were torn between the old safety-and-soundness regulatory requirements and the new affordable-housing regulations, did not sound the alarm. There is absolutely no evidence that if financial regulators had possessed even more resources or authority to intervene, anything would have been different.

THE TROUBLED ASSET RELIEF PROGRAM

Another myth of the financial crisis is that the bailout was required because some banks were too big to fail.[47] Had the government's massive injection of capital—the Troubled Asset Relief Program, or TARP—been only about bailing out too-big-to-fail financial institutions, at most a dozen institutions might have received aid. Instead, such assistance was doled out to 954 financial institutions, with more than half the money going to small banks.

Many of the largest banks did not want or need aid, and Lehman's collapse was not a case of a too-big-to-fail institution spreading the crisis. The entire financial sector was already poisoned by the same subprime assets that felled Lehman. The subprime bailout occurred because the US financial sector was—and always will be—too important to be allowed to fail.

One government response to the financial crisis does deserve some credit. According to the Congressional Budget Office, the 1980s bailout of depositors of insolvent savings and loans (S&Ls) cost taxpayers, on net, $258 billion in 2009 dollars. In contrast, of the $245 billion disbursed by TARP to banks, 67 percent was repaid within fourteen months and 81 percent within two years. The final totals show that taxpayers earned $24 billion on the banking component of TARP. The rapid and complete payback of TARP funds by banks strongly suggests that the financial crisis was more a liquidity crisis than a solvency crisis.[48]

What turned the subprime crisis and ensuing recession into the *Great Recession* was not a failure of policies to address the financial crisis. Instead, it was the failure of subsequent economic policies that impeded the recovery.

THE FAILED RECOVERY

The financial crisis is often referred to as the Great Recession. It is so labeled not because it generated the highest unemployment level since the Great Depression—the highest unemployment level occurred in 1982—but because the ensuing recovery was so weak. Recovery after the crisis was the weakest both in postwar history and in American history (other than the recovery following the Great Depression).

In early 2010, after the recession formally ended, the Office of Management and Budget projected a 3.7 percent average annual increase in GDP over the next seven years. The Congressional Budget Office projected 3.3 percent growth for the same period, while the Federal Reserve predicted growth between 3.4 and 4.3 percent through 2013.[49] And these estimates were conservative compared to the actual recovery patterns that had followed every major recession (except the Great Depression in the 1930s). Contrary to all predictions and historical precedents, average annual growth for the remainder of the Obama administration slumped to an eighty-year low of 2.2 percent as its policies kicked in.[50] During the 2010 to 2016 recovery, the CBO was repeatedly forced to slash its growth and revenue projections. As growth faltered, federal revenues fell, and government debt soared.

Three years after the financial crisis began, real GDP per person was still down $1,288 from the prerecession level, and 7.1 million fewer Americans were working than when the recession had started. Four years after the financial crisis began, real GDP per person was down $878 from the prerecession level, while 5.6 million fewer Americans were working than when the recession started.[51] Never before in postwar America had either real per capita GDP or employment still been lower four years after a recession began than when the recession started. If the economy had grown and generated jobs at the average annual percentage rate achieved following the ten previous postwar recessions, by the end of Obama's first term, GDP per person would have been $6,417 higher, and 12.5 million more Americans would have been working.[52]

As the recovery faltered, President Obama first blamed the weakness of the recovery on the recession's depth, saying that it was "going to take a while for us to get out of this. I think even I did not realize the magnitude . . . of the recession until fairly far into it."[53]

It's true that by most measures the financial crisis was the worst economic downturn in America since the Great Depression. But this comparison conceals more than it reveals. When put into historical context, the downturn caused by the financial crisis is seen as much closer in severity to other postwar downturns than to the Great Depression. The Great Depression, after all, lasted for at least twelve years and, arguably, in terms of real purchasing power of American families, didn't end until the postwar expansion.[54] As we note in chapter 3, from 1929 to 1933, real GDP fell by 29 percent, and the unemployment rate rose to 25 percent. In stark contrast, the financial crisis formally lasted nineteen months, with GDP falling by only 3.8 percent and unemployment peaking (in October 2009) at 10 percent.

The financial crisis is more accurately compared with the recession of 1981–1982. This downturn in the early 1980s lasted seventeen months, with GDP falling by 2.6 percent. Unemployment then peaked at 10.8 percent in November and December of 1982. Compared to the downturn of 1981–1982, the financial crisis lasted two months longer and knocked 1.6 more percentage points off GDP, but its peak unemployment was nearly a full percentage point lower.[55]

Important differences nevertheless distinguish these two postwar downturns from each other. Not the least of these differences is the fact that the 1982 recovery was constrained by a contractionary monetary policy that pushed interest rates above 21 percent, a tough but necessary step to break inflation.[56] It was also a recovery that required American businesses to undergo a painful restructuring to become more competitive in the increasingly globalized economy. By way of comparison, the financial crisis recovery had benefited from the most expansionary monetary policy to that point in the peacetime history of the United States. Nevertheless, recovery from the downturn in the early 1980s was significantly faster and fuller than was the recovery from the financial crisis.

Consider employment. Use as your starting point total nonfarm employment in the month before the start of each recession: For the 1981–1982 recession, total employment took twenty-nine months to recover to its prerecession level. For the Great Recession, it took total employment an astonishing seventy-eight months to recover, much more than twice as long as it had taken to recover from the downturn in the early 1980s.[57]

Personal income followed a similar pattern. In 2007, real median personal income was (in 2022 dollars) $36,370. It then fell in each of the next five years, bottoming out in 2012 at $33,510. Although it rose a bit in 2013, it remained below its 2007 level until 2015, when it reached $36,610. All told, real median personal income took seven years to recover fully.[58]

Despite the significant disadvantages the economy faced in 1982, President Ronald Reagan's policies—reductions in domestic spending, significant reductions in marginal tax rates, and a continuation of the deregulatory movement that had begun under President Carter— ignited a recovery so powerful that if it had been equaled in the wake of the financial crisis, four years after recovery from the beginning of the Great Recession real per capita GDP would have been $6,567 higher than it actually was. For a family of four, that would have been an extra $26,268. Also, some 12.5 million more Americans would have had jobs.[59]

Things were very different under President Obama's program. By 2017 the Bureau of Labor Statistics reported that annual labor-productivity growth since 2010 had plummeted to less than one-quarter of the average growth rate for the previous twenty, thirty, and forty years. This productivity fall occurred not during the actual recession but during the recovery. New investment was large enough only to offset depreciation, so the value of the capital stock per worker, a major engine of the American economic colossus, stopped expanding and so contributed nothing to growth.

Chief among the causes of the weakness of the Obama "recovery" was what Calomiris and Haber describe as "the unprecedented steps that the Federal Reserve and the U.S. government took."[60] The American economy was hit with a tidal wave of new rules and regulations across health care, financial services, energy, and manufacturing. Companies were forced to spend billions on new capital and labor that served the government but not consumers. Banks hired compliance officers rather than loan officers. Energy companies spent billions on environmental-compliance costs, none of which produced energy more cheaply or abundantly. Health insurance premiums skyrocketed—but with no additional benefits for the vast majority of covered workers.

In 2007 the BLS predicted that demographic changes alone would lower the labor-force participation rate from 66.2 percent in 2006 to 65.5

percent in 2016.[61] But under President Obama's policies, it actually fell much further, to 62.8 percent, by the end of his second term.[62]

In July 2012 most Americans were shocked to discover that 246,000 new people had qualified for disability benefits during the previous three months, while only 225,000 people had found new jobs. A total of 471,000 Americans left the unemployment rolls—but the difference between qualifying for disability benefits and getting a job is profound for the economy and the people involved. In contrast, fifty-five months after the 1981 recession began, the number of Americans drawing disability benefits had actually dropped by 655,000, or 14.3 percent.[63]

The explosion of disability payments is only the tip of the iceberg. Fifty-five months after the 1981 recession began, the number of people on the Supplemental Nutrition Assistance Program (SNAP)—formerly known as food stamps—had fallen by three million, or 13.4 percent. In contrast, the number of food stamp recipients in the fifty-five months after the start of the Great Recession *grew* to more than 46 million, up from 26 million.[64] That's a mind-boggling increase of 77 percent. While much of the growth in SNAP and disability benefits was due to a lowering of qualification standards, some of the increase is attributable to the failed recovery.

The number of beneficiaries of the Aid to Families with Dependent Children (AFDC) program had declined by 1 percent, or 42,000 people, fifty-five months after the start of the 1981–1982 recession. But during the Obama recovery, over the same time period, the number of beneficiaries in AFDC's successor program, the Temporary Assistance for Needy Families program (TANF), *rose* by 467,000, or 12 percent.[65] This growth resulted from the administration's decision to waive work requirements for these welfare recipients. As the University of Chicago economist Casey Mulligan documented in 2012, after 2007, more than a dozen government programs meant to help the poor and unemployed became more generous. This "generosity" greatly diminished many Americans' incentives to work and produce.[66]

The absence of a strong recovery following the financial crisis is similar to that of the Great Depression not because of the financial events that triggered the disease or the depth of the downturn but, rather, because of the similar policy prescriptions of the doctor. Under Pres. Franklin

Roosevelt, federal spending jumped by 3.6 percent of GDP from 1932 to 1936, an unprecedented spending spree, as the New Deal was implemented. Under President Obama, spending exploded by 4.6 percent of GDP from 2008 to 2011. In 2009, federal spending as a share of GDP surged by an enormous 4.1 percentage points, reaching 24.3 percent, the highest level since World War II.[67] Spending was 23.2 percent of GDP in 2010. In the entire postwar era through 2008, federal spending averaged about 20 percent of GDP. For comparison, consider that in 1952, the Korean War pushed federal spending to only about 19 percent of GDP, even as defense spending then made up 68 percent of federal budgetary outlays. This financial crisis spending surge, which started during the recession, continued long after the recession was over. In 2011 federal spending was still 23.4 percent of GDP, the second-highest level since World War II—over one-fourth higher than the postwar average before the Obama era. [68] While advocates of increased federal spending during the pandemic would argue that the Obama recovery was stunted by ending spending stimulus too soon, in 2012 federal spending was 21.9 percent of GDP—less than in the stimulus years but still the fourth-highest level in the postwar period prior to the Obama presidency. And 2012 was three *after* the recession formally ended.

In perhaps the most important similarity between the Great Depression and Great Recession, the regulatory burden exploded under Obama as it had under Roosevelt. The expansion of government control of the economy under President Obama reached levels not experienced since the Roosevelt era. Winston Churchill's scathing critique of the Roosevelt administration's regulatory "machinery of voluminous codes," which created conditions where "wages, prices and labour conditions have been grasped in muscular hands and nailed to an arbitrary framework," would have applied to the Obama regulatory onslaught as well.[69] Furthermore, tax policy during both Great Depression and the Great Recession was destructive, with rising marginal tax rates on ordinary income and capital gains.

Moreover, the Obama administration's populist tirades against private business were hauntingly similar to those of the Roosevelt administration. FDR's demagoguery against "the privileged few" and "economic royalists" was echoed in Mr. Obama's expression of his disdain for "the richest 1%" and America's "millionaires and billionaires."[70] Just as the rise of economic policy uncertainty had eroded confidence, reducing both investment and consumption during the implementation of the New Deal in the 1930s, the Obama-era policy uncertainty generated by dramatic increases in federal spending, taxes, and regulatory burdens—along with the president's growing hostility toward business and the accumulation of wealth—caused economic policy uncertainty to spike and investment to lag. Scott Baker of Northwestern University, Nicholas Bloom of Stanford University, and Steven Davis of the University of Chicago, using an index of economic policy uncertainty based on mentions of uncertainty related to government action in the nation's leading newspapers, found that economic policy uncertainty—which had reached a peak for the twentieth century during the Roosevelt New Deal—reached its second highest level during the Obama era.[71]

CONCLUSION

America's historic ability to economically outperform Europe is well documented; it is part of what is called American exceptionalism. It has always been based on the fact that the United States has benefited from more competitive, more market-driven economic policies, and our economy therefore has worked better. But as the US economy was Europeanized through higher taxes and heavier regulatory burdens during the Obama years, the American economy's exceptionalism faded, taking economic growth down with it.

The Obama program represented the most dramatic change in US economic policy in over three-quarters of a century. We know from the experience of our individual states and the historic performance of other nations that policy choices have profound effects on economic outcomes.

US states and foreign nations tend to prosper when tax rates are low, regulatory burdens are relatively light, the rule of law protects private property, contractual rights and creditors' rights are secure, labor markets are flexible, and capital markets are dominated by private decision-making. While many other factors are important, economists generally agree that these conditions are essential for economic growth. As measured by virtually every economic policy known historically to promote growth, the structure of the US economy became less conducive to growth under Obama's policies than it had been for the entire post–World War II period.

Despite the largest fiscal stimulus program and the most expansive monetary policy (to that point) in postwar history, the US economy vastly underperformed during the recovery from the 2008 financial crisis. America succeeded in the Reagan and the immediate post-Reagan era because of sound economic policies. Economic policies have consequences. Whether we call them liberal, progressive, populist, or socialist, bad policies produce bad results. They do so not just sometimes in some places, but at all times in all places, even in America.

With better economic policies, America was like the fabled farmer with the goose that laid golden eggs. He kept the pond clean and full, he erected a nice coop, threw out corn for the goose, and every day the goose laid a golden egg. President Obama drained the pond, burned down the coop, and let the dogs loose to chase the goose around the barnyard. Not surprisingly, the goose stopped laying golden eggs. Administration apologists—blaming "secular stagnation" —added insult to injury by suggesting that something was wrong with the goose.

Six

THE MYTH AND REALITY
OF INCOME INEQUALITY
IN AMERICA

W HEN THOMAS JEFFERSON WROTE in the Declaration of
Independence that "all men are created equal,"[1] neither he
nor any of the other founders believed that people had equal
abilities and ambitions or that the government could or should seek to
engineer equal outcomes in Americans' efforts to succeed. A commitment to equality of outcome in the competition of life is totally alien
to the American ethos. America, in the words of Abraham Lincoln, is
committed to "an open field and a fair chance for your industry, enterprise and intelligence."[2] Recognizing the truth in the words of historians
Will and Ariel Durant—that "freedom and equality are sworn and ever-
lasting enemies, and when one prevails the other dies"—Americans have
chosen freedom.[3]

From the very beginnings of recorded history, pervasive inequality
has spawned cries for income and wealth redistribution, as well as unleashed envy's corrosive force against prosperity and freedom. While
economic success is not a zero-sum game in a market economy such as
we continue to enjoy in America, the appeal of income redistribution as
a response to claimed injustice in the distribution of income still exerts
political power in the modern world.

In ancient times massive inequality repeatedly unleashed the forces of
revolution and redistribution. Because trying to impose equality where it

doesn't exist and cannot be sustained is unworkable, Plato saw inequality as the Achilles' heel of democracy. In Plato's world, ownership of land in a city-state was the primary source of wealth. This reality, combined with the fact that economic growth was virtually nonexistent, meant that income and wealth were indeed largely distributed and not created. Plato could not have envisioned the post-Enlightenment world, as described by Adam Smith, in which economic growth made it possible for everyone to have more. Elon Musk became the richest man in the world not by taking wealth away from anyone but by *creating* it. New college graduates earn, on average, twice the income of those who have only high school diplomas. College graduates do so not because they take income away from those who are less educated but because the acquisition of human capital increases their ability to produce goods and services that consumers—including those with less education—value.

Much of the discussion of income redistribution in America is based on the implicit assumption that the share of overall income earned by an individual or group of individuals is generated, at least in part, by taking income away from other individuals or groups; however, in a growing economy, the primary driver of income distribution is the ability to earn wages and accrue earnings through thrift, accumulation, and entrepreneurial creativity. In modern America the distribution of income is also profoundly affected by the government's imposition of taxes and its disbursal of transfer payments. The distribution of income is the confluence of all these forces and is a relevant economic indicator of how broadly prosperity is being shared. Income distribution is, therefore, worthy of our attention.

THE MYTH

"It is a truth universally acknowledged that inequality in the rich world is high and rising."[4] That is how, in 2020, the *Economist* magazine summed up public opinion. While the political reaction to the level of income inequality varies between America's two major political parties, the claim that income inequality in America is high and rising on a secular basis is almost universally accepted as true. According to Sen. Bernie

Sanders (I-Vermont), "the obscene and increasing level of wealth and income inequality in this country is immoral, un-American and unsustainable."[5] In his 2014 digital project, *Growing Apart, A Political History of American Inequality*, Colin Gordon, professor of American history at the University of Iowa, gave an academic imprimatur to Bernie Sanders's political assessment.[6] Gordon writes, "First, American inequality is *exceptional*. By any measure, we are more unequal now than we have ever been, and we are more unequal—by a longshot—than our peers among developed and democratic nations."[7] Thomas Piketty goes one step further by concluding that income inequality in the United States "is probably higher than that in any other society at any other time in the past, anywhere in the world."[8]

The drumbeat of complaints about high and rising economic inequality is unrelenting. For example, in 2020 Pope Francis described today's distribution of income as "dismal," "a sickness," and "a social disease."[9] He encourages his flock to combat it, insisting, "We cannot stand and watch."[10] Likewise, Disney heiress Abigail Disney declares that "extreme wealth is eating our world alive." Ms. Disney is part of a group of wealthy celebrities, including the movie star Mark Ruffalo, who argue—as reported by CBS News—"that the rich aren't paying their fair share, allowing them to become even richer while inequality widens across the globe."[11]

This same theme is sounded even by some Nobel laureate economists. The 2015 Nobel laureate Angus Deaton reports being shocked, upon moving from Britain to the United States in 1983, that so many American economists were unconcerned about American economic inequality. Deaton complains that "the top 10 percent of incomes in the United States account for nearly half of all income, compared with only 14 percent for the bottom half of incomes."[17] In 2023 he insisted that "the United States has become a darker society since I arrived in 1983."[13] Among Deaton's other grievances about the "darkening" American economy is the alleged fact that "less well-educated Americans have seen little or no improvement in their material circumstances for more than fifty years. For men without a four-year college degree, median real wages have trended downward since 1970."[14] Joseph Stiglitz, cowinner of the 2001 Nobel Prize, believes that "growing inequality in our society undermines the strength of the American economy."[15] Not to be outdone, Paul Krugman, the 2008 Nobel laureate in economics, warns that

the reality of rising American inequality is stark. Since the late 1970s real wages for the bottom half of the work force have stagnated or fallen, while the incomes of the top 1 percent have nearly quadrupled (and the incomes of the top 0.1 percent have risen even more). While we can and should have a serious debate about what to do about this situation, the simple fact—American capitalism as currently constituted is undermining the foundations of middle-class society—shouldn't be up for argument.[16]

These worries and warnings are not without support in the nation's official economic statistics. According to the US Census Bureau, the top 20 percent of households in America in 2017 had an average income that was 16.7 times higher than the average income of the bottom 20 percent of households.[17] The official Census data also show that income inequality has grown on a secular basis, and by 2017 was 22.9 percent higher than in 1947.[18] In addition, data from the Organisation for Economic Co-operation and Development (OECD) show that the United States has the most unequal distribution of income of any developed nation in the world and that the level of inequality is rising.[19]

THE MYTH VS. THE REALITY OF INCOME DISTRIBUTION IN AMERICA

Careful inspection reveals numerous clues that something is profoundly wrong with the above-mentioned Census measure of household income, which is the fundamental building block of American statistics on the distribution of income and poverty. Every year, the Census Bureau issues an official measure of household income, which is broken up into quintiles. The official numbers for 2017 are presented in column 1 of table 6.1. The Bureau of Labor Statistics releases official data on annual consumption expenditures by American households, which are also broken out into quintiles. Those data are presented in column 2 of table 6.1.

Column 3 shows the ratio of the Bureau of Labor Statistics measure of annual *consumption* compared to the Census measure of annual household *income*. According to the official statistics of the nation's two leading statistical agencies, the bottom 20 percent of American households had an average income of $13,258 in 2017 yet, in that same year, consumed $26,091 of goods and services. This fact raises the obvious question of how the bottom 20 percent of households can consume twice their income. This extraordinary gap between the official measure of income and the official measure of consumption has grown more or less steadily since 1967, when funding for the War on Poverty began to ramp up.

Table 6.1. The Official Census Measure of Household Income and the Official Bureau of Labor Statistics Measure of Household Consumption in 2017

	OFFICIAL CENSUS MEASURE OF HOUSEHOLD INCOME	OFFICIAL BLS MEASURE OF HOUSEHOLD CONSUMPTION	RATIO OF EXPENDITURES TO INCOME
Bottom	$13,258	$26,091	1.97
Second	$35,401	$39,300	1.11
Third	$61,564	$50,470	0.82
Fourth	$99,030	$67,604	0.68
Top	$221,846	$116,988	0.53

Source: US Census Bureau, "Historical Income Tables: Households," last updated August 30, 2024, https://www.census.gov/data/tables/time-series/demo/income-poverty/histori cal-income-households.html; Bureau of Labor Statistics, "Table 1101. Quintiles of Income Before Taxes: Annual Expenditure Means, Shares, Standard Errors, and Coefficients of Variation, Consumer Expenditure Survey, 2017," published September 2018, https:// www.bls.gov/cex/tables/calendar-year/mean-item-share-average-standard-error/cu -income-quintiles-before-taxes-2017.pdf.

Comparisons of average income with consumption in the other quintiles are also revealing. The second quintile's average income was $35,401, but its members consumed $39,300—11 percent more than their income. The middle-income quintile consumed 82 percent of their income, the fourth quintile consumed only 68 percent of their income, and the top quintile consumed only slightly more than half of their income, even though no official statistics on household savings show anything like these levels of thrift. Something here screams for an explanation.

UNCOUNTED INCOME

All of these anomalies occur for the simple reason that the Census Bureau does not count two-thirds of all transfer payments to the recipients as income, instead counting only $0.9 trillion of $2.8 trillion of government transfer payments. In addition, the Census Bureau neither adjusts household income for taxes paid nor counts tax credits as income received by the recipients, even though they receive checks from the Treasury. Census does not count SNAP benefits as income, despite beneficiaries receiving debit cards to pay for groceries. Also not counted as income are benefits received from Medicaid, under which the government pays for each beneficiary's health care. And also uncounted as income are the transfer payments dispensed through more than one hundred other federal, state, and local programs.[20]

In 2017, prior to the pandemic, Americans paid $4.6 trillion in federal, state, and local taxes.[21] Of these taxes, 83.1 percent were paid by the top 40 percent of income earners; the top 1 percent of earners alone paid 23.8 percent of these taxes.[22] Most households never see this money because it is withheld from their paychecks. Yet in measuring household income, poverty, and income inequality, the Census Bureau neither reduces household income by the amount of taxes paid nor increases household income by the amount of refundable tax credits received. The extraordinary result is that by not counting two-thirds of all transfer payments, net of the cost of making the transfer, as income received—and by also not counting taxes paid as income lost to taxpayers—the official Census measure of household income fails to take into account most of the impact that government policy has on income distribution. Because the Census Bureau excludes $1.9 trillion of transfer payments as income received and fails to count $4.4 trillion of taxes paid as income lost to taxpayers, the Census measure of household income ignores some 40 percent of national income which is either gained in transfer payments or lost in taxes.[23]

The Census Bureau's bizarre process of measuring household income dates back to the origin of the statistical measurement of household income, which began in 1947. At that time, the great majority of all payments were made in cash or cash equivalents. Given the Census Bureau's statistical capacity in 1947, it decided, for simplicity purposes, to count as income only cash and cash-equivalent payments. Since businesses paid few fringe benefits and virtually all government benefits were paid in cash, the 1947 measure was reasonably accurate. However, with the coming of the War on Poverty in the mid-1960s, almost all new benefits were payments in kind. The government paid for those benefits directly rather than giving the beneficiaries money to purchase them. In the fifty years between 1967 and 2017, inflation-adjusted government transfer payments to the average household in the bottom 20 percent of the income distribution rose from $9,677 to $45,389.[24]

Yet the official Census measure of poverty showed that the percentage of Americans living in poverty did not change significantly, rising to as high as 15 percent during recessions and falling to as low as 11 percent during periods of prosperity.[25]

When refundable tax credits were first created by Congress in 1975, even though these payments were made in the form of a check from the Treasury, the Census Bureau did not count the Treasury checks as income because the Census, as a matter of policy, did not take taxes into account. Yet despite issuing warnings about the limitations of its data, the Census Bureau nevertheless uses its own incomplete measure of household income to calculate the official measures of inequality and the poverty rate. Since the government's official definition of poverty is based on a multiple of the cost of a nutritionally adequate diet, it is astonishing that a measure of income that does not count SNAP benefits is used to calculate the official poverty rate.

The Census Bureau also uses its household-income data to measure income inequality without considering the income lost in paying taxes and the income gained by the receipt of the two-thirds of all transfer payments that are not counted as income. Payments for medical care, housing, and food consume over half the income of the average middle-income household. Yet the Census measure of the inequality of middle-income households as compared to bottom-income quintile households fails to take into account the fact that middle-income households must pay for medical care, housing, and food out of their own incomes; meanwhile, the government provides those benefits to low-income households in the form of Medicaid, housing subsidies, and SNAP benefits. Footnotes and caveats found in official statistical reports largely explain all of these limitations of the Census measure of household income, but the government nevertheless uses these measures of household income to calculate and report the poverty rate and income inequality as if those limitations do not exist. Others who use the Census measure of household income follow the same practice.[26]

Whereas the Census Bureau's official numbers tell us that the average household in the top quintile has 16.7 times as much income as the average household in the bottom quintile, when you count (1) all income, including fringe benefits and realized capital gains, which are not counted in the official Census household income numbers; (2) all transfer payments as income to their recipients; and (3) all taxes paid as income lost to the taxpayers, the ratio of the income of the average household in the top quintile to the average household in the bottom quintile falls from the official Census Bureau number of 16.7 to 1 to the significantly lower number of 4 to 1. Of course, you can argue that 4 to 1 is still too high. But the debate is very different when this ratio is recognized as 4 to 1 than when it's believed to be 16.7 to 1.

Figure 6.1, originally developed by economist John Early, former assistant commissioner of the Bureau of Labor Statistics, shows earned income as the dashed line. Income after taxes and transfer payments is shown as the solid line. Where transfer payments exceed taxes paid, the difference is shown in the vertically shaded area. Where taxes exceed the value of transfer payments, the difference is shown by the diagonally shaded area.[27]

In addition to the fall in the ratio of the top-to-bottom-quintile income ratio from 16.7 to 1 to 4 to 1, figure 6.1 also notably shows how flat the income distribution is among the bottom three quintiles. In 2017 the after-tax income of the bottom quintile amounts to $49,613 when all income sources, including all transfer payments, are counted. In that same year, the average household in the second quintile had an income of only $53,924, while the average income of the middle-income quintile was $65,631.[28]

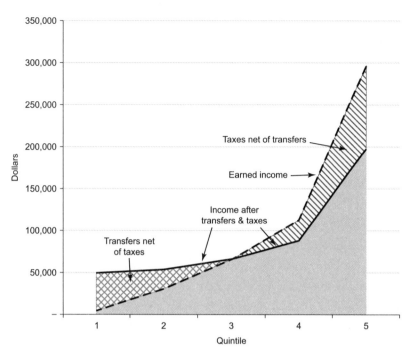

Figure 6.1. Contributions of Earned Income, Government Transfer Payments, Private Transfer Payments, and Taxes to After-Tax Income, 2017. *Sources:* US Census Bureau, "Current Population Survey, Annual Social and Economic Supplement, March 2018 (Data for 2017)," census.gov; Congressional Budget Office, "The Distribution of Household Income, 2015," published March 2018, https://www.cbo.gov/publication/54646#:~:tex; Washington, DC, Extreme poverty adjustments based on Bruce D. Meyer, Derek Wu, Victoria Mooers, Carla Medalia, "The Use and Misuse of Income Data and Extreme Poverty in the United States," NBER Working Paper No. 25907 (May 2019); US Bureau of Economic Analysis, "Table 3.12 Government Social Benefits," National Income and Product Accounts," last revised September 27, 2024, https://apps.bea.gov; Social Security Administration, *Annual Statistical Supplement to the Social Security Bulletin, 2017* (SSA, 2018); The Board of Trustees, Federal Old-Age and Survivors Insurance and Federal Disability Insurance Trust Funds, *The 2018 Annual Report of the Board of Trustees of the Federal Old-Age and Survivors Insurance and Federal Disability Insurance Trust Funds* (SSA, 2018), table II.B1, 7; The Boards of Trustees, Federal Hospital Insurance and Federal Supplementary Medical Insurance Trust Funds, *2018 Annual Report of the Boards of Trustees of the Federal Hospital Insurance and Federal Supplementary Medical Insurance Trust Funds* (SSA, 2018), table II.B1, 11; Jeff Sessions, *CRS Report: Welfare Spending the Largest Item in the Federal Budget* (United States Senate Budget Committee, 2013); Congressional Research Service, "Spending for Federal Benefits and Services for People with Low Income, FY 2001–2011: An Update of Table B-1 from CRS Report R41625," published October 16, 2012, https://digital.library.unt.edu/ark:/67531/metadc227630/; US Census Bureau, American Housing Survey, "2017 National—Housing Costs—All Occupied Units, Tenure Filter: Renter," https://www.census.gov/programs.

But even these numbers for household income overstate income inequality by failing to account for differences in the number of individuals living in the average-sized household of each income quintile. The bottom quintile has, on average, only 1.69 people living in each household. The conception of a poverty-stricken household headed by a mother caring for a bunch of children is fifty years out of date. The second quintile has, on average, 2.23 people living in the household, and the middle, fourth, and top quintiles have 2.51, 2.81, and 3.10, respectively.[29] When you calculate per capita income, or you use the OECD or Census technique for adjusting for household size, the net result of taking account of the number of people living in the household is that *individuals* living in the bottom 60 percent of American households all have roughly the same level of income. This near-equality occurs even though only 36 percent of prime working-age persons in the bottom quintile actually work compared to 85 percent in the second quintile and 92 percent in the middle-income quintile.[30]

The average second-quintile household earned almost five times as much as the average household in the bottom quintile because it had 2.4 times as many working-age members working, and, on average, each worker worked 80 percent more hours. The average middle-quintile household earned almost 10 times as much and had 2.6 times the percentage of its working-age persons working, each working twice as many hours. Yet the bottom 60 percent of American households all received essentially the same income after accounting for taxes, transfer payments, and household size.[31]

While official statistics don't count two-thirds of those transfer payments and don't show the income equality they produce, Americans who work hard to make ends meet are well aware of it. Despite widespread efforts to provoke resentment against the rich, when was the last time you heard working people complain that some people in America are rich? The hostility of working people increasingly focuses on a system in which those who don't break a sweat are about as well off as they are. This resentment is a major cause of the wave of populist sentiment that has swept across the nation in the last decade and spawned political support for a new and more comprehensive welfare reform.

IS INCOME INEQUALITY GROWING IN AMERICA?

Not only do the official Census numbers overstate the difference between the top and bottom quintile household incomes by over 300 percent, but the Census Bureau's failure to count two-thirds of all transfer payments and all taxes further distorts the measure of the growth in income inequality over time. Figure 6.2 shows the growth in income for all five quintiles from 1947 through 2017, taking into account income gained through transfer payments and income lost through payment of taxes.

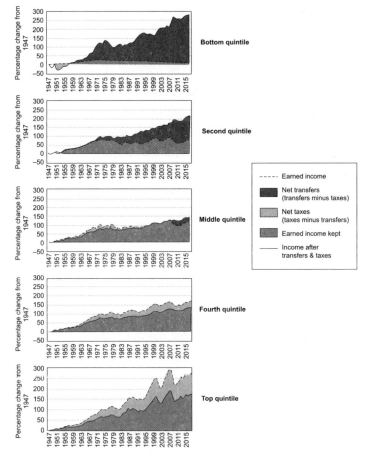

Figure 6.2. Cumulative Percentage Change from 1947 in Real Household Income Components, by Quintile.[33] *Source:* Phil Gramm, Robert Ekelund, and John Early, *The Myth of American Inequality* (Rowman & Littlefield, 2022), 45.[32]

Over the seventy years from 1947 to 2017, after adjusting for infla-tion, the real value of all transfer payments grew 212.2 percent, faster than earned personal income had grown. Taxes grew less dramatically, rising only 7 percent faster than earned income over these seventy years. Income and payroll taxes rose 21 percent faster than income. Sales, ex-cise, and property taxes rose 8.3 percent slower than income.[33] The net result was that the US income-tax system became significantly more progressive in the seventy years leading up to the COVID-19 pandemic as an ever-larger share of the tax burden has been shifted from low- and middle-income households onto higher-income households, reducing income inequality.

As presented in figure 6.2, the *earned* income of bottom-quintile households, shown by the dashed line, rose from 1947 to 1967 and then steadily declined through 2017. As the number of prime working-age persons who actually worked in the bottom quintile of households fell from 67 percent in 1967 to 36 percent fifty years later, the level of earned income for the average household in the bottom quintile fell, even though real wages and benefits rose for those individuals who continued to work. Taking into account all transfer payments and taxes shown in figure 6.2, the average real income of bottom-quintile households rose by 285 percent, faster than in any other quintile. The average real income of the second quintile rose by 217 percent despite the small decline in earned income due to a decline in labor-force participation after 1967. The middle-income quintile saw its real income rise by 146 percent and received, on average, about the same amount of transfer payments as it paid in taxes. It is important to note that Medicare and Social Security make up a significant share of transfer payments going to the middle- and higher-income quintiles. The fourth quintile saw its after-tax real income grow by 137 percent while its earned income rose along with the taxes it paid. The top quintile saw its earned real income rise dra-matically, but its taxes rise even faster, resulting in its after-tax income growing by 174 percent.

The conventional measure of income inequality is the Gini coeffi-cient, which ranges from 0 to 1. A Gini coefficient of 0 means that every household in the nation has the same income, while a coefficient of 1 means that a single household has all of the nation's income. Because the Census Bureau fails to count as income approximately two-thirds of all transfer payments, including 88 percent of all transfer payments to the bottom 20 percent of income earners, and fails to deduct from income measures the taxes paid, using Census Bureau numbers to calculate the Gini coefficient for America produces a highly inaccurate result. The calculated Gini coefficient for America in 2017—0.482—significantly overstates the reality of household-income differences.[34]

According to the Census Bureau, the US Gini coefficient grew by 21.4 percent over the fifty-year period from 1967 to 2017.[35] Yet much of this increase was due simply to two very significant changes made in the way the Census Bureau collects and records data. The most significant change in the Census Bureau's data-collection process occurred in 1993. Before that year, when a respondent to the Census survey reported an income source greater than $249,999, the interviewer entered only $249,999 for that income category—no matter how high that respondent's actual income was. In 1993 this artificial reporting limit was raised to $999,999, and subsequently the cap was eliminated altogether.[36] The 1993 change alone added $52.7 billion to the estimated aggregate 1993 income of high-income households, causing the Gini coefficient to balloon strictly due to this change in the way data are collected and recorded.[37] The differences in income shown in the 1993 measure and in subsequent years had existed in earlier years but had not been counted. The Census reported in detail on the methodological discontinuity that this change produced; it warned that "the change in the questionnaire causes a break in the time series for some income measures . . . mean income, per capita income, shares of aggregate income by quintile and the index of income concentration (Gini Index) were all affected by the revisions, and caution should be used when comparing the 1993 data to earlier years."[38] Yet this warning did not stop the Census Bureau from using pre- and post-1993 data in calculating the Gini coefficient. Nor did it prevent those using the data from leaping to the mistaken conclusion that income inequality ballooned in America in 1993.

A similar discontinuity occurred in 2013, when a new set of questions was added to probe for and encourage more complete reporting of income. But as was the case in 1993, the Census continued to calculate the Gini coefficient using the unadjusted data for the years before 2013. Astonishingly, as much as 42.1 percent of the measured increase in the Gini coefficient between 1947 and 2017 is due solely to these two changes in the way data are collected and recorded.[39] Correcting only for these two statistical anomalies causes the Gini coefficient to rise, over the past seventy years, by only 16.1 percent rather than by the reported 22.9 percent.[40]

When these corrections are made *and* all transfer payments and taxes are counted, the Gini coefficient is actually slightly lower today than it was in 1947. Over the fifty years from 1967 to 2017, the level of inequality fell by slightly more than 3 percent. We now are having a debate about the threat that growing income inequality poses to both our economic and political systems when, in fact, income inequality has actually *declined* over the past seventy years instead of having risen by nearly 23 percent, as reported by the Census Bureau. The most important thing to know about the growth of income inequality in America is that it is *not* growing and that our official statistics present a grossly distorted picture of reality by not correcting for statistical anomalies in the Bureau's collection and reporting process, as well as by not counting all transfer payments as income to recipients and all taxes paid as income lost to taxpayers. When all of those things are taken into account, income inequality in the last seventy years has slightly declined.

HOW DOES US INEQUALITY STACK UP INTERNATIONALLY?

The Census Bureau submits incomplete data to the OECD, which do not include most of the transfer payments, as these payments are not counted in measuring household income in the United States. Those incomplete data are then used by OECD to reach the mistaken conclusion that the United States has a higher level of income inequality than any other developed country. When the Census Bureau data submitted to the OECD are corrected for the missing transfer payments—the

OECD already takes most taxes into account—America's Gini coefficient falls to a level roughly in the middle of the seven largest developed
countries.[41]

It is also important to note that having a lower Gini coefficient—that
is, a more equal distribution of incomes—by no means indicates that a
nation is better off than other nations with higher Gini coefficients or
even that low-income individuals in that more "equal" nation are better
off than are low-income people in countries with higher Gini coefficients. Major developed nations that have more equal distributions of
income than the United States have significantly lower incomes overall,
so their populations at all levels might have more equally distributed
incomes, but they are equally poorer. According to the standards for
poverty measurement used by international organizations, developed
nations with more equal income distributions than America also have
larger portions of their populations that are poor. (These are the results
when the income levels used to determine poverty for America are also
used for the other countries.)[42]

USING STATISTICAL TRICKERY TO OVERSTATE INCOME INEQUALITY

To "prove" massive income inequality, advocates of greater redistribution, in addition to not taking into account most transfer payments and
all taxes, focus on the earnings of a small number of very high-income
earners. Thomas Piketty uses both tactics in his 2014 best seller, *Capital
in the Twenty-First Century*.[43] The numbers he uses do not count any
transfer payments as income to the recipients, since he excludes even the
transfer payments that are counted as income by the US Census Bureau.
This maneuver alone lowers the income of America's bottom quintile by
some 90 percent. And by not reducing the incomes of the top 1 percent
of earners by the amount of taxes they pay, Piketty increases the income
of top earners by 39 percent. The net result of both maneuvers is to vastly
overestimate the share of income the top 1 percent of earners are said—
not to earn—but to "take."[44]

While Piketty claims that the share of national income going to the top 1 percent of earners more than doubled between 1962 and 2019, Gerald Auten of the Office of Tax Analysis at the US Treasury and David Splinter of the Joint Committee on Taxation, in their 2024 study "Income Inequality in the U.S.: Using Tax Data to Measure Long-term Trends," show that when all transfer payments and taxes are counted, the share of national income going to the top 1 percent of American households is about the same as it was in the mid-1960s.[45]

Like many critics of capitalism and the contemporary distribution of income in America, Piketty is obsessed with top-percentile earners. This obsession has a long history. American progressives were so obsessed with the 4,050 American millionaires in the Gilded Age that they turned a blind eye to the 66 million Americans whose economic well-being was improving faster than that of any other people who had ever lived.[46] The relevance to public policy of the top 1 percent of earners, especially given that they already pay a larger share of the total income tax burden compared to their share of earned income than any other taxpayers in the world, boils down mostly to the demagogic value of the numerical comparison of their incomes to those of everybody else.[47]

Moreover, in the debate about income inequality and the fairness of the tax code, the deception is even greater than simply not counting transfer payments and taxes in income comparisons. Emmanuel Saez and Gabriel Zucman seek to show that low-income Americans face an effective tax rate that is higher than the rate faced by the highest-income earners in the country.[48] They perform this astonishing feat by not counting any transfer payments as income to the recipients *and* by changing the definition of income for high-income households. In refusing to count transfer payments as income for low-income households, Saez and Zucman swell the level of state and local taxes paid by these households to 25 percent of their "income." Because of the standard deduction and various tax credits, low-income households don't pay federal income taxes. It should also be noted that, to avoid having to explain how low-income households paid taxes in excess of their incomes, these researchers arbitrarily exclude from their statistics very low-income households, which are more than 16 percent of all households and four-fifths of those in the bottom quintile.

What Saez and Zucman do at the opposite end of the income distribution is equally distorting: they change the definition of income to include appreciation of unsold assets. This move is the equivalent of measuring your income in any given year by estimating what your earnings would be that year if you sold your house, cashed out your retirement investments, and liquidated all of your other financial and physical assets. Since the average top earners paid over 40 percent of their income (as income is defined by the IRS) in federal, state, and local taxes, it is only by grossly understating the income of low-income households and inflating what is meant by "income" for high-income households that Saez and Zucman are able to claim that the rich pay taxes at lower rates than poor people do.

When the journalism organization ProPublica obtained the stolen tax returns of ultra-high earners, the actual tax rates obviously did not support the point ProPublica sought to make, inducing them to engage in a classic bait and switch. From ProPublica's exposé, it appears that figures on actual taxes paid are taken from the stolen tax returns, but in fact, ProPublica does not use the reported taxable income. Instead, it makes up an income figure by estimating what the taxpayers *would have earned* if all of their assets had been sold and the resulting capital gains taxed. By this definition of income, which is applied in the taxing system of no country in the world, ProPublica claims that the titans of industry and finance "don't pay their fair share."[49]

INDIVIDUALS SUCCEED IN MARKETS BY ENRICHING OTHERS

Piketty, like other collectivists, not only focuses on economic outliers but speaks of their higher incomes as what they "take," "claim," or "absorb" instead of what they earn or create. The clear implication is that the rich are taking something away from someone else, as if we live in a zero-sum world in which someone earning more means that someone else must be earning less. How are we worse off because Bill Gates today owns 0.53 percent of Microsoft?[50] His products enrich our lives, he created hundreds of thousands of jobs, and our pension funds are more valuable because we own many times more shares of Microsoft than he does. And, of course, the government took a large share of Gates's creation in taxes.

While at Yale, Fred Smith got a C on a research paper he'd written on the feasibility of an overnight-delivery service. In the real world, he got an A+ when FedEx's customers made him a billionaire, and he created six hundred thousand jobs worldwide. Just how did his success make you poorer?

Likewise, what exactly did Warren Buffett's investment genius take away from us? He made the economy more productive by improving the employment of capital. He made his investors rich and built companies that carried thousands of people to the top of the financial mountain with him. The Buffett case allegedly illustrates the left's argument that the megarich avoid taxes by simply avoiding taking income. Fair-minded people can debate whether a chronic wealth accumulator like Mr. Buffett, who spends so little of his wealth, is paying his fair share of taxes. But there's a strong case to be made that his living a modest lifestyle only further increases the benefits he bestows on the public.

What is the purpose of taxation if not to serve the general welfare? To the degree that Mr. Buffett simply accumulates and does not consume, his wealth is devoted to expanding and improving the capital bases of the companies in which he invests. He thereby creates better jobs and promotes the general prosperity rather than increasing his own consumption. What he creates but doesn't consume, he leaves for the rest of us to consume. Though sweeter and more generous than Ebenezer Scrooge, Mr. Buffett resembles the Victorian-era financier in his restrained consumption. Money was of no use to Scrooge, because he didn't spend it, but accumulators like Scrooge financed the investments in railroads and factories that gave nineteenth-century England the highest living standards in the world at that time and, not incidentally, also helped to enrich Americans when their funds were invested across the Atlantic. Would the public really be better off if the government diverted Mr. Buffett's billions from promoting general prosperity? When he dies, he will either give his wealth away or the government will take 40 percent of it in death taxes. But he has benefited mankind more in making the money than he ever will ever giving it away or having it spent by the government.

In a society based on voluntary exchange, only governments and criminals take without giving. Those with skills and accumulated capital can earn vast incomes only by employing those skills and that capital to produce things others are willing to buy. Competition for consumer patronage fuels the process that generates greater value. In engaging in this productive process, managers, entrepreneurs, and investors don't just earn, they *create*, and we all benefit from the value-creation process as consumers of the goods and services it produces. Nobel laureate economist William Nordhaus of Yale University estimates that innovators in America during the second half of the twentieth century captured a mere 2.2 percent of the total social value of their innovations.[51] By any plausible criteria, this entrepreneurial deal is an incredible bargain for ordinary people. High-income earners in the market economy are not taking, claiming, or absorbing; they are instead *creating*, producing, sharing, and giving. We are not made poorer by this process; we are enriched by it.

THE AMERICAN DREAM IS ALIVE AND WELL

Finally, much of the income-inequality debate implies that the system is rigged and that children who are born and grow up in poor families don't have an opportunity to succeed in America. This claim is totally refuted by the data. It is of course better to be born rich, beautiful, and brilliant than to come into this world poor, ugly, and ordinary. But in America, being poor, ugly, and ordinary disqualifies no one from participating in the American dream.

It is important to understand the extraordinary progress that has occurred in America in just the last fifty years. In real purchasing-power dollars, median household income from 1967 to 2017 rose by 40.3 percent.[52] An income level that put you into the middle quintile in 2017 would have put you in the top quintile in 1967, even after adjusting for inflation.[53]

The American Dream, stated in its simplest economic form, is the dream that our children will do better economically than we have done. Using data from the Panel Survey of Income Dynamics, analysts for the Pew Charitable Trusts calculated the percentage of adult children who, at the age of forty-five, lived in a family with an average real income higher than their parents' income at a similar age. The American dream comes true for the overwhelming majority of American families. Of children born in a bottom-quintile household from 1967 through 1971, 93 percent of them, as adults between 2000 and 2008, lived in households with higher real incomes than their parents. Children who were born and grew up in second-, middle-, and fourth-quintile households lived in households as adults with higher incomes than their parents some 86 percent of the time. Those who were born and grew up in the top quintile exceeded their parents' real income 70 percent of the time. This level of economic achievement is, of course, only possible in a country that experiences significant and sustained economic growth.[54]

In addition to measuring absolute mobility, several major studies have investigated relative mobility—that is, the probability that a child who was born and grew up in a household in a certain income quintile would remain in that quintile as an adult, rise to a higher quintile, or fall to a lower quintile. Three major studies—one by the Pew Charitable Trusts, another led by Raj Chetty of Harvard University, and a third by economist Michael Strain of the American Enterprise Institute—look at slightly different time periods, but their results are almost identical.

The Pew Charitable Trusts study used data from the University of Michigan's Panel Study of Income Dynamics to compare the quintiles of average adult children's income from the period 2000 to 2008, when the children were between thirty-two and fifty-eight years of age, with the quintile of their parents' income in 1967 to 1971, when they were children between zero and eighteen years old.[55] The study led by Raj Chetty, using IRS data taken from income-tax returns, compared the income rank of children in their early thirties in 2011–2012 with the rank of their parents' income in 1996–2000, when the children were between the ages of fifteen and twenty.[56]

The final study, by Michael Strain, used the same data as the Pew study and compared the income rankings of those children who were in their forties in the years 2013–2017 with their parents' income rankings during the years when their parents were in their forties.[57] The findings of the three studies are very similar, but the Strain study covers a longer period of time, and therefore the ages of the parents and the adult children are more similar, so we focus on its findings. The findings of the Strain study are presented in figure 6.3.

It is important to note that if parents' income had no relationship to the income of their adult children, the children, when grown, would fall randomly into the five quintiles. If, instead, the parents' incomes were totally determinative of the children's incomes, 100 percent of the children who were born and grew up in any given quintile would end up as adults

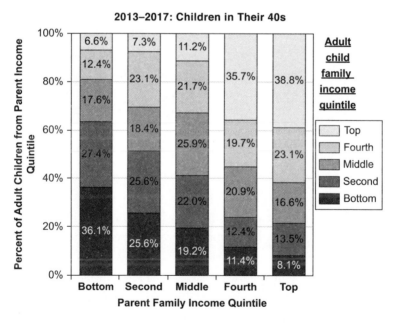

Figure 6.3. Strain Study Comparing Average Annual Income Quintiles for Adult Children with Income Quintiles for Their Parents. *Source:* Michael R. Strain, *The American Dream Is Not Dead* (Templeton Press, 2020), as corrected after first printing, figure 16.

with incomes in that same quintile. With these points of reference, the Strain study indicates significant intergenerational mobility, as do the Pew and Chetty studies.

Using five bar charts, figure 6.3 shows children born in each of the five quintiles. Children who were born and grew up in the bottom quintile are presented in the bar chart on the far left, and children who were born and grew up in the top quintile are represented in the bar chart on the far right. Of the children born in the bottom quintile, 36.1 percent ended up living in households as adults that had bottom-quintile incomes. Of that same group of children, 27.4 percent rose to the second quintile, 17.6 percent rose to the middle-income quintile, 12.4 percent rose to the fourth quintile, and 6.6 percent lived as adults in households with top-quintile incomes. The results for children who were born and grew up in the top quintile are virtually a mirror image of the bottom quintile. Of the children who were born and grew up in the top quintile, 38.8 percent lived, as adults, in households with a top-quintile income. Of this same group, 23.1 percent fell to the fourth quintile, 16.6 percent fell to the middle-income quintile, 13.5 percent fell to the second quintile, and 8.1 percent fell all the way to the bottom quintile. About half of the children born in the second quintile rose to a higher quintile, and about a quarter fell to the bottom quintile. About a quarter of the children born and raised in the middle quintile stayed in the middle quintile as adults, 33 percent rose to the fourth or top quintile, and 41 percent fell to the second or bottom quintile.

Figure 6.3 clearly shows that while the income quintile of parents has some effect on their children's economic success, there is nevertheless significant mobility across all quintiles, with the mobility in the middle three quintiles being closer to what you would expect if parental income had no effect. Professors, pundits, and politicians who have criticized economic mobility in America have focused almost exclusively on the bottom and top quintiles, noting the large number of children—36 percent and 39 percent, respectively—who were born and raised in the bottom and top quintiles and who remained in those quintiles as adults. However, at least some of this clustering at the bottom and the top of the distribution is due to what statisticians call *truncation*. Because there is no cap on the top-income quintile, children born in the top quintile remain in the top quintile no matter how much more they earn than their parents. For example, from all outward appearances, Elon Musk was born and grew up in the top quintile, but in becoming the richest man in the world, he could not earn his way out of the top quintile, since there is no penthouse category. A similar truncation occurs for children born in the bottom quintile. No matter how little income they have, there is no basement quintile, and so they are recorded as having stayed in the same quintile as their parents, even though they might have significantly less income.

We expect children of highly successful parents to have some clear advantages over children born to less economically successful parents, as they have their parents' genes and live in economically successful households. Their parents can afford to send them to private schools and hire tutors and counselors to promote their success. But the ability of parents to nurture their children is a product of more than the parents' income. Anyone who believes that parental income is the dominant factor in nurturing of children and promoting their success has clearly not met many American mothers. The extraordinary success of countless immigrant families' children in contemporary America is ample proof that parental support and nurturing are very important to the development of children—and parental support is only marginally related to the parents' monetary income. Even more important are parental devotion, attention, and nurturing.

It is clear from figure 6.3 that the American dream is alive and well, but even these impressive numbers understate real income mobility in America. The Strain study and similar studies, including those by Pew and Chetty, measure the relative mobility of children born and raised in one quintile against the mobility of children initially from other quintiles. Yet between the time that children were growing up in their parents' household and when they became adults, the American economy grew significantly, changing the quintiles in that the children's incomes being measured are significantly higher than were the incomes that defined the quintiles of their parents' generation. Between 1982, the beginning of the parents' era in the Strain study, and 2017, the ending of the measurement period for the children's era, real median household income rose by 38 percent. To rise out of the bottom quintile, since the ceiling of the bottom quintile was significantly higher for these children in 2017 than it had been for their parents in 1982, a child had to receive 35 percent more income to escape the bottom quintile than would have been required for their parents to escape the bottom quintile years before. Children reared in any other quintile had to see their real income as adults rise as much as 50 percent above their parents' income simply to avoid falling into a lower quintile than their parents. The climb to a higher quintile was steeper as well.

Fortunately, data from the Strain study can be used to measure mobility in a way that considers the income growth that occurred in America between the parents' generation and the adult children's generation. When comparing the children's income with their parents' inflation-adjusted income using the real-income quintiles of their childhood in 1982–1986 rather than the changed income quintiles of their adult years, 2013–2017, these researchers found measured mobility to be dramatically greater. Based on the real-income quintiles of the parents, only 28 percent of children reared in the bottom quintile had adult incomes that kept them in the bottom childhood quintile. Twenty-six percent rose all the way to their childhood top quintile, which required a minimum childhood income of only $111,416 (in 2016 dollars) for a family of four in 1982–1986. A family of four with that income, using the income quintiles of 2013–2017, would have been in the middle quintile, but compared to the real income of their parents' era, they had real incomes that put them in the top quintile.

During the thirty-five years covered by the Strain study, adult children who worked enjoyed the impact of the rapid economic growth that occurred during that period. Those who worked harder or acquired more skills saw their incomes rise even faster. And those who dropped out of the labor market missed the increase in income altogether. Those who didn't work had their progress stunted, as it was limited to the growth in welfare payments. The Strain study shown in figure 6.3 captures the effect of how well adult children did compared to other adult children, but it completely misses the fact that, on average, adult children born in every income quintile were earning real incomes that were significantly greater than their parents.'

This incredible income mobility is measured only over one generation. Parents struggle and sacrifice to provide their children with education and opportunities they themselves lacked, and millions of parents live out their own dreams through the achievements of their children. American mobility is impressive over one generation, but it becomes even more clearly pronounced over multiple generations. Historians believe that George Washington's grandmother came to America as an indentured worker. In turn, Washington became one of the richest men in Colonial America, and in the words of King George III, he was "the greatest man in the world."[58] That was America then; it is America still today.

Seven

THE MYTH THAT POVERTY
IS A FAILURE OF AMERICAN
CAPITALISM

———

THERE HAS ALWAYS BEEN something anomalous about poverty in America. In the closest place to Eden in human imagination, how could this land of milk and honey with its commodious harbors, ample rivers, fertile fields, and boundless forests have poverty in the midst of such natural and human wealth and unparalleled freedom and opportunity? In no other country has poverty seemed so unnatural, and therefore, it has been viewed as the great failing of American capitalism.

At the peak of the postwar boom, which had reduced the poverty rate from 32 percent of the nation's population in 1947 to 14.7 percent in 1965—an astonishing 54 percent decline in less than a generation— President Lyndon B. Johnson declared war on poverty in America. In an address before a joint session of Congress, he set the goal of eliminating the scourge of poverty in America. His stated goal was not just to provide a helping hand but to help America's poor find a way to share in and contribute to the nation's bounty. "The War on Poverty," he declared, "is not a struggle simply to support people, to make them dependent on the generosity of others. It is a struggle to give people a chance. It is an effort to allow them to develop and use their capacities as we have been allowed to develop and use ours, so that they can share, as other share, in the promise of this nation."[1]

The stated goal of the War on Poverty was to bring poor people into the mainstream of the economy. In that effort, by any objective measure, the War on Poverty has been an abject failure, as it has increased dependency and largely severed the bottom fifth of income recipients from the rewards and responsibilities of work. In 1967, as funding for the War on Poverty began to ramp up, so broadly based was the work ethic that 68 percent of prime working-age persons in the bottom income quintile worked. The second quintile actually had proportionately more of its prime working-age persons who worked than the middle quintile—89 percent compared to 85 percent. But despite LBJ's stated intent, the rapid growth in antipoverty transfers has been accompanied by a dramatic drop in the number of working-age persons in low-income households who actually work. By 2017 the number of working-age persons in the bottom quintile who actually worked had fallen to only 36 percent. The percentage of working-age persons in the second quintile who worked had fallen to 85 percent, while the percentage of working-age persons in middle-income America who worked had risen to 92 percent.[2]

By increasing dependency on government, the War on Poverty failed in its primary objective of bringing poor people into the mainstream of the American economy. Government programs replaced deprivation with idleness, stifling human flourishing. It happened just as Pres. Franklin Roosevelt predicted in 1935: "The lessons of history show conclusively that continued dependency upon relief induces a spiritual and moral disintegration fundamentally destructive to the national fiber. To dole out relief in this way is to administer a narcotic, a subtle destroyer of the human spirit. It is inimical to the dictates of a sound policy. It is in violation of the traditions of America."[3]

THE MYTH

The Marxian view that, under capitalism, the capitalists seize ever larger shares of society's wealth remains widespread. In 2014 the French economist Thomas Piketty, in his *Capital in the Twenty-First Century*, argued that as economic growth slows in developed countries, the rate of return on investment will exceed the rate of economic growth and ensure that, over time, an ever-larger share of the economic pie will be seized by the owners of capital. Piketty assumes that ownership of capital in society is concentrated in a small, closed group and that "inherited wealth will dominate wealth amassed from a lifetime's labor by wide margin."[4]

A similar story is told by Pulitzer Prize–winning Princeton sociologist Matthew Desmond. In his best-selling 2023 book, *Poverty, by America*, he insists that the poverty rate in America remains stubbornly high.[5] He pins much of the blame on the cruelties he believes naturally arise when corporations are lightly regulated, lightly taxed, and successful at keeping labor unorganized. As Desmond wrote in the *New York Times Magazine*, "with unions largely out of the picture, corporations have chipped away at the conventional midcentury work arrangement which involved steady employment, opportunities for advancement and raises and decent pay with some benefits."[6] Favorably reviewing Desmond's book in the *Guardian*, Yale professor of law and history Samuel Moyn remarked that

> one cause [of poverty's persistence] is a labour market that forces workers to help companies achieve profits while underpaying them, simply because they can. Desmond shows that the American economy has increasingly allowed business to enjoy power to coerce people into earning less for doing more. He insists he's not a Marxist—though he writes that raising the spectre of exploitation always makes him sound like he is. Yet Desmond's argument foregrounds precisely the extraction of surplus value that Marxists describe. The changing nature of work opportunities in America, along with the collapse of union density in the last 50 years, mean the forces of capitalism are winning. "Capitalism is inherently about workers trying to get as much, and owners trying to give as little, as possible," Desmond observes—and poverty endures because the first group has lost many battles against the second.[7]

The prolific author Joel Blau, a professor of social work at Stony Brook University, is of a similar opinion. Reviewing Washington University sociologist Mark Robert Rank's 2005 volume, *One Nation, Underprivileged:*

Why American Poverty Affects Us All, Blau applauds Rank for recognizing "that the causes of poverty lie in the workings of the U.S.'s particularly dogmatic brand of free market capitalism."[8] Also among those who share this negative view of capitalism is the founder of the People's Policy Project, Matt Bruenig, who declared in the pages of the *Washington Post* that "capitalism is a coercive economic system that creates persistent patterns of economic deprivation."[9]

With only a cursory look at the data, this negative assessment of capitalism seems justified. Statistics from the US Census Bureau, trumpeted by the Organisation for Economic Co-operation and Development, the United Nations, and the International Monetary Fund, show that a higher percentage of Americans live in poverty than in any other developed country in the world. Furthermore, the difference between the general level of prosperity in America and the living standards of its poor is larger than in other developed nations. A 2018 United Nations General Assembly report by the Special Rapporteur on Extreme Poverty proclaims that in America, "immense wealth and expertise stands in shocking contrast with the conditions in which vast numbers of its citizens live. About 40 million live in poverty, 18.5 million in extreme poverty, and 5.3 million live in Third World conditions of absolute poverty."[10] A 2017 report on America by the International Monetary Fund found that "job opportunities are deteriorating, prospects for upward mobility are waning and economic gains are increasingly accruing to those who are already wealthy."[11] Defining a nation's poverty rate as two-thirds of its median income, the Pew Research Center finds that the percentage of Americans living in poverty is significantly higher than in any other major developed nation.[12]

All of these damning conclusions are buttressed by the US Census Bureau's official measure of poverty, which shows that the poverty rate has not declined on a secular basis for more than fifty years. While the poverty rate plunged by over 50 percent from 1947 to 1967, from 1967 to the present the percentage of Americans living in poverty has simply oscillated from a low of 11 percent during periods of broad prosperity to a high of 15 percent during deep recessions.[13] It's no surprise, therefore, that Matthew Desmond laments that "when it comes to poverty reduction, we have had 50 years of nothing."[14] "Poverty will be abolished in America," Desmond concludes, "only when a mass movement demands it"—by which he means a mass *political* movement consciously devoted to eliminating poverty.[15]

GETTING THE FACTS STRAIGHT

The US government established a poverty threshold in 1963 that defined the minimum economic needs for each of the forty-eight family types and sizes.[16] Families that could not meet those needs were defined as poor. Beginning with US Department of Agriculture estimates of the cost of an economically, nutritionally adequate diet, the Social Security Administration set the poverty threshold for each family type at three times the cost of the economically, nutritionally adequate diet for the relevant family type and size. That number was based on a 1955 USDA food-consumption survey that showed that families spent, on average, roughly a third of their after-tax income on food. That fixed threshold of poverty consumption has been adjusted for inflation each year since 1963 using the Consumer Price Index for all urban consumers, thus increasing the nominal-dollar poverty level by 701 percent by 2017.[17]

It is important to note that the US definition of poverty, established in 1963, is based on the capacity to consume a level of goods and services deemed to be the minimum adequate amount. The dollar value of those goods and services has been adjusted over time to compensate for inflation. It seems strange that the poverty rate would have fallen by more than 50 percent in less than a generation, but then, when the War on Poverty began and its programs were funded at significant levels, beginning in 1967, the poverty rate then remained essentially unchanged for over a half-century. Counting the value of all transfer payments made to the bottom 20 percent of households in America, net of the cost of making those transfers, the average bottom-quintile household has seen the inflation-adjusted value of government transfer payments rise from $9,700 per year in 1967 to $45,400 in 2017, just three years before the pandemic.[18] Obviously, something is wrong here.

The same incongruous results occurred more recently when the explosion of pandemic spending sent means-tested government transfer payments, which mostly support low-income households, skyrocketing by 103 percent—or by $1.4 trillion—between 2019 and 2021.[19] The subsequent Census poverty measure then failed the most important statistical test: the laugh test. Following this $1.4 trillion explosion in social benefits that went mostly to low-income beneficiaries, the poverty rate—incredibly!—*rose* from 10.5 percent to 11.6 percent. President Biden claimed that the pandemic-era increase in the refundable child tax credit would cut child poverty in half, but when the Census subsequently reported the official child poverty measure, it showed that childhood poverty had actually risen from 14.4 percent to 15.3 percent.[20]

These absurd results were produced by the fact that the official Census measure of poverty fails to count 88 percent of all the benefits that poor American families receive from the government as part of their income, including refundable tax credits where the beneficiary receives a check from the Treasury, debit cards loaded with SNAP allowances, and benefits from over a hundred other major programs, including Medicaid and housing subsidies in which the government simply pays bills that are incurred by the programs' beneficiaries.[21] This extraordinary failure to take into account the vast majority of welfare transfers is rooted in an accounting practice adopted in 1947, when most public and private payments were made in cash or cash equivalents, and for simplicity purposes, the Census Bureau counted only payments in cash or cash equivalents as household income. This measure of household income was, in turn, used to calculate the percentage of Americans living below the poverty threshold.

As explained in chapter 6, counting only cash and cash-equivalent payments in 1947 initially produced a fairly accurate estimate of the poverty rate because, in the immediate postwar period, virtually all earned income and government benefits were paid in cash and cash equivalents. But with the ramping up of War on Poverty expenditures in 1967, almost all new benefits were paid in kind, as the federal government provided benefits that it paid for directly. The Census Bureau has never taken into account taxes paid as income lost to the taxpayer and, therefore, to this day, does not count refundable tax credits as income to households in poverty, even though these households receive checks from the Treasury. By the beginning of the pandemic, the Census definition of income counted only 12 percent of benefits paid to poverty households as part of their income.[22] The poverty rate has not fallen in over 50 years largely because the Census Bureau does *not* count some 88 percent of all benefits provided to poverty households as part of their income, and the benefits that *are* counted have been largely offset by the reduction in earned income produced by the dramatic decline in the labor-force participation rate of prime-working age persons in poverty households, which has fallen since 1967 from 67 percent to 36 percent.[23]

As Gramm, Ekelund, and Early show in their 2022 book, *The Myth of American Inequality*, today the average household in the bottom 20 percent of earners has an earned annual income from wages, fringe benefits, and private retirement income of only $4,908. But these households also receive, on average, annual government transfer payments of $45,389.[24] It is easy to understand that simplified procedures were used in 1947 given that almost all payments then were in cash or cash equivalents, and our sampling capacity was rudimentary compared to our current capacity. What is harder to understand is how these simplifying assumptions were continued after 1967, when a growing percentage of all poverty benefits were not paid in cash. Data on each of the subsidy programs are collected and reported by statistical agencies of the federal government, but the US Census Bureau does not use those government figures when calculating the percentage of American households living in poverty. When all transfer payments, net of the costs of making those payments, are counted as income to the recipients of the transfers, the poverty rate for 2017 falls from its official level of 12.3 percent to only 2.5 percent.[25]

The poverty rate calculated by the Census Bureau is based on annual income, but the number of people who are classified as poor changes dramatically over time. Less than a quarter of families classified as being poor have been poor for two years or more.[26] It should also be understood that twice as many families were poor for only some part of the year as those families who were poor the entire year. Experiences such as being laid off, suffering illness, or being employed in seasonal work contribute to people alternating between being on the poverty rolls and rising off them.

In the analysis of poverty numbers, special attention is given to children and the elderly. When all transfer payments are counted as income, the percentage of children living in poverty plummets from 17.5 percent to only 3.1 percent.[27] In the senior population, when all transfer payments are counted as income, the poverty rate for those sixty-five and over falls from 9.2 percent to a mere 1.1 percent.[28] For statistical purposes, Social Security, Medicare, Supplemental Security Income, SNAP benefits, and other transfer payments have all but eliminated senior poverty in America.

In 2017, according to official statistics, 13.6 percent of women were living in poverty as compared to 11 percent of men. Yet if we count all transfer payments, the poverty level among women falls to 2.4 percent and, for men, to 2 percent. Counting all transfer payments also eliminates most of the huge differences in the poverty rate that exist among the races. Census data show that 10.7 percent of Whites and 21.2 percent of Blacks are poor. The poverty rate of a conglomerate of other races averages about 13 percent. But when counting all transfer payments as income received, one finds that the relative poverty numbers fall to 2.3 percent for Whites, 3.5 percent for Blacks, and 2.5 percent for other races.[29] Poverty differentials on a geographic basis also decline dramatically when all transfer payments are counted.

It is likely not an overstatement to say that most of the 2.5 percent of the population who truly are living in poverty—even after accounting for government support—are people who have specific problems and have fallen through the cracks in the welfare system. Research on the homeless shows that mental and physical problems, together with alcohol and drug addiction, are major reasons why government welfare programs do not reach a significant number of people who remain in poverty.[30] Increasing SNAP funding and easing eligibility for Medicaid generally do not, in practice, affect these people. These individuals have particular problems that need to be understood and dealt with at the individual level. In this sense, it is legitimate to argue that much of the recent growth in welfare spending has not reached the very people who are most in need.

VERIFICATION OF THE 2.5 PERCENT POVERTY RATE

Further verification of the 2.5 percent poverty rate can be found in a comprehensive study by Bruce Meyer of the University of Chicago and James Sullivan of Notre Dame University, who arrive at a very similar poverty number by comparing the goods and services actually consumed by poor households in 1980 with the actual level of consumption of households that were counted as poor in 2017.[31] Remembering that poverty is officially defined as the ability to consume a fixed quantity of goods and services—a quantity that does not change over time—the Meyer-Sullivan study finds that only 2.8 percent of households were consuming at or below the poverty level in 2017. Their study shows that many households counted as poor in 2017 consumed far more than the minimum level of consumption below which a household is defined as being poor. A similar number was found in a recent Federal Reserve Bank study headed by Cornell University economist Richard Burkhauser, which attempted to take into account all income sources for poverty households. These researchers found the actual poverty rate in 2017 to be 2.3 percent.[32] These findings also comport with the Census Bureau's *American Housing Survey* showing that 42 percent of poor households own their own homes, the average of which has three bedrooms, one and a half baths, a garage, and a porch or patio. Of the households considered to be poor, 88 percent have air-conditioning, and the average poor American family lives in a home that is larger than that of the average middle-income family in France, Germany, and Britain.[33]

Some mention should be made of the often-heard claims that rampant hunger exists in America. On its website, the nonprofit group Feeding America tells us that "44 million people face hunger in the United States—including more than 13 million children."[34] These claims, however, are based on a misrepresentation of the US Department of Agriculture survey that attempts to calculate "food insecurity."[35] The

USDA clearly defines food insecurity as there being some level of concern about having adequate food, as opposed to actually being hungry. In calculating the food-insecurity measure, the USDA asked survey participants if, at any time in the last twelve months, they ever worried about being unable to buy the food they needed. If, for even a single day in the entire year, someone reported having worried that his or her family might not have been able to buy food, that respondent's entire family was counted as being "food insecure." Based on this survey, advocacy groups routinely claim that millions of people in American are going hungry.

In 2013 researchers at the Harvard School of Public Health conducted an experiment to test the connection between actual food availability and the responses received on questionnaires about food insecurity. They found that when a household received new and continued subsidies of extra money to buy food, the response of the family on food-security questionnaires did not improve.[36] A USDA report titled "What We Eat in America" showed that for the years 2013 and 2014, there was no statistical difference in the calorie consumption per person for a family with an annual income of $25,000 compared to a family with an annual income of $75,000.[37] And by 2017 the total real value of SNAP benefits received had risen by 43 percent since that study was done.[38] There is certainly some hunger in America, and one hungry person is one too many, but the food-insecurity questionnaire is a very poor guide for accurately determining how many Americans are actually hungry.

INTERNATIONAL ASSESSMENTS OF US POVERTY

In 2017 the Pew Research Center, using data from the Luxembourg Cross-National Data Center—which generally omits many of the same transfer payments excluded by the US Census Bureau—defines low-income households as those with less than two-thirds of the national median income after transfers and taxes, adjusted for household size. Using two-thirds of their national median income levels as the poverty level, European countries such as France and Germany have 17 and 18 percent of their populations, respectively, living below the poverty level, as compared to 26 percent for the United States. But it is important to note that two-thirds of the median income in the United States is a significantly higher real income level than two-thirds of the median income in France or Germany. If you use two-thirds of the median income of the United States to define poverty in both Europe and the United States, then, by the American standard, 33 percent of the populations of both France and Germany are living in poverty households, compared to 26 percent of households in the United States. When using the same level of income to define poverty in all three countries, you will find that 27 percent more of the populations in France and Germany are living in poverty than in the United States.[39] The higher poverty level for the United States, as reported by Pew and found in most other international comparisons, is due exclusively to the fact that poverty is defined in these studies as a portion of median income, and median income in America is substantially higher than in other large developed countries.

Simply by not counting transfer payments, the United Nations' *Report of the Special Rapporteur on Extreme Poverty* is able to find that 40 million Americans are living in poverty, 18 million in extreme poverty, and 5.3 million in third-world conditions of absolute poverty. Bruce Meyer and his academic colleagues, in a 2021 *Journal of Labor Economics* paper, show that the United Nations' findings of poverty in America grossly misrepresent the well-being of the lowest-income Americans: "More than 90% of those reported to be in extreme poverty are not, once we include in-kind transfers, replace survey reports of earnings and transfer receipt with administrative records, and account for ownership of substantial assets."[40] According to Meyer's study, "more than half of all misclassified households have incomes from the administrative data above the poverty line, and many have middle-class measures of material well-being."[41] In short, the UN study, like other international comparisons, presents a distorted picture by not counting US transfer payments when comparing the income of Americans to the income of people of other nations that *do* count similar transfer payments. This distortion is aided and abetted by the US Census Bureau's data. When all transfer payments are counted as the recipients' income, only France redistributes a larger share of its GDP than the United States.[42]

And there is scant evidence to support Thomas Piketty's argument that when the rate of return on capital exceeds the economic growth rate, income and inherited wealth become increasingly concentrated and "potentially incompatible with the meritocratic values and principles of social justice fundamental to modern democratic societies."[43] Tellingly, inherited wealth is not a dominant factor in the Forbes 400, which lists the four hundred richest people in the country, or in any other measure of income and wealth concentration in America.[44] The accumulation of massive wealth in America is overwhelmingly produced by those who create or implement new and powerful ideas and technologies that, in turn, spawn economic growth and raise the nation's standard of living. Piketty uses the net earnings of nonprofit foundations as a proxy for the rate of return on capital. But foundations don't pay taxes, while individuals and families in America face the most progressive income tax system in the world, as well as significant death taxes. In addition, foundations can diversify their investments, whereas owners of active businesses have their wealth highly concentrated and subject to the creative destruction of competition and technological change.

Most importantly, Piketty implicitly assumes that ownership of capital is highly concentrated and largely acquired through inheritance. But 74 percent of the ownership of corporate America is held by pension funds, 401(k)s, IRAs, and life insurance companies that fund death benefits and annuities.[45] Since the Second World War, the percentage of Americans who own shares of corporate stock has grown consistently. Finally, Piketty's measure of capital is based only on physical capital and not human capital. Yet the percentage of Americans without a high school diploma over the last fifty years has fallen by over two-thirds. The percentage of Americans with four-year college degrees has almost tripled, and those with advanced and professional degrees have more than tripled.[46] Human capital in America has soared in the last fifty years, and access to that capital has become increasingly available across all of American society. To ignore the value of human capital in a country such as the United States is to ignore one of the most important sources of income and wealth.

OBSTACLES TO ESCAPING POVERTY

The obstacles to escaping poverty are numerous, but several measurable factors warrant special attention. In 2017 the average hourly earnings of a worker in the bottom 20 percent of earners was $11.76, slightly lower than the average wage of workers in the second quintile and only 34 percent lower than the average hourly wage of middle-income workers. But because the average household in the bottom 20 percent had only 36 percent of its prime working-age persons—defined as someone who is eighteen to sixty-six years of age, not a full-time student, and not disabled or retired—working, in contrast to 85 percent in the second quintile and 92 percent in the middle quintile, the earned-income differences were a multiple of the wage differential.[47]

President Johnson's War on Poverty failed because the payout of benefits was accompanied by a collapse in the percentage of low-income, working-age persons who actually worked. Had the same percentage of working-age persons in the bottom quintile worked as much as did those in the middle quintile, the income differential for the two quintiles would have fallen from 14 to 1 to 4 to 1.[48] In short, the largest source of disparity in earned income between the two quintiles is labor-force participation. This differential was made even bigger by the fact that average bottom-quintile workers work only seventeen hours a week, whereas the average middle-income household worker works over thirty-six hours a week. Any significant narrowing of earned-income differentials between poor and middle-income American households would require a dramatic increase in both labor-force participation among non-elderly members of low-income American households and an increase in the average number of hours they work.

Over the past half century, there has been only one significant attempt to reverse the collapse of labor-force participation among poor Americans—namely, the Personal Responsibility and Work Opportunity Act of 1996, also known as the Clinton Welfare Reform.[49] This bipartisan effort focused on only one part of the welfare program, Aid to Families with Dependent Children (AFDC). The reform of AFDC and the work requirement it imposed was the most successful social reform in postwar history. The number of families receiving payments under AFDC and its successor program, Temporary Assistance for Needy Families, declined by more than half, and much of this decline came because more prime working-age adults went to work. As a result, employment among low-income single parents rose sharply.[50]

From the ramp-up of funding for the War on Poverty in 1967 until the Clinton reform of AFDC in 1996, the inflation-adjusted value of transfer payments to the bottom 20 percent of income households rose by 3.9 percent per year.[51] During the four years after the welfare reform was implemented, that annual growth in real transfers fell to only 0.6 percent. But the reduction in the growth of benefits going to the bottom 20 percent of households began to reverse and rise rapidly as other welfare benefits spiraled. The percentage of households receiving SNAP benefits jumped from 9.5 percent to 13 percent between 1996 and 2017 due to a significant loosening of eligibility standards. Even though the unemployment rate was 18 percent lower in 2017 than in 1996, the percentage of households getting SNAP benefits was 36.7 percent higher. Likewise, the number of Americans receiving Social Security Disability Insurance benefits grew by 50 percent between 1996 and 2017, despite the dramatic fall in workplace accidents, rapid improvements in the quality of health care, dramatic decreases in morbidity and mortality rates, and the passage of the Americans with Disabilities Act, which forced American business to better accommodate disabled workers.[52]

Even though the work requirements of welfare reform were subsequently waived during both the financial crisis and the pandemic, and numerous states have been granted the power to waive the work requirements during other periods, the poverty rate for single mothers not only declined after the 1996 welfare reform but continues to remain significantly lower than it was before that reform.[53] Replicating the 1996 welfare-reform program and expanding its work requirements to all means-tested programs would dramatically increase labor-force participation among recipients of public assistance.

As noted in the previous chapter on income inequality, after you count all transfer payments as income for the recipients, and also counting taxes paid as income lost to the taxpayers, you see that the bottom 60 percent of households have very similar incomes. Contrary to conventional wisdom, the most dramatic and consequential change in the distribution of income in America in the past half century isn't rising income inequality but the extraordinary growth in income *equality* among the bottom 60 percent of household earners. Real government transfer payments to the bottom 20 percent of household earners surged by 269 percent between 1967 and 2017, while middle-income households saw their real earnings after taxes rise by only 154 percent during the same period.[54] This growth of transfer payments to the bottom quintile has far outpaced the rise in the income of middle-income households, and it is the main reason for the largely equalized incomes of the bottom 60 percent of American households.

In 2017, among working-age households, the bottom 20 percent earned, on average, only $6,941, and only 36 percent of the working-age persons in those households were employed. But after transfer payments and taxes, those same households had an average income of $48,806. The average working-age household in the second quintile earned $31,811, and 85 percent of the working-age persons were employed. However, after transfers and taxes, they had an income of $50,492, a mere 3.5 percent more than the bottom quintile. The middle quintile earned $66,453, and 92 percent of working-age persons were employed. But after taxes and transfers, they kept only $61,350—just 26 percent more than the bottom quintile.[55]

Since the households in the bottom 60 percent all have similar after-tax, after-transfer incomes, the incentive for low-skilled working-age individuals in low-income households to find employment is virtually nonexistent. Figure 7.1 shows average quintile incomes with the sources of income derived from transfer payments and earnings after taxes. Both the massive loss of transfer payments and the rise in tax payments as households move from the bottom quintile to the middle quintile clearly show that the amazing thing about our current welfare system is not that the proportion of prime working-age persons who hold jobs has collapsed to 36 percent among bottom-income households but that 36 percent of the prime working-age persons in the bottom quintile are actually willing to work, given the small rewards for doing so.

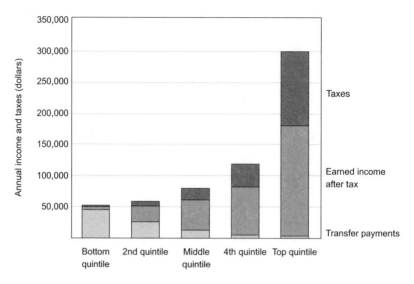

Figure 7.1. Components of Income after Transfers and Taxes for Non-Elderly Households by Earned Income Quintile in 2017. *Source:* Gramm, Ekelund, and Early, *The Myth of American Inequality,* figure 5.1, 69.

Second only to work effort, the most important factor affecting income inequality is education and worker training. Over time the importance—and, hence, the value—of human capital has been rising, causing the incomes earned by workers with more human capital to rise more than those of workers with less human capital. For example, in the fifty years from 1967 to 2017, the average real wage of high school dropouts rose by only 32 percent; the average real wage for high school graduates rose by 50 percent, while it rose by 77 percent for college graduates; and for individuals with advanced degrees, the average rise in the real wage was 107 percent.

Primary and secondary public schools that performed well in the immediate postwar period have increasingly succumbed to the disease that plagues government monopolies. They are increasingly run to benefit those who staff school systems and the teachers' unions; less and less are they run to benefit students and their parents. An education debate is raging intensely in America today, but no one argues that our public school systems, especially those in inner cities, are now performing well. The argument that the problem is a lack of financial support has been largely discredited, as there is no correlation between the amount of money spent by states on a per-student basis and the academic performance of its students. The same is true for comparisons of various nations' standardized test scores and their education expenditures per student.[56]

Charter schools, operating in the public school system but outside of many restraints set by school system bureaucracy and the teachers' unions, have shown some promise in increasing academic performance. School-choice, or voucher, programs that allow the students and their parents to take some portion of the state funds provided for the child's education in public schools and use those funds to attend private schools have expanded across the country. The performance of school-choice programs have been encouraging, and access to school choice will no doubt continue to grow. With only one-quarter of high school seniors now proficient in mathematics and only one-third in reading, our failing public schools are a major impediment to equality of opportunity in America.[57]

If the nation is ever to achieve the objective of its War on Poverty, it will have to find a way to incite low-income people to work and improve the education system in order to better equip them with the tools they need to compete. We know from American history and from the data in the previous chapter on income inequality that the American dream is alive and well, but unfortunately our poverty programs have left too many poor Americans outside the great driver of American prosperity: the American economy.

FIFTY YEARS OF PROGRESS

No discussion of poverty in America would be complete without some reference to the extraordinary economic progress made by working Americans in the last fifty years. Though few periods in American history have been more maligned than the last fifty years, the economic progress made especially by middle and low-income Americans is extraordinary. This fact is made clear in figure 7.2.

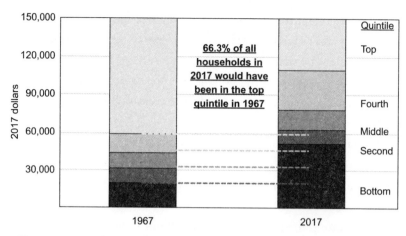

Figure 7.2. Distribution of Earned Income Plus Transfer Payments Minus Taxes, 1967 and 2017 (2017 Dollars, Using the Census Adjustment for Inflation in Income). *Sources:* Gramm, Ekelund, and Early, *The Myth of American Inequality*, 142.

Figure 7.2 shows the income brackets that defined the quintiles of American household income in 1967 in the bar chart on the left. The bar chart on the right shows the income levels that defined household income quintiles in 2017, fifty years later, adjusted for inflation using 2017 dollars. As shown in figure 7.2, to rise out of the bottom quintile (counting all earned income, all transfer payments, and all taxes paid), a household in 2017 had to have an income of $51,469.[58] A household with that real income level in 1967 would have been in the fourth quintile. In real purchasing power, the income required to be counted in the middle-income quintile in 2017 would have put that household in the top quintile fifty years earlier. This extraordinary growth has transformed America. Of all American households in 2017, 66.3 percent had real incomes, after transfers and taxes, that only the top 20 percent enjoyed in 1967.

It is often lamented that in recent decades America has not created more blue-collar jobs. But with almost 60 percent of Americans in 2017 having attended college, blue-collar workers make up only about half the percentage of the labor force than they did 50 years earlier. In 1967, 45.5 percent of all American workers had not graduated from high school. That number is now 15.1 percent.[59] In reality, the accumulation of human capital through the spread of education has priced many Americans out of the market for blue-collar jobs.

You might ask, if America really is so prosperous today relative to a half century ago, why are so many Americans still having trouble making ends meet? The answer is that the ends today's Americans are trying to make meet are significantly larger than the ends people were trying to make meet in the 1960s. There is no comparability between the first house that most families buy today and the first house their parents bought. Less than half of houses in 1967 had either central air-conditioning or a window unit.[60] Today virtually all houses are air-conditioned. In the 1960s half of poverty households did not have complete indoor plumbing. Today, for all practical purposes, every house in America has indoor plumbing.[61]

GOVERNMENT AND POVERTY

The more than half-century-long ballooning of government spending on means-tested welfare programs has provided a standard of living for low-income households that, today, is roughly equivalent to the standard of living enjoyed by middle-income Americans. If the objective of the War on Poverty was to banish want, it has been a resounding success. We now count as poor 11.5 percent of the US population, even though, when transfer payments and tax credits are considered, only 2.5 percent of Americans meet the Census Bureau's definition of poverty. Counting all of the transfer payments and tax credits that go to poor households, over 78 percent of those receiving benefits are no longer poor.[62]

The objective of the War on Poverty, however, was not just taking care of people. And it certainly wasn't to foster dependence on the government. The objective was to help people help themselves. That goal entailed helping people to become self-supporting and contributing members of society. According to the objective stated by President Johnson, the War on Poverty has been an abject failure. In operating the current welfare system for almost sixty years, our government has never found a way to help people without also diminishing their incentive to help themselves.

By failing to count 88 percent of all transfer payments that go to American families classified as poor, the Census Bureau continues to overstate dramatically the number of Americans living in poverty. Not surprisingly, therefore, over and over again, the number of Americans officially counted as poor has been used as an argument to further expand benefits. Today almost 80 percent of welfare benefits go to families classified as poor who have long since ceased to be poor. This fact raises a fundamental question: At what point does bureaucratic and political bias become an actual fraud when it leads to the expenditure of hundreds of billions of dollars and, in turn, causes millions of Americans to leave the labor force?

The explosion in poverty benefits since 1967 caused the prepandemic employment rate among the bottom 20 percent of income earners to plummet from 67 percent to 36 percent, as well as the employment rate among the second quintile of earners to fall by almost 6 percent. So generous were the benefits provided during the pandemic that, for the first time, the labor-force participation rate among middle-income Americans was affected and only returned to its prepandemic level when pandemic-era benefits had sun-setted.[63] The growth in the welfare program has largely delinked the bottom 20 percent of income earners from the American economy and diminished the labor-force participation rate of the earners in the second quintile of income. Our experience during the pandemic clearly shows that we might be approaching a level of welfare benefits at which middle-income Americans find it more attractive not to work than to work.[64] Clearly, there is a price at which you can pay people not to work, and they will take you up on the offer. If the growth in welfare benefits continues and, in the process, diminishes work effort among middle-income Americans, we will not only erode self-reliance and assault worker pride, we will also undermine the very foundations of American prosperity.

CONCLUSION

It is a myth that poverty is the great failure of American capitalism. Poverty and dependence are the great failures of the US government.

Banishing want at a price of idleness kept the poor dependent on the government and severed their link to the economy, their avenue for success and personal achievement. Our welfare system might serve the political interests of the government, but it does not serve the interests of those who are victimized by the dependency the program breeds. Our welfare program cries out for reform that, at a minimum, would institute work incentives and mandatory work requirements for able-bodied working-age adults receiving benefits from means-tested programs, as well as a wholesale reform of America's now-failing public education system.

Eight
LESSONS AND CONCLUSIONS

FOR MORE THAN A thousand years, from the fall of Rome until the Enlightenment, economic growth stagnated on a secular basis. Generation after generation lived more or less in the same way as their grandparents had, eking out subsistence livelihoods with back-breaking work. And then something that bordered on miraculous oc-curred. An intellectual consensus formed in Europe that ordinary people should have the right to worship God in their own way, think their own thoughts, and own the fruits of their labor and thrift.

The right of people to worship as they chose brought the religious wars of Europe to an end, reducing the oppression of religious intol-erance and the coercive power of the medieval church. The right of ordinary people to think their own thoughts evolved into a system of government in which an increasing number of people had a voice in how they were governed. Treating the fruits of the workers' labor and thrift as their property reduced the leeching power of the crown, church, guild, and village, incentivizing work and thrift and unleashing a productive energy that the world had never known. Confirming, through the most dramatic change in recorded history, that ideas have consequences, a thousand years of stagnation was converted in less than three centuries into a burst of sustained economic growth that lifted the oppression of Malthusian arithmetic by empowering people to produce faster than they procreate.

In England in 1215, the Magna Carta gave the church a degree of independence from the crown, generating a check and balance on each entity and opening space for the freedom that would fuel the rise of the West. Moreover, Magna Carta guaranteed property, legal, and commercial rights for the nobility and protected creditors' rights. During the Enlightenment these rights were extended to ordinary people as the government recognized common law practices. Legal procedures were formalized, further strengthening the protection of property and contract rights and providing fertile ground for a system of pooling capital for investment. The social status of those engaged in profit-seeking industry and enterprise rose, ushering in a new commercial age. From these foundations, the modern world took wings.

The economic manifestation of the Enlightenment, the Industrial Revolution, changed everything. However, this freedom unleashed not just creativity but disturbance. As the economist David McCord Wright explains, "growth comes through change and causes change."[1] And change brings uncertainty and fear as old products and methods of production are swept away by waves of creative destruction, upending the social and economic order. Economic changes of biblical proportions in a world that had been little changed for a thousand years proved to be beyond the comprehension of most people and their governments. Partly out of fear and partly out of vested interest—especially among the landed gentry and the writers and political leaders who benefited from their patronage—those losing economic and political power rose to decry and impede these changes, attempting to escape the need to adapt to them.

The Industrial Revolution and the opportunities it created uprooted millions, launching a massive exodus from rural areas and swelling the population of manufacturing cities far beyond their immediate capacity to house such populations. The poor, who had previously remained largely hidden in the countryside, became all too visible when they exercised their new freedom, voting with their feet to join the Industrial Revolution in search of the better life they saw in the factories and cities. And as the Industrial Revolution took hold and the level of prosperity soared, the human suffering that had been the norm and accepted as an inevitable part of life suddenly became unacceptable. The success of the Industrial Revolution in creating prosperity on a scale never before experienced in human history, thereby, paradoxically, gave rise to a revolt against the very system that made the new prosperity possible. Looking back from the heights of material well-being we enjoy in the twenty-first century, the standard of living at the dawn of the Industrial Revolution looks like abject poverty, and we are moved by those who denounced it.

Some of the most moving lines in world literature were written in condemnation of the Industrial Revolution, the very system that made the modern world. But while that literature still touches our hearts, English literature and British statistics tell very different stories. The overwhelming evidence from the Industrial Revolution shows that by every measured index of wages, nutrition, literacy, morbidity, mortality, and human flourishing, the Industrial Revolution, while not putting workers back in the Garden of Eden, broke the stagnation and crippling poverty that had always been their lot. And the history of the Industrial Revolution should reassure us that if humankind could not only endure but prevail in the face of those traumatic changes, we can surely cope with the changes that new technology will produce in areas like artificial intelligence.

In nineteenth-century America, as production tripled and the population doubled in only two generations, critics of the Industrial Revolution sought to bring the most productive parts of the economy under government regulation. The rise of nationwide economic giants, or "trusts," brought not only prosperity but their own waves of creative destruction that swept away smaller, less efficient competitors. As prices fell and living standards rose, those who could not compete sought political influence to thwart the dramatic economic changes transforming their world. The combination of vested interests, envy, economic uncertainty, and the efforts of progressives, whose agenda was one of greater government control over the economy, created the political movement that persuaded the government to adopt what we now know as Progressive Era regulations. Whether the trusts covertly supported Progressive regulations or coopted the regulations once they were in place, during the seventy years of Progressive Era regulations production was impeded and prices driven higher as regulations came to protect producers and not consumers.

As evidence of the failure of Progressive Era regulations to benefit the consumer became undeniable, these regulations were either repealed or dramatically refocused on protecting consumers' interests. With the deregulation of transportation, energy production, and communications in the late 1970s, the economy found a new life. Transportation costs plummeted, innovation flourished, and America became a world leader in each of these areas.

As Demosthenes says, "the time for extracting a lesson from history is ever at hand for them who are wise."[2] America's failed experiment with Progressive Era regulations and subsequent success in focusing antitrust enforcement solely on consumer welfare strongly encourage caution in empowering the government to exercise discretionary authority over private economic activities. Without the constraint that government antitrust regulation be used only when there is clear evidence of it promoting the consumers' welfare, antitrust regulatory powers give the government the dangerous discretion to pick winners and losers, punish and reward, and, in the process, unbridle powers inimical to a free society.

In retrospect, President Clinton wisely chose to let the internet develop competitively by following his policy of doing no harm. In stark contrast, the Biden administration's plan to heavily regulate artificial intelligence, requiring it to serve numerous interests other than those of consumers, imperils a new and powerful technology. Surely, history proves that governments given broad powers to do good often abuse those powers in order to promote the interests of those who control the government, and even officials with great knowledge and the best intentions can never match the cumulative knowledge of private decision-makers spending their own money.

Whereas Americans are diligent in protecting political and religious rights, unfortunately their diligence often does not extend to protecting economic rights. But without economic freedom, other freedoms lose their effectiveness, as people who do not control their own livelihoods can too easily be coerced into giving up their political and religious freedoms. Economic freedom is constantly under the greatest assault because people understand it the least.

Looking at the hard evidence of the causes of both the Great Depression and the 2008 financial crisis reveals a pattern: When failed government policies produce a crisis, government blames capitalism and then uses the crisis to expand the very powers that initially caused the crisis. The failure of the Federal Reserve Bank to perform its basic function of providing liquidity to stop a financial panic from turning into a depression triggered the Great Depression. Government intervention, first under Hoover and then Roosevelt, exacerbated the downturn by preventing markets from adjusting to the crisis. The uncertainty created by Roosevelt's assault on private business, seen against a backdrop of growing totalitarianism worldwide, stifled investment and the recovery. Not until America was an active belligerent in the war did unemployment subside. The pre-Depression availability of consumer goods did not return until the late 1940s, and the value of the nation's equity market did not fully recover until the Eisenhower administration.

The root cause of the financial crisis was the government policy to promote public objectives with private capital, which destroyed mortgage-lending standards. Government regulatory policy pressured banks to make bad loans and forced government-sponsored enterprises to purchase and securitize those loans. In addition, the government manipulated financial institutions' capital standards to encourage banks to hold massive quantities of mortgage-backed securities. When the housing bubble burst and subprime loan defaults soared, the authors of the very housing policy that caused the crisis blamed capitalism and greed and, in the process, expanded the very governmental powers that caused the crisis in the first place. Our experiences with the Great Depression and the financial crisis suggest that when future crises occur, it would behoove the American people to first look closely at what the government had to do with causing the crises before they allow any further expansion of the government's power to deal with them.

Of all areas of the economy, the one most subject to exploitation and demagoguery is international trade. Nationalism is always a powerful force that can be tapped to stoke support for protectionism, and significant benefits can be granted to a small number of economic interests, with the costs spread almost imperceivably across society as a whole. Adam

Smith and other Enlightenment economists discredited the economic system of mercantilism, a system through which the government manipulates trade to benefit the government's treasury and favored constituencies. But the power of special interests is ever present. Protectionism has reared its head throughout American history. It reached a zenith with the Smoot-Hawley Tariff of 1930, which deepened the Great Depression. So painful were the lessons learned from the Smoot-Hawley Tariff, and so great were the challenges of the postwar world, that America led the effort to open world trade. The facts demonstrate conclusively that with the expansion of postwar trade, working Americans prospered, and most of the world escaped from pervasive poverty.

Our recent experiments with protectionism in the name of revitalizing American manufacturing have proven abject failures, even on their own terms. Manufacturing production—the focus of the current wave of protectionism—is slightly *lower* today (October 2024) than when the 2018 tariffs were first implemented. Employment in manufacturing as a percentage of the nonfarm workforce is also lower, and the trade deficit is significantly higher. Protectionism persists because the public does not understand who loses and who benefits from tariffs, though the evidence continues to build that with the increasing economic integration of the world economy, the percentage of people who benefit from protectionism is declining while the percentage who lose is increasing. The decline in manufacturing employment as a share of total employment is nothing new. It has been going on for eighty years, even as manufacturing output has continued to rise. What's happening now in manufacturing is what happened a hundred years ago in agriculture, which, of course, also saw a dramatic fall in employment as agricultural output soared. Technology eliminates jobs in agriculture and manufacturing and creates new and better jobs in IT, health care, and other service-sector industries. Wages rise as progress occurs, but nostalgia and special interests cry out in alarm. Protectionism is a loser in every arena except that from which it draws its driving force: the political arena.

Inequality is a product of freedom. Theoretically, the government could produce total equality by ever more radical redistribution of income, though it has never come close to achieving that result. And in societies whose governments proclaim the goal of income equality, both poverty and inequality are more pervasive than in societies promising freedom and opportunity. As a whole, the people are much better off in nations that choose freedom. Income inequality is grossly overstated in the official statistics of the United States because the Census Bureau chooses not to count two-thirds of all transfer payments as income paid to the recipients, while it fails to treat taxes paid as income lost to the taxpayers. When these corrections are made, the measured level of income inequality is reduced by three-quarters. Counting all transfer payments and taxes, income inequality in America is lower today than it was in 1947.

Those who earn the most in America are those who contribute the most, as only criminals and the government can take more than they give in a free society. Did Elon Musk, Bill Gates, and Warren Buffett make America poorer by becoming richer? The clear answer is no; they became richer by making us richer.

A comprehensive analysis of income inequality shows that the two greatest causes of income inequality in America today spring from two failed government policies. The first cause is the explosion in government welfare payments, which has induced two-thirds of low-income, working-age Americans to stop working. Capitalism is said to be failing the poor, but in reality, except in consuming its bounty, most poor Americans today live almost entirely outside the capitalistic system. The second cause is that, without accountability or competition, public education has succumbed to the disease that plagues government entities. It now serves the interests of those who run it, the teachers and administrators, and not the students and their parents. Work incentives and mandatory work requirements for welfare program recipients, as well as a wholesale reform of public education that brings the power of competition and innovation to bear in America's classrooms, would significantly reduce income inequality and poverty.

Poverty has no causes; prosperity has many. As history attests, poverty is humanity's default condition. No effort, thrift, creativity, or risk-taking is necessary to produce poverty. Where property rights, the rule of law, and economic freedom are absent, the rewards for working and sweating are drained away, and poverty reigns. Only where property is secure and the rule of law is enforced will economic freedom reign and unleash the extraordinary store of human energy to create general prosperity. Adam Smith, writing at the apex of the economic awakening that made the modern world, titled his seminal 1776 book *An Inquiry into the Nature and Causes of the Wealth of Nations.* In his world, when most of humanity was still mired in poverty, Smith would have thought it mad to inquire into the causes of poverty. It was prosperity and wealth, which were just beginning to produce a cornucopia of abundance, that Smith sought to understand and explain.

In the richest countries in history's most prosperous age, it is poverty, not affluence, that looks unnatural. But prosperity is not natural; it does not just happen. Prosperity and wealth must be actively and continuously produced. In America, poverty is abetted by failed government policies that decouple poor people from the very system that creates prosperity. Welfare payments discourage work, failed public education deprives children of human capital, and inadequate law enforcement stunts the power of market forces to generate prosperity in poor neighborhoods.

There are certainly poor people in America, but if you count all transfer payments as income to the recipients of those transfers, only about 2.5 percent of Americans are poor by the official definition of poverty, not 11.5 percent. No area of government is more ripe for reform than the welfare system, which, as currently constituted, pays massive benefits to people who have long since ceased to be poor. At the same time, it fails to reach those genuinely in need who suffer from mental and physical health problems or alcohol and drug addiction. Welfare spending is the elephant in the room in terms of the federal deficit, public debt, and the crowding out of defense and other essential government services. While Social Security and Medicare are almost always highlighted in any discussion of the nation's budgetary challenges, to this point in American history, Social Security has more than paid for itself through Social Security payroll taxes, and Medicare is at least partially self-funded by its payroll taxes. Social Security and Medicare will become major problems in the future if they are not reformed, but today, the major fiscal problem of the nation, the elephant in the room, is the explosive growth of means-tested social welfare spending that now absorbs 57.4 percent of general revenues, minus the payroll taxes set aside to fund Social Security and Medicare, which are available to fund general government operations after interest is paid on the national debt.[3] Through the disincentives they create, welfare programs have idled tens of millions of potential workers.

To paraphrase Winston Churchill, capitalism is highly imperfect—except when compared to any other economic system that has ever been implemented. Our challenges come from many sources, such as natural scarcity and human error, but any student of history should be struck by the fact that so many of our problems result from failed government policies. At a minimum, an appeal to the facts reveals that popular history both underestimates the benefits Americans have reaped from free markets and overestimates the benefits we have received from government interventions.

There will always be work to do, and we are unlikely to ever get something for nothing. But freedom has been the key to the great progress we have made in the past, and it is the key to our progress in the future. If we can preserve freedom, especially economic freedom, there is no limit to the future of America.

NOTES

Preface and Introduction

1. See National Historical Publications & Records Commission, "From Thomas Jefferson to John Adams, 11 July 1786," National Archives, accessed December 2, 2024, https://founders.archives.gov/documents/jefferson/01-10-02-0058.
2. Thomas Sowell, *A Conflict of Visions* (William Morrow, 1987; repr., Basic Books, 2002), 3, 6.
3. Sowell, *A Conflict of Visions*, 3, 6.
4. Sowell, *A Conflict of Visions*, 124.
5. F. A. Hayek, ed., *Capitalism and the Historians* (University of Chicago Press, 1954), 3–4.
6. Alexander Hamilton, *Selected Writings and Speeches of Alexander Hamilton*, ed. Morton J. Frisch (American Enterprise Institute, 1985), 390.
7. Adam Smith, *An Inquiry into the Nature and Causes of the Wealth of Nations* (Liberty Fund 1776; repr., 1981), 26–27.
8. Thomas Babington Macaulay, "Southey's Colloquies" (Jan. 1830), The Online Library of Liberty, last updated 2024, https://oll.libertyfund.org/pages/macaulay-southey-s-colloquies-1830.
9. Milton and Rose Friedman, *Free to Choose* (Harcourt Brace Jovanovich, 1980), 148.
10. On the tendency of emergency powers to persist after emergencies end, see Robert Higgs, *Crisis and Leviathan* (Oxford University Press, 1987).
11. John Stuart Mill, *On Liberty* (Appleton-Century-Crofts, 1859; repr., 1947), 36.

One: The Genesis Myth

1. We agree with Deirdre McCloskey that the term *capitalism* does not adequately capture the essence of the dynamic and innovative free market system that it is widely used to denote. But because *capitalism* is so entrenched as the name of the modern market order, we elect here to stick with this common usage.
2. Karl Marx and Friedrich Engels, *The Communist Manifesto*, ed. Samuel H. Beer (Appleton-Century-Crofts, 1848; repr., 1955), 14. On the key role that the embrace of bourgeois values played in the industrial revolution, see Deirdre Nansen McCloskey, *Bourgeois Equality* (University of Chicago Press, 2016).
3. By "empowered to pursue their own private interests," we do not mean that ordinary individuals were freed merely to chase greater material betterment for themselves and their families. The empowerment to which we refer is more general: individuals

gained greater freedom to pursue whatever peaceful ends, low or high, they chose without having to get permission to do so from their alleged superiors. The freedom to pursue one's own peaceful ends is what University of Chicago law professor Richard Epstein calls "the autonomy principle." Respect for this principle reflects "not any belief that people live in small social islands uninfluenced by and unconcerned with the interests and the behavior of others. It is that no other principle matches power with interests to the same degree." Richard A. Epstein, *Simple Rules for a Complex World* (Harvard University Press, 1995), 59.

4. W. H. Hutt, "The Factory System of the Early Nineteenth Century," in *Capitalism and the Historians*, ed. F. A. Hayek (University of Chicago Press, 1954), 156–84. The quoted passage here is found on page 167.
5. UK Parliament, "The 1833 Factory Act," last updated 2024, https://tinyurl.com/2xcddmz4.
6. F. A. Hayek, "History and Politics," in *Capitalism and the Historians* (University of Chicago Press, 1954), 18.
7. The historian Stephen Davies even calls it "the wealth explosion." See Davies, *The Wealth Explosion* (Edward Everett Root, 2019).
8. Arnold Toynbee, *Lectures on the Industrial Revolution in England* (The Beacon Press, 1884; repr., 1956), 57, 66.
9. E. P. Thompson, *The Making of the English Working Class* (Vintage, 1965), 198.
10. Thomas Hood, "The Song of the Shirt," *Punch*, Christmas 1843.
11. Hood, "The Song of the Shirt."
12. Thomas Piketty, *Capital in the Twenty-First Century*, trans. Arthur Goldhammer (Harvard University Press, 2014), 7.
13. William Blake, "London," in *Songs of Innocence and Experience* (London, 1794).
14. Friedrich Engels, *The Condition of the Working Class in England* (John W. Lovell, 1845; repr., 1887), 3.
15. Engels, *The Condition of the Working Class*, 76.
16. Marx and Engels, *The Communist Manifesto*, 46.
17. Bertrand Russell, *The Impact of Science on Society* (Columbia University Press, 1951), 19–20.
18. Deirdre McCloskey, "The Great Enrichment," *Discourse*, July 13, 2020, https://www.discoursemagazine.com/p/the-great-enrichment.
19. Carlo M. Cipolla, *Before the Industrial Revolution*, 3rd ed. (W. W. Norton, 1993), 276.
20. Gregory Clark, *A Farewell to Alms* (Princeton University Press, 2007), 92.
21. "Anne, Queen of Great Britain," Wikipedia, last updated October 28, 2024, https://en.wikipedia.org/wiki/Anne,_Queen_of_Great_Britain.
22. Robert William Fogel, *The Escape from Hunger and Premature Death, 1700–2100* (Cambridge University Press, 2004), 6.
23. Fogel, *The Escape from Hunger*, 9.
24. Frances and Joseph Gies, *Life in a Medieval Village* (Harper & Row, 1990), 35.
25. Gies and Gies, *Life in a Medieval Village*, 34.
26. William Manchester, *A World Lit Only by Fire* (Little, Brown & Company, 1992), 52–53. In his mid-nineteenth century *History of England*, Thomas Babington Macaulay describes the interior of a seventeenth-century highland Scot's residence:

    > His lodging would sometimes have been in a hut of which every nook would have swarmed with vermin. He would have inhaled an atmosphere thick with peat smoke, and foul with a hundred noisome exhalations. At

supper grain fit only for horses would have been set before him, accompanied by a cake of blood drawn from living cows. Some of the company with which he would have feasted would have been covered with cutaneous eruptions, and others would have been smeared with tar like sheep. His couch would have been the bare earth, dry or wet as the weather might be; and from that couch he would have risen half poisoned with stench, half blind with the reek of turf, and half mad with the itch.

See Macaulay, *The History of England*, vol. 3 (John C. Winston Co., n.d., ca. 1858), 279.

27. Deirdre Nansen McCloskey, *Bourgeois Dignity* (University of Chicago Press, 2010).
28. McCloskey, *Bourgeois Dignity*.
29. Clark, *A Farewell to Alms*, 276.
30. Clark, *A Farewell to Alms*, 276. Some historians find that real wages began rising even earlier, in the latter half of the eighteenth century. Few researchers, however, doubt that these wage increases were underway by 1840. See, for example, Mark Koyama and Jared Rubin, *How the World Became Rich* (Polity Press, 2022), 177; Stephen Broadberry an Bishnupriya Gupta, "The Early Modern Great Divergence: Wages, Prices and Economic Development in Europe and Asia, 1500–1800," *Economic History Review*, February 2006, 2–31.
31. N. F. R. Crafts, "Economic Growth in France and Britain, 1830–1910: A Review of the Evidence," *Journal of Economic History* 44 (March 1984): table 1, 51.
32. Office for National Statistics, "How Has Life Expectancy Changed Over Time?," published September 9, 2015, https://www.ons.gov.uk/peoplepopulationandcom munity/birthsdeathsandmarriages/lifeexpectancies/articles/howhaslifeexpectancy changedovertime/2015-09-09.
33. Matthew Ingleby, "Charles Dickens and the Push for Literacy in Victorian Britain," Queen Mary University of London, published June 10, 2020, https://www.qmul .ac.uk/media/news/2020/hss/charles-dickens-and-the-push-for-literacy-in-vic torian-britain.html.
34. Thomas E. Jordan, "An Index of the Quality of Life for Victorian Children and Youth, the VICY Index," *Social Indicators Research* 27 (November 1992): 257–77, specifically 274–75.
35. Carolyn Tuttle and Simone A. Wegge, "Regulating Child Labor: The European Experience," in *Institutions, Innovation, and Industrialization: Essays in Economic History and Development*, ed. Avner Greif, Lynne Kiesling, and John V. C. Nye (Princeton University Press, 2015), 337–78; the quoted passage is on p. 337.
36. Carolyn Tuttle, "Child Labor During the British Industrial Revolution," Economic History Association Encyclopedia, ed. Robert Whaples, published August 14, 2001, https://eh.net/encyclopedia/child-labor-during-the-british-industrial-revolution/.
37. Jane Humphries, "Childhood and Child Labour in the British Industrial Revolution," *Economic History Review* 66 (May 2013): 395–418; the quoted passage is on page 400.
38. Humphries, "Childhood and Child Labour," 406.
39. Clark Nardinelli, *Child Labor and the Industrial Revolution* (Indiana University Press, 1990), 115. See also Clark Nardinelli, "Child Labor and the Factory Acts," *Journal of Economic History* 40 (December 1980): 739–55.
40. Chelsea Follett, "Scrooge and the Reality of the Victorian Home: Why, for Young Women Especially, Factory Work Was Preferable to Domestic Labor in Dickensian

Times," *Human Progress* (blog), December 12, 2018, https://www.humanprogress
.org/if-you-thought-scrooge-was-bad-consider-the-victorian-home/.

41. Judith Flanders, *Inside the Victorian Home: A Portrait of Domestic Life in Victorian England* (W. W. Norton, 2005).

42. An anonymous woman who ran a lodging house, reported by Jessie Boucherett, "Legislative Restrictions on Women's Labour," *Englishwoman's Review*, 1873; she is cited by Flanders, *Inside the Victorian Home*; Follett, "Scrooge and the Reality of the Victorian Home."

43. Edwin Chadwick, *Report on the Sanitary Conditions of the Labouring Population and on the Means of Its Improvement* (London, 1842), 105–6, https://s3.amazonaws.com/aspphwebassets/delta-omega/archives/ChadwickClassic.pdf.

44. T. S. Ashton, "The Standard of Life of the Workers in England, 1790–1830," in *Capitalism and the Historians*, ed. F. A. Hayek (University of Chicago Press, 1954), 123–55; the quoted passage is on page 154.

45. T. S. Ashton, *The Industrial Revolution*, rev. ed. (Oxford University Press, 1948; repr., 1964), 110–11. Ashton does not identify the historian whom he quotes, but it is probably George Norman Clark, who used this phrase on page 156 of his article "Early Capitalism and Invention," *Economic History Review* 6 (April 1936): 143–56.

46. Deirdre McCloskey, "The Industrial Revolution 1780–1860: A Survey," in *The Economics of the Industrial Revolution*, ed. Joel Mokyr (George Allen & Unwin, 1985), 56.

47. Peter H. Lindert and Jeffrey G. Williamson, "'English Workers' Living Standards During the Industrial Revolution: A New Look," in *The Economics of the Industrial Revolution*, ed. Joel Mokyr (George Allen & Unwin, 1985), 198.

48. Matt Ridley, *The Rational Optimist* (Harper Perennial, 2010), 218.

49. Stanley Lebergott, after noting Wordsworth's contempt for humankind's vulgarity— as Wordsworth put it, "getting and spending"—drolly points out that the poet "inherited much. And his sister did the housework." Lebergott, *Pursuing Happiness: American Consumers in the Twentieth Century* (Princeton University Press, 1993), xi.

50. Hayek, "History and Politics," 19.

51. Donald Boudreaux and Douglas Irwin, "Donald Boudreaux and Douglas Irwin on Free-Trade Tips from 1846," *The Economist*, June 25, 2021, https://www.econ omist.com/by-invitation/2021/06/25/donald-boudreaux-and-douglas-irwin-on -free-trade-tips-from-1846.

52. Douglas A. Irwin and Maksym G. Chepeliev, "The Economic Consequences of Sir Robert Peel: A Quantitative Assessment of the Repeal of the Corn Laws," *Economic Journal* 131 (November 2021): 3322–37.

53. Emma Griffin, *Liberty's Dawn: A People's History of the Industrial Revolution* (Yale University Press, 2013).

54. Griffin, *Liberty's Dawn*, 19.

55. Griffin, *Liberty's Dawn*, 243.

56. Britannica Editors, "Gilded Age," in *Encyclopedia Britannica*, accessed May 20, 2023, https://www.britannica.com/event/Gilded-Age.

57. Howard Zinn, *A People's History of the United States* (Harper & Row, 1980), 251.

58. Henry Demarest Lloyd, *Wealth Against Commonwealth* (Harper & Bros., 1894).

59. Quoted in Richard Hofstadter, *Great Issues in American History, Volume 2, 1864–1957* (Vintage Books, 1959), 100.

60. Ray Ginger, *The Age of Excess: The United States from 1877 to 1914* (Macmillan, 1965).

61. Richard Hofstadter, *The Age of Reform* (Alfred A. Knopf, 1955).

62. C. Vann Woodward, "The Ordeal of Industrialization," in *The National Experience*, 8th ed., eds. John M. Blum, William S. McFeeley, Edmund S. Morgan, Arthur M. Schlesinger Jr., Kenneth M. Stampp, and C. Vann Woodward (Harcourt Brace College Publishers, 1993), 471.

   According to Hillsdale College historian Burton Folsom, "Woodward wrote the whole chapter, 'The Ordeal of Industrialization.'" See Folsom, *The Myth of the Robber Barons* (Young America's Foundation, 2007; repr., 2018), 171.

63. "The Gilded Age," *American Experience*, directed by Sarah Colt, aired February 6, 2018, on PBS; see also "Our Plan," *The Prize: The Epic Quest for Oil, Money, and Power*, directed by Willian Cran and Stephanie Tepper, aired 1992, on PBS.

64. Lindsay Graham, host, *American History Tellers*, podcast, season 24, episode 7, "What America Failed to Learn from the Gilded Age," Wondery+, September 2, 2020, https://podcasts.apple.com/nz/podcast/the-gilded-age-what-america-failed -to-learn-from/id1313596069?i=1000489819560. The blurb for this episode pro-claims that "greed and disregard for the working class defined the Gilded Age."

65. Piketty, *Capital in the Twenty-First Century*, 350.

66. Matthew Josephson, *The Robber Barons* (Harcourt, Brace & Co., 1934), 29.

67. Josephson, *The Robber Barons*, 52–53.

68. Josephson, *The Robber Barons*, 253.

69. Susan B. Carter, Scott S. Gartner, Michael R. Haines, Alan L. Olmstead, Richard Sutch, and Gavin Wright, eds., *Historical Statistics of the United States: Millennial Edition*, vol. 3 (Cambridge University Press, 2006), table Ca-19, 24–25.

70. Carter et al., *Historical Statistics of the United States*, vol. 3, table Ca-C, 5.

71. Carter et al., *Historical Statistics of the United States*, vol. 3, table Ca-19, 24–25.

72. Carter et al., *Historical Statistics of the United States*, vol. 3, table Ca-169-183, 57.

   1869 is the earliest year for which these data on consumer goods are available.

73. Data on nominal earnings are from Susan B. Carter, Scott S. Gartner, Michael R. Haines, Alan L. Olmstead, Richard Sutch, and Gavin Wright, eds., *Historical Statistics of the United States: Millennial Edition*, vol. 2 (Cambridge University Press, 2006), table Ba-4280-4282, 265.

   We converted these nominal dollars into real dollars using the Minnesota Federal Reserve's index of prices dating back to 1800. See Federal Reserve Bank of Minneapolis, "Consumer Price Index, 1800–," last updated 2024, https://www .minneapolisfed.org/about-us/monetary-policy/inflation-calculator/consumer -price-index-1800- .

74. Lawrence H. Officer, *Two Centuries of Compensation for U.S. Production Workers in Manufacturing* (Palgrave Macmillan, 2009), table 7.2, 170

75. Robert W. Fogel and Jack Rutner, "The Efficiency Effects of Federal Land Policy, 1850–1900: A Report of Some Provisional Findings," in William Aydelotte, Robert William Fogel, and Allan G. Bogue, *The Dimensions of Quantitative Research in History* (Princeton University Press, 1972), 390–418. See also Douglass C. North, Terry L. Anderson, and Peter J. Hill, *Growth & Welfare in the American Past: A New Economic History*, 3rd ed. (Prentice Hall, 1983).

   After confirming that, from 1865 until at least 1900, "the farmer . . . was in fact get-ting more for his money" (128), these authors go on to attribute the agrarian unrest of the era largely to American farmers becoming far more integrated into the global economy: "When farmers suffered from a period of drought and poor crops, the higher prices they had learned to expect in such a case might not be forthcoming" (131). While the absolute number of agricultural workers increased in the latter half of the nineteenth century, as a portion of America's growing labor force, the number of agricultural workers fell. In 1860, 53 percent of American workers toiled on farms; by 1900, only 40 percent did so. By 1910 this figure was down to 31 percent. See Carter et al., *Historical Statistics of the United States*, vol. 2, table Ba-814-830, 110.

76. U.S. Department of Commerce, *Historical Statistics of the United States: Colonial Times to 1970* (U.S. Bureau of the Census, 1975), Series E40-51 and E52-63, 200–201.

77. Susan B. Carter, Scott S. Gartner, Michael R. Haines, Alan L. Olmstead, Richard Sutch, and Gavin Wright, eds., *Historical Statistics of the United States: Millennial Edition*, vol. 1 (Cambridge University Press, 2006), table Ab1-10, 391.

78. Carter et al., *Historical Statistics of the United States*, vol. 1, table Ab1-10, 391. These data on infant mortality are for White births. Consistent data on Black births are not available until 1900. These data show that between 1900 and 1910, the rate of Black infant mortality fell by 16.3 percent.

79. Carter et al., *Historical Statistics of the United States*, vol. 2, table Bc793-797, 468.

80. Carter et al., *Historical Statistics of the United States*, vol. 2, table Ba4545-4551, 301.

81. U.S. Department of Commerce, *Historical Statistics of the United States*, 200–201.

82. Thomas J. Schlereth, *Victorian America: Transformations in Everyday Life* (Harper Perennial, 1991), 141.

83. Hugh Rockoff, "Great Fortunes of the Gilded Age," Research Working Paper No. 14555 (National Bureau of Economic, December 2008), table 6, 37. In 1892 dollars, $1 million is the equivalent of $32.8 million in 2023 dollars. This sum today obviously isn't what it was in the late nineteenth century, as a dollar today has only a fraction of the purchasing power that it had long ago. In 2022 about 23.7 million— or 18 percent—of US households had a net worth of at least $1 million (in 2022 dollars). See Adam Levy, "Here's How Many Millionaires There Are in America," *The Motley Fool*, May 27, 2024, https://www.fool.com/retirement/2024/05/27/heres-how-many-millionaires-there-are-in-america/.

Two: Progressive Era Regulation

1. U.S. Department of Commerce, *Historical Statistics of the United States: Colonial Times to 1970* (U.S. Bureau of the Census, 1975), Series F1-5 and F238-249, 224, 239.

2. David Emory Shi, *America: A Narrative History* (W. W. Norton, 2019).

3. Shi, *America*, 708.

4. Shi, *America*, 871.

5. Shi, *America*, 871–72. The quotations are from *The Jungle*.

6. Shi, *America*, 872.

7. Shi, *America*, 864.

8. Shi, *America*, 702.

9. Shi, *America*, 701.

10. Shi, *America*, 728.

11. Jack London, *The Iron Heel* (Hill & Wang, 1908; repr., 1957), 74–75.

12. Herbert Croly, *The Promise of American Life* (Transaction Publishers, 1909; repr., 1993), 108.

13. Croly, *The Promise of American Life*, 115.

14. Croly, *The Promise of American Life*, 190.

15. Charles A. Beard and Mary R. Beard, *History of the United States* (Macmillan, 1921).

16. Beard and Beard, *History of the United States*, ch. XXI.

17. The quotation is from the "Platform of the People's Party, Omaha, Nebraska," *The American Yawp Reader*, 1892, https://www.americanyawp.com/reader/16-capital -and-labor/the-omaha-platform-of-the-peoples-party-1892/.

18. Beard and Beard, *History of the United States*, ch. XXI, sec. "The Great Riches and Taxation," p. 9, https://www.marxists.org/archive/beard/history-us.

19. U.S. Department of Commerce, *Historical Statistics of the United States*, 200–201.

20. See any textbook on the principles of microeconomics—for example, Paul Heyne, Peter Boettke, and David Prychitko, *The Economic Way of Thinking*, 13th ed. (Prentice Hall, 2013), ch. 9, "Competition and Monopoly."

21. Thomas J. DiLorenzo, "The Origins of the Sherman Act: An Interest-Group Perspective," *International Review of Law and Economics* 5 (1985): 73–90.

22. DiLorenzo, "The Origins of the Sherman Act," 78–80.

23. Robert Higgs, *The Transformation of the American Economy, 1865–1914* (John Wiley & Sons, 1971), 23.

24. Stanley Lebergott, *The Americans: An Economic Record* (W. W. Norton, 1984), 312.

25. Gabriel Kolko, *The Triumph of Conservatism* (The Free Press, 1963), 18.

26. Kolko, *The Triumph of Conservatism*, p. 31.

27. Kolko, *The Triumph of Conservatism*, 30.

28. Kolko, *The Triumph of Conservatism*, 30.

29. Kolko, *The Triumph of Conservatism*, 54. Joseph Schumpeter famously—and approvingly—identified "the process of creative destruction" as an essential feature of capitalism. See Joseph A. Schumpeter, *Capitalism, Socialism, and Democracy* (Harper, 1942), 81–86.

30. Kolko, *The Triumph of Conservatism*, 18.

31. Kolko, *The Triumph of Conservatism*, 39.

32. Kolko, *The Triumph of Conservatism*, 5.

33. Using the Minnesota Federal Reserve's index of prices dating back to 1800, we converted the 1870 price of a gallon of kerosene ($0.26) into 1885 dollars, yielding an 1870 "real" price of $0.20. A fall in this real price from $0.20 to $0.08 is a fall of 60 percent. A similar adjustment for deflation is done for each of the other real price changes reported in the text. See Federal Reserve Bank of Minneapolis, "Consumer Price Index, 1800–," last updated 2024, https://www.minneapolisfed.org/about-us/ monetary-policy/inflation-calculator/consumer-price-index-1800-.

34. 51 Cong. Rec. H2558 (daily ed. June 20, 1890).

35. John S. McGee, "Predatory Price Cutting: The Standard Oil (N.J.) Case," *Journal of Law & Economics* 1 (October 1958): 137–69; the quoted passage is on page 168.

36. Dominick T. Armentano, *Antitrust and Monopoly: Anatomy of a Policy Failure* (John Wiley & Sons, 1982), 58–64; Donald J. Boudreaux and Burton W. Folsom, "Microsoft and Standard Oil: Radical Lessons for Antitrust Reform," *Antitrust Bulletin* 44 (Fall 1999): 555–76.

37. Armentano, *Antitrust and Monopoly*, 62. See also William F. Shughart II and Michael Reksulak, "Of Rebates and Drawbacks: The Standard Oil (N.J.) Company and the Railroads," *Review of Industrial Organization* 38 (May 2011): 267–83.

38. Armentano, *Antitrust and Monopoly*, 66.

39. *Standard Oil Company of New Jersey v. United States*, 221 U.S. 1 (1911).

40. Armentano, *Antitrust and Monopoly*, 67. By producing and distributing its products with exceptional efficiency, Standard Oil outdid its rivals for decades. (Not incidentally, these rivals included both the father and brother of muckraking journalist Ida Tarbell.) The rivals' difficulties were, in turn, mistaken by Tarbell and countless other critics of Rockefeller as damage inflicted on the American people as a whole. However, economic competition is *supposed* to press producers to be efficient and to serve the interests of consumers—or uncompetitive firms will be driven out of business. By focusing on the travails of Standard's rivals, writers such as Henry Demarest Lloyd and Matthew Josephson either failed to notice that consumers were reaping huge benefits in the form of lower prices and greater varieties of products, or they presumed that these consumer benefits did not justify the sheer size of Standard Oil, since, in their view, bigness in and of itself is bad. The view that big is bad remains the cornerstone of the progressive ethos to this day. In the mind of America's progressives, only the government should be big.

41. Gary D. Libecap, "The Rise of the Chicago Packers and the Origins of Meat Inspection and Antitrust," *Economic Inquiry* 30 (April 1992): 242–62; the quotation is on page 246.

42. Mary Yeager, *Competition and Regulation: The Development of Oligopoly in the Meat Packing Industry* (JAI Press, 1981), 70. Yeager reports that the nominal price per pound of beef tenderloins fell from $0.275 in 1883 to $0.1675 in 1889. In 1889 the price level was 3.6 percent lower than it was in 1883. Adjusting Yeager's nominal prices for the deflation that occurred yields a real-price decline of 37 percent.

43. Rudolf A. Clemen, *The American Livestock and Meat Industry* (The Ronald Press, 1923), 255.

44. Libecap, "The Rise of the Chicago Packers," 248. Although no evidence exists that the big slaughtering houses were colluding either to raise the prices charged to consumers or to lower the prices paid to cattlemen, belief in such collusion persisted into the early years of the twentieth century. See David Moss and Mark Campasano, "*The Jungle* and the Debate over Federal Meat Inspection in 1906," Harvard Business School Case 716-045, published February 2016, p. 12:

> In 1904, the U.S. Bureau of Corporations began investigating the wide gap between low cattle prices and high beef prices. Roosevelt supported the investigation, hoping to find evidence of meatpacker misconduct, but the resulting 1905 report disappointed him and his antitrust allies. Instead of revealing meatpacker wrongdoing, it concluded that their profits were entirely reasonable and that industry leaders had not restricted competition. The report found, for example, that while Swift's 1904 sales were about $200 million, its profits were only $3.85 million, or 1.93% of sales, far lower than popularly believed.

45. See Libecap, "The Rise of the Chicago Packers"; Donald J. Boudreaux, Thomas J. DiLorenzo, and Steven Parker, "Antitrust Before the Sherman Act," in *The Causes and Consequences of Antitrust*, ed. Fred S. McChesney and William F. Shughart II (University of Chicago Press, 1995), 255–70.

46. Libecap, "The Rise of the Chicago Packers," 246.

47. See Maxwell L. Stearns and Todd J. Zywicki, "Antitrust and Public Choice," Law & Economics Center, George Mason University, published 2011, 15–16, https://mason lec.org/site/rte_uploads/files/Antitrust_FINAL.pdf.

48. U.S. Congress, *Journal of the Senate of Missouri*, 35th General Assembly, 1889, 407.

49. In a May 1890 ruling, the U.S. Supreme Court declared Minnesota's version of this inspection statute to be an unconstitutional obstruction of interstate commerce. *Minnesota v. Barber*, 136 U.S. 313 (1890).

50. U.S. Congress, Senate, *Senate Report No. 829 from the Select Committee on the Transportation and Sale of Meat Products, Report to Accompany S3717, 3718, 3719, and Senate Joint Resolution 78*, 1890, 51st Congress, 1st Session, S. Rep. 2705, 3.

51. U.S. Congress, Senate, *Senate Report No. 829*.

52. Stearns and Zywicki, "Antitrust and Public Choice," 17.

53. In "The Origins of the Sherman Act," DiLorenzo argues that among the motives of Sen. John Sherman and other Republican supporters of the antitrust act was a desire to defuse criticism of their support for protective tariffs, which, of course, protect favored domestic producers from competition. DiLorenzo's argument is compelling because, a mere three months after enactment of the Sherman Antitrust Act, Congress—with the support of Sen. Sherman—passed the McKinley Tariff, one of the largest tariff hikes in American history.

54. DiLorenzo, "The Origins of the Sherman Act," 78–80.

55. Phil Gramm and Jerry Ellig, "'Big Bad Trusts' Are a Progressive Myth," *Wall Street Journal*, October 2, 2019, https://www.wsj.com/articles/big-bad-trusts-are -a-progressive-myth-11570056543.

56. Marxist Internet Archive, "The Appeal to Reason," last updated August 12, 2019, https://www.marxists.org/history/usa/pubs/appeal-to-reason/-:~:text=Upton Sinclair%27s novel The Jungle,the novel%27s protagonist, Jurgis Rudkus.

57. Moss and Campasano, "*The Jungle* and the Debate," 13. See also Patrick Newman, "The Big Meat: The Beef Trust, Regulatory Capture, and Government Intervention," SSRN Working Paper No. 3213676 (the University of Tampa, July 13, 2018), 37. Soon after the USDA's report, President Roosevelt sent two other investigators to Chicago: Charles Neill and James Reynolds. The Neill-Reynolds report claimed to verify the truth of Sinclair's descriptions. But we agree with Newman that there are good reasons to credit the USDA's report and to discount this report. Not the least among the reasons for the latter is that both Neill and Reynolds were noted anticapitalists.

58. Quoted in Newman, "The Big Meat," 39.

59. Quoted in Newman, "The Big Meat," 39.

60. Quoted in Newman, "The Big Meat," 39.

61. Lawrence W. Reed, "Of Meat and Myth," Foundation for Economic Education, published February 8, 2013, https://fee.org/articles/of-meat-and-myth/.

62. Libecap, "The Rise of the Chicago Packers," 246.

63. Kolko, *The Triumph of Conservatism*, 98–101.

64. See Newman, "The Big Meat," 52.

65. Gramm and Ellig, "'Big Bad Trusts.'"

66. United States Industrial Commission, *Preliminary Report on Trusts and Industrial Combinations: Vol. 1* (Government Printing Office, 1900), 215.

67. Lebergott, *The Americans*, 292.

68. Using nominal figures from the Federal Reserve Bank of St. Louis (FRED) and adjusting them for deflation yields a real fall in these freight rates of 34.7 percent. See Federal Reserve Bank of St. Louis, "Revenue Per Freight Ton-Mile," FRED Economic Data, accessed September 2024, https://fred.stlouisfed.org/series/A0303 FUSA259NNBR.

69. See George Hilton, "The Consistency of the Interstate Commerce Act," *Journal of Law & Economics* 9 (October 1966): 187–13; Gabriel Kolko, *Railroads and Regulation, 1877–1916* (W. W. Norton, 1970).

70. Lebergott, *The Americans*, 293.

71. Thomas Gale Moore, *Freight Transportation Regulation: Surface Freight and the Interstate Commerce Commission* (American Enterprise Institute, 1972), 15.

72. Moore, *Freight Transportation Regulation*, 15.

73. Moore, *Freight Transportation Regulation*, 16. Even this third piece of regulatory tightening left the railroads unsatisfied. A fourth statute in this vein, the Mann-Elkins Act of 1910, gave the ICC additional powers, most of which were desired by the railroads but some of which pleased shippers. See Moore, *Freight Transportation Regulation*, 16–18.

74. Thomas Gale Moore, "Surface Freight Transportation Deregulation," in *The Concise Encyclopedia of Economics*, ed. David R. Henderson (Liberty Fund, 2006), 485–88; the quotation is on page 485. See also Randall G. Holcombe, *Liberty in Peril: Democracy and Power in American History* (Independent Institute, 2019). On page 120 Holcombe, an economist at Florida State University, reports that

> the railroads saw advantages to regulation. Unstable prices, disliked by rail customers, could also be detrimental to the railroads. A recession in 1884 led to the failure of a number of railroads, and the railroads wanted to undertake pooling arrangements for their mutual profitability. Thus, the railroad industry, which was very competitive, wanted the ICC to stabilize rates, regulate routes, and protect their profitability. Essentially, the ICC cartelized the industry, allowing it to be more profitable than it could have been in a more competitive unregulated environment.

75. Moore, "Surface Freight Transportation Deregulation," 485.

76. Moore, "Surface Freight Transportation Deregulation," 485.

77. Federal Trade Commission, 15 U.S.C. §§ 41–58 (1914).

78. The Clayton Antitrust Act, 15 U.S.C. §§ 12–27 (1914).

79. The Robinson-Patman Price Discrimination Act, 15 U.S. Code § 13 (1936).

80. William F. Shughart II, "Don't Revise the Clayton Act, Scrap It!" *Cato Journal* 6 (Winter 1987): 925–32.

81. See, for example, D. Daniel Sokol, "Analyzing Robinson-Patman," *George Washington Law Review* 83 (November 2015): 2064–2100.

82. Robert H. Bork, *The Antitrust Paradox* (The Free Press, 1978).

83. Bork, *The Antitrust Paradox*, 7.

84. Franklin H. Giddings, "The Persistence of Competition," *Political Science Quarterly* 2 (March 1887): 62–78; this quotation is found on page 65.

85. John Bates Clark and Franklin H. Giddings, *The Modern Distributive Process* (Ginn, 1888), 111.

86. Frank Taussig, *Principles of Economics* (Macmillan, 1917), 425. For a useful survey of the skeptical attitudes of late nineteenth- and early twentieth-century economists toward antitrust, see Thomas J. DiLorenzo and Jack C. High, "Antitrust and Competition, Historically Considered," *Economic Inquiry* 26 (July 1988): 423–35.

87. "Statement of Senator Edward M. Kennedy Before the Senate Subcommittee on Aviation—Hearings on S. 689, The Air Transportation Regulatory Reform Act of

1977," *Congressional Record*, Senate, March 22, 1977, 8569, https://www.govinfo.gov/content /pkg/GPO-CRECB-1977-pt7/pdf/GPO-CRECB-1977-pt7-5-2.pdf.

88. "Statement of Senator Edward M. Kennedy on the Airline Deregulation Act of 1976—Conference Report," *Congressional Record*, Senate, October 14, 1978, 37419, https://www.congress.gov/95/crecb/1978/10/14/GPO-CRECB-1978-pt28-1-1.pdf.

89. See Douglas W. Caves, Lauritis R. Christensen, and Joseph A. Swanson, "The Staggers Act, 30 Years Later," *Regulation* (Winter 2010–2011): 28–31, https://www.cato.org/sites/cato.org/files/serials/files/regulation/2010/12/regv33n4-5.pdf.

90. Jimmy Carter, "Motor Carrier Act of 1980 Statement on Signing S. 2245 into Law," The American Presidency Project, delivered July 1, 1980, https://www.presidency.ucsb.edu/documents/motor-carrier-act-1980-statement-signing-s-2245-into-law.

91. Kenneth Burton and David Christensen, "Unleashing Innovation: The Deregulation of Air Cargo Transportation," Mercatus Center, published December 15, 2014, https://www.mercatus.org/research/policy-briefs/unleashing-innovation-deregulation-air-cargo-transportation.

92. Fred Smith, personal communication in 2022 to author Phil Gramm.

93. Robert Reich, "Warren is Correct About Busting Up Big Tech," *Robert Reich Substack* (blog), March 11, 2018, https://robertreich.org/post/183389236450.

94. As of May 2024, Bill Gates owned only 2.79 percent of Microsoft shares. Tipranks, "Microsoft (MSFT) Ownership—Who Owns It?," accessed September 2024, https://www.tipranks.com/stocks/msft/ownership# .

95. Federal Reserve Bank of St. Louis, "Producer Price Index by Commodity: Advertising Space and Time Sales: Internet Advertising Sales, Excluding Internet Advertising Sold by Print Publishers (WPU365)," FRED Economic Data, accessed September 2024, https://fred.stlouisfed.org/series/WPU365.

96. Gabe Alpert, "Top 10 S&P 500 Stocks by Index Weight," *Investopedia*, August 29, 2023, https://www.investopedia.com/top-10-s-and-p-500-stocks-by-index-weight-4843111.

97. See U.S. Bureau of Labor Statistics, "73 Percent of Civilian Workers Had Access to Retirement Benefits in 2023," *TED: The Economics Daily*, September 29, 2023, reporting that "in March 2023, 73 percent of civilian workers had access to retirement benefits, with 56 percent of workers participating in these plans." See also U.S. Bureau of Labor Statistics, table A-1: "Employment status of the civilian population by sex and age." This shows civilian employment in 2023 was at roughly 160 million. Fifty-six percent of 160 million is 89.6 million workers.

98. Ted Cruz and Phil Gramm, "Biden Wants to Put AI on a Leash," *Wall Street Journal*, March 25, 2024, https://www.wsj.com/articles/biden-wants-to-put-artificial-intelligence-on-a-leash-progressive-regulation-45275102.

99. U.S. Bureau of Labor Statistics, "Consumer Price Index for All Urban Consumers: Recreational Books in U.S. City Average," FRED Economic Data, published June 27, 2024, https://fred.stlouisfed.org/series/CUUR0000SERG02; U.S. Bureau of Labor Statistics, "Consumer Price Index for All Urban Consumers: Video and Audio Products in U.S. City Average," FRED Economic Data, published July 8, 2024, https://fred.stlouisfed.org/series/CUUR0000SERAC; U.S. Bureau of Labor Statistics, "Consumer Price Index for All Urban Consumers: Recorded Music and Music Subscriptions in U.S. City Average, All Urban Consumers," accessed September 2024, https://data.bls.gov/PDQWeb/cu.

100. "Telephone hardware, calculators, and other consumer information items in U.S. city average, all urban consumers," U.S. Bureau of Labor Statistics, "Databases, Tables & Calculators by Subject," accessed September 2024, https://data.bls.gov/timeseries/CUUR0000SEEE04?output_view=data.

101. Erik Brynjolfsson, Avinash Collis, W. Erwin Diewert, Felix Eggers, and Kevin J. Fox, "GDP-B: Accounting for the Value of New and Free Goods," NBER Working Paper No. 25695 (March 2019), see especially pages 43–45, https://www.nber.org/system/files/working_papers/w25695/w25695.pdf.

102. Brynjolfsson et al., "GDP-B: Accounting for the Value," 30.

103. Importantly, the kind of innovation at work here is what the tech scholar Adam Thierer calls "permissionless innovation." Under a regime of permissionless innovation, entrepreneurs are free to innovate without first needing to get permission from the government. Adam Thierer, *Permissionless Innovation: The Continuing Case for Comprehensive Technological Freedom* (Mercatus Center, 2016).

104. Ceren Kurban, "World's 22 Biggest Tech Companies of 2024," UserGuiding, published January 4, 2024, https://userguiding.com/blog/biggest-tech-companies/.

105. Sam Bowman, "What Lina Khan's Appointment Means for the House Antitrust Bills," *Truth on the Market*, June 22, 2021, https://truthonthemarket.com/2021/06/22/what-lina-khans-appointment-means-for-the-house-antitrust-bills/.

   Commissioner Slaughter asserts that if "Black-owned businesses and Black consumers are systematically underrepresented and disadvantaged, we know our markets are not fair." This assertion, however, does nothing to justify the abandonment of the consumer-welfare standard. If the underrepresentation and disadvantage alleged here are real and caused by market monopolization, reliance on the consumer-welfare standard is sufficient to solve the problem. If, instead, the problem is not caused by market monopolization, the problem isn't one that antitrust is equipped to address. Its solution must be found elsewhere.

106. Prohibiting Anticompetitive Mergers Act of 2022, S. 22464, 117th Congress. (2022). https://www.warren.senate.gov/imo/media/doc/SIL22464.pdf.

107. Prohibiting Anticompetitive Mergers Act of 2022, S. 22464, 117th Congress. (2022).

108. "Joe Biden Signs Executive Order Promoting Competition in U.S. Economy Speech Transcript," *rev* (blog), July 9, 2021: https://www.rev.com/blog/transcripts/joe-biden-signs-executive-order-promoting-competition-in-u-s-economy-speech-transcript.

109. "Joe Biden Signs Executive Order," *rev* (blog).

Three: The Myth that the Great Depression Was a Failure of Capitalism

1. Jewish Telegraph Agency, "Judge Brandeis Says Crisis Is Worse than War," *Daily Bulletin*, April 7, 1932, https://www.jta.org/archive/judge-brandeis-says-crisis-is-worse-than-war.

2. The unemployment rate fell to 14.3 percent in 1937 before rising again. See Jim Rose, "How Great Was the Great Depression Unemployment? The Official and Darby Estimates of US Unemployment in the 1930s," *Utopia, you are standing in it!* (blog), June 17, 2015, https://utopiayouarestandinginit.com/2015/06/17/how-great-was-the-great-depression-unemployment-the-official-and-darby-estimates-of-us-unemployment-in-the-1930s/.

Because a chief concern in this chapter is to take stock of the performance of the economy, we count among the unemployed all workers on government work-relief programs, such as the Works Progress Administration (WPA) and the Civilian Conservation Corps (CCC). An alternative measure of Great Depression unemployment, developed by UCLA economist Michael Darby, counts workers on work-relief programs as employed and thus finds lower rates of unemployment for much of the Depression. By Darby's measurement, the unemployment rate in 1937 was not 14.3 percent but 9.1 percent. See Michael R. Darby, "Three-and-a-Half Million U.S. Employees Have Been Mislaid: Or, an Explanation of Unemployment, 1934–1941," *Journal of Political Economy* 84 (February 1976): 1–16.

3. George Selgin, *False Dawn: The New Deal and the Promise of Recovery* (University of Chicago Press, 2025), 6. Wesleyan University economic historian Stanley Lebergott is the source of the unemployment figure of 11.7 percent. Stanley Lebergott, *Manpower in Economic Growth* (McGraw-Hill, 1964), table A-3, 512.

4. George Selgin, "The New Deal and Recovery, Part 1: The Record," *Alt-M* (blog), June 16, 2020, https://www.cato.org/blog/new-deal-recovery-part-1-record.

5. On the percentage of the workforce employed in nonfarm jobs, see HSUS; on the unemployment rate of nonfarm workers as reported by Marquette University economist Gene Smiley, see Gene Smiley, "Great Depression," in *Concise Encyclopedia of Economics*, ed. David R. Henderson (Liberty Fund, 2006), 230. Again, these numbers include workers on government work-relief programs.

6. David Wheelock, "How Bad Was the Great Depression? Gauging the Economic Impact," Federal Reserve Bank of St. Louis, accessed September 2024, https://www.stlouisfed.org/the-great-depression/curriculum/economic-episodes-in-american-history-part-3.

7. Selgin, *False Dawn*, 11. For these figures, Selgin cites Lester V. Chandler, *America's Greatest Depression, 1929–1941* (Harper & Row, 1970), 4.

8. Milton Friedman and Anna Jacobson Schwartz, *A Monetary History of the United States, 1867–1960* (Princeton University Press, 1963), 301.

9. Federal Reserve Bank of St. Louis, "Industrial Production: Total Index (INDPRO)," FRED Economic Data, accessed September 2024, https://fred.stlouisfed.org/series/INDPRO.

10. Robert Higgs, *Neither Liberty nor Safety* (Independent Institute, 2007), 109.

11. Marriner S. Eccles, *Beckoning Frontiers* (Alfred A. Knopf, 1951), p. 76.

12. William E. Leuchtenberg, quoted in John Garraty's conversation with William Leuchtenberg, in John A. Garraty, *Interpreting American History: Conversations with Historians, Part II* (Macmillan, 1970), 171.

13. Arthur M. Schlesinger Jr., *The Crisis of the Old Order, 1919–1933* (Houghton Mifflin, 1957), 159–60.

14. Schlesinger, *The Crisis of the Old Order*, 67.

15. David Emory Shi, *America: A Narrative History*, 11th ed. (W. W. Norton, 2019), 1004.

16. John Kenneth Galbraith, *The Great Crash 1929* (Houghton Mifflin, 1955).

17. Robert L. Heilbroner, *The Worldly Philosophers* (Simon & Schuster, 1953) 227.

18. Shi, *America: A Narrative History*, 1011.

19. Conor Clarke, "An Interview with Paul Samuelson, Part One," *The Atlantic*, June 17, 2009, https://www.theatlantic.com/politics/archive/2009/06/an-interview-with-paul-samuelson-part-one/19572/.

Samuelson's full quotation reads, "I came to the University of Chicago on the morning of January 2, 1932. I wasn't yet a graduate of high school for another few months. And that was about the low point of the Herbert Hoover/Andrew Mellon phase after October of 1929. That's quite a number of years to have inaction."

20. Galbraith, *The Great Crash 1929*, 138–41.

21. Franklin D. Roosevelt, "Oglethorpe University Address," Pepperdine School of Public Policy, delivered May 22, 1932, https://publicpolicy.pepperdine.edu/aca demics/research/faculty-research/new-deal/roosevelt-speeches/fr052232.htm.

22. Shi, *America: A Narrative History*, 1019–20.

23. Joseph R. Conlin, *The American Past*, 6th ed. (Wadsworth, 2001), 833.

24. Samuel Eliot Morison, *The Oxford History of the American People* (Oxford University Press, 1965), 953.

25. Heilbroner, *The Worldly Philosophers*, 252.

26. Heilbroner, *The Worldly Philosophers*, 252.

27. Eric Rauchway, "(Very) Short Reading List: Unemployment in the 1930s," *The Edge of the American West*, October 10, 2008, https://edgeofthewest.wordpress .com/2008/10/10/very-short-reading-list-unemployment-in-the-1930s/.

28. Leigh Haber, "Jane Fonda's New Book *What Can I Do?* Is a Climate Crisis Call to Arms," Oprah.com, last updated 2024, https://www.oprah.com/inspiration/ jane-fonda-talks-climate-change-and-her-new-book.

29. Prohibitions on branch banking artificially diminish banks' abilities to diversify their portfolios and thus dampen the competition that weeds out weak banks. Such prohibitions unnecessarily increase the banking system's fragility. See Mark Carlson and Kris James Mitchener, "Branch Banking as a Device for Discipline: Competition and Bank Survivorship During the Great Depression," *Journal of Political Economy* 117 (April 2009): 165–210.

Restrictions on banks' ability to issue paper currency were also important. Currency withdrawals are not problematic for banks that can issue their own notes on the same terms as those required to write up demand deposit balances.

30. Friedman and Schwartz, *A Monetary History*, 157.

31. Friedman and Schwartz, *A Monetary History*, 157.

32. Jon R. Moen and Ellis W. Tallman, "The Panic of 1907," Federal Reserve History, published December 4, 2015, https://www.federalreservehistory.org/essays/panic -of-1907.

33. Andrew J. Jalil, "A New History of Banking Panics in the United States, 1825–1929: Construction and Implications," *American Economic Journal: Macroeconomics* 7 (July 2015): 295–330; see especially page 308.

34. Robert F. Bruner and Sean D. Carr, *The Panic of 1907: Lessons Learned from the Market's Perfect Storm* (John Wiley & Sons, 2007), 141–42.

35. Jalil, "A New History of Banking Panics," 308, 312; Moen and Tallman, "The Panic of 1907."

36. Richard H. Timberlake, "The Central Banking Role of Clearinghouse Associations," *Journal of Money, Credit, and Banking* 16, no. 1 (1984): 1–15, https://www.jstor.org/ stable/1992645. Timberlake tracks the evolution of this role of clearinghouse associations from 1857 to its "full flowering" during the panic of 1907. This role was brought to an abrupt end with the opening of the Federal Reserve in 1914.

37. Steven Horwitz, "Competitive Currencies, Legal Restrictions, and the Origins of the Fed: Some Evidence from the Panic of 1907," *Southern Economic Journal* 56, no. 3

(1990): 639–49, https://www.jstor.org/stable/1059365; the passage quoted is on page 646.

38. Federal Reserve Bank of Boston, "Panic of 1907," accessed September 2024, https://www.bostonfed.org/publications/economic-education/panic-of-1907.aspx.

    Since the close of the Second Bank of the United States in 1836, the US Treasury regularly played a central-banking role by redirecting many of its funds into deposits in banks located in regions that were at rising risk of experiencing runs.

39. Federal Reserve Bank of Boston, "Panic of 1907," 11.

40. Tim Sablik, "Liquidity Requirements and the Lender of Last Resort," *Econ Focus*, Fourth Quarter 2015, https://www.richmondfed.org/publications/research/econ _focus/2015/q4/federal_reserve.

41. See, for example, William G. Dewald, "The National Monetary Commission: A Look Back," *Journal of Money, Credit, and Banking* 4 (November 1972): 930–56; George Selgin, "New York's Bank: The National Monetary Commission and the Founding of the Fed," *Policy Analysis* (Cato Institute), June 21, 2016. Selgin is critical of the commission's chairman, Nelson Aldrich, for successfully maneuvering to ensure that any central-banking system created by Congress would promote the interests of big New York banks.

42. Friedman and Schwartz, *A Monetary History*, 231.

43. Federal Reserve Bank of St. Louis, "Industrial Production." Victor Zarnowitz's estimate of the peak-to-trough decline in "business activity" in 1920–1921 is 38 percent; see Zarnowitz, *Business Cycles* (University of Chicago Press, 1996), table 7.4, 226.

44. Federal Reserve Bank of St. Louis, "Industrial Production."

45. The lower estimate of the unemployment rate is from Christina D. Romer, "World War I and the Postwar Depression: A Reinterpretation Based on Alternative Estimates of GNP," *Journal of Monetary Economics* 22 (July 1988): 91–115, especially table 4, page 100. The higher estimate is from Lebergott, *Manpower in Economic Growth*, table A-3, 512.

46. James Grant, *The Forgotten Depression* (Simon & Schuster, 2014), 69.

47. Grant, *The Forgotten Depression*, 67. Nominal GNP fell by 24 percent. Estimates of the fall in the GNP during this downturn vary wildly. The US Department of Commerce estimates the fall in the GNP to have been 7 percent, while Romer estimates that the GNP fell by only 2.4 percent. See Romer, "World War I," 100, 104.

48. Grant, *The Forgotten Depression*, 2–3: "The recognized arbiter of the cyclical calendar, the National Bureau of Economic Research, dates the start of the downturn of 1920–21 in January 1920 and its conclusion in July 1921, which is to say that things stopped getting better in January 1920, and they stopped getting worse in July 1921. The elapsed time was 18 months." See also Davis Kedrosky, "In the Shadow of the Slump: The Depression of 1920–1921," *Berkeley Economic Review*, March 18, 2021, https://econreview.berkeley.edu/in-the-shadow-of-the-slump-the-depression -of-1920-1921/. He claims that this downturn lasted only fourteen months.

49. Grant, *The Forgotten Depression*.

50. Stanley Lebergott, *The Americans: An Economic Record* (W. W. Norton, 1984), 432.

51. Ellis Tallman and Eugene Nelson White, "Why Was There No Banking Panic in 1920–21?," ASSA Annual Meetings, Unpublished manuscript, 2020, 6. See also p. 20: "The district banks in areas exposed to dramatic commodity price shocks resisted demands that they adhere to a policy of austerity until the middle of the recession," by which time the risk of a bank panic had been avoided.

52. Grant, *The Forgotten Depression*, 1. Grant argues that Wilson ignored the downturn only because he was incapacitated by a stroke. Harding ignored it because he believed in limited government. In addition to there being no fiscal-policy response in 1920–1921 to the downturn, there also were no regulatory measures aimed at artificially preventing wages and prices from falling.

53. On the start of the Great Depression, see also Gary Richardson, "The Great Depression," *Federal Reserve History*, November 22, 2013, https://www.federalreserve history.org/essays/great-depression.

> "The Great Depression began in August 1929, when the economic expansion of the Roaring Twenties came to an end."

54. Gene Smiley, "The U.S. Economy in the 1920s," Economic History Association Encyclopedia, ed. Robert Whaples, published June 29, 2004, https://eh.net/encyclopedia/the-u-s-economy-in-the-1920s/.

55. Smiley, "The U.S. Economy in the 1920s."

> Milton Friedman and Anna Schwartz agree that while the crash didn't start the Depression, it sharpened the downturn. They write, "Partly, no doubt, the stock market crash was a symptom of the underlying forces making for a severe contraction in economic activity. But partly also, its occurrence must have helped to deepen the contraction." Friedman and Schwartz, *A Monetary History*, 306.

56. Smiley, "The U.S. Economy in the 1920s."

57. Stanley Lebergott, "Wages and Working Conditions," in *Concise Encyclopedia of Economics*, ed. David R. Henderson (Liberty Fund, 2006), table 1, https://www.econlib.org/library/Enc/WagesandWorkingConditions.html.

58. Simon Kuznets, *National Income and Its Composition, 1919–1938* (National Bureau of Economic Research, 1941), 218.

59. Stanley Lebergott, *Consumer Expenditures: New Measures & Old Motives* (Princeton University Press, 1996), 19.

60. Lebergott, *Consumer Expenditures*, table 3.1, 19.

61. Lebergott, *Consumer Expenditures*, 432. Elsewhere, Lebergott writes that "there is . . . no evidence that the proportion of personal income going to consumption fell below that of any prior decade. Indeed, it actually rose during the decade. Moreover, 98 of the 100 categories into which consumption is classified (e.g., food, tobacco, rent) did not slow down before the crash. They gained quite as much from 1925 to 1929 as from 1920 to 1924." See Stanley Lebergott, *The Americans: An Economic Record* (W. W. Norton, 1984), 432. Citing the pioneering work of John Kendrick, Lebergott reports that "personal consumption accounted for 68 percent of the value of GNP in the prosperity of 1919–20 and 76 percent in 1928–29."

62. Burton Folsom Jr., *New Deal or Raw Deal? How FDR's Economic Legacy Has Damaged America* (Threshold Editions, 2008), 35.

63. Alan Greenspan and Adrian Wooldridge, *Capitalism in America: A History* (Penguin Press, 2018), 236.

64. Friedman and Schwartz, *A Monetary History*, 307–8.

65. Friedman and Schwartz, *A Monetary History*, 307–8.

66. See Tallman and White, "Why Was There No Banking Panic," 2:

> The period we consider [1920–1921] preceded the Federal Reserve Board's famous Tenth Annual Report (1923). That report recognized the need to coordinate discounting and open market operations for a consistent general credit policy and led to the formation in the Spring of 1923 of the Open

Market Investment Committee and a system-wide account that pro-rata allocations to the Reserve banks of centrally determined open market operations. Thus, we examine the pre-1923 period when the Reserve banks had the greatest latitude for pursuing their own policies, even resisting directions from the Board of Governors and pressure from other Reserve banks.

67. Friedman and Schwartz, *A Monetary History*, 299. See George Mason University economist Lawrence White, *The Clash of Economic Ideas: The Great Policy Debates and Experiments of the Last Hundred Years* (Cambridge University Press, 2012), 128: "They [Friedman and Schwartz] pointed out that the Federal Reserve, having taken over superintendence of the banking system from private clearinghouse associations, failed to do what the clearinghouses had done in previous crises to shore up the banks, stem bank runs, and prevent such a large monetary contraction." Charles Calomiris and Joseph Mason find that, of the four distinct banking panics that occurred between 1929 and 1933, only one—the last of these, starting in January 1933—was unambiguously nationwide. They further argue that this crisis was likely caused not by depositor fears of bank insolvency but by a run on the dollar sparked by fears that Roosevelt would prevent private persons from converting their dollars into gold following his inauguration that March. See Charles W. Calomiris and Joseph R. Mason, "Fundamentals, Panics, and Bank Distress During the Depression," *American Economic Review* 93 (December 2003): 1615–47.

68. Friedman and Schwartz, *A Monetary History*.

69. Allan H. Meltzer, *A History of the Federal Reserve: Volume 1, 1913–1951* (University of Chicago Press, 2003), 277, 412.

70. See William P. Gramm, "The Real-Balance Effect in the Great Depression," *Journal of Economic History* 32 (June 1972): 499–519.

71. Jennifer Burns, *Milton Friedman: The Last Conservative* (Farrar, Straus & Giroux, 2023), 255.

72. Richard H. Timberlake, "The Federal Reserve's Role in the Great Depression and the Subprime Crisis," *Cato Journal* 28 (Spring/Summer 2008): 303–12; Thomas M. Humphrey and Richard H. Timberlake, *Gold, the Real Bills Doctrine, and the Fed: Sources of Monetary Disorder 1922–1938* (Cato Institute, 2019). Also blaming the Fed for believing in the false real-bills doctrine is Allan Meltzer; see Allan Metzer, *A History of the Federal Reserve*, 273–82.

73. Remarks by Governor Ben Bernanke at the conference to honor Milton Friedman, University of Chicago, Chicago, Illinois November 8, 2002. The Federal Reserve Board (emphasis added), https://urldefense.com/v3/__https://www.federalreserve .gov/boarddocs/speeches/2002/20021108/__;!!O5VZiZhZuxILryEb!ecziUHM mZ51DfttX_gd5NtJ77QxNLU0u-lB_JI3Gk8wLNr44yZUnMFeKMhDzSVGgWfV J1Rc-QdBx2HY_GMpxEBSx$.

74. Herbert Hoover, "Address Accepting the Republican Presidential Nomination," The American Presidency Project, delivered August 11, 1932, https://www.presidency .ucsb.edu/documents/address-accepting-the-republican-presidential-nomination.

75. According to Steven Horwitz,

Hoover had long been a critic of laissez faire. As president, he doubled federal spending in real terms in four years. He also used government to prop up wages, restricted immigration, signed the Smoot-Hawley tariff, raised taxes, and created the Reconstruction Finance Corporation—all interventionist measures and not laissez faire. Unlike many Democrats today, President Franklin D. Roosevelt's advisers knew that Hoover had started the New Deal. One of them [Raymond Moley] wrote, "When we all burst into Washington . . . we found every essential idea [of the New Deal] enacted in the 100-day Congress in the Hoover administration itself."

Horwitz, "Herbert Hoover: Father of the New Deal," Briefing Paper No. 122 (Cato Institute, September 29, 2011), https://www.cato.org/briefing-paper/herbert-hoover -father-new-deal. See also Selgin, *False Dawn*, 68.

76. Selgin, *False Dawn*, 68.
77. Selgin, *False Dawn*, 68.
78. "Revenue Act of 1932," Wikipedia, last updated May 10, 2023, 16:38 (UTC), https:// en.wikipedia.org/wiki/Revenue_Act_of_1932; Horwitz, "Herbert Hoover," 8; Chris Edwards, "Tax Increases and the Great Depression," Cato Institute, published November 16, 2022, https://tinyurl.com/4byees6b. Although signed in June 1932, this tax increase acted retroactively back to January.
79. Horwitz, "Herbert Hoover," 4. Horwitz observed that in "no year between 1933 and 1941 under Roosevelt had a deficit been that large."
80. Veronique de Rugy, "High Taxes and High Budget Deficits: The Hoover–Roosevelt Tax Increases of the 1930s," *Cato Institute Tax & Budget Bulletin*, no. 14 (March 2003), https://www.cato.org/sites/cato.org/files/pubs/pdf/tbb-0303-14.pdf.
81. Franklin D. Roosevelt Presidential Library and Museum, "FDR: From Budget Balancer to Keynesian," FDR Library National Archives, last updated 2016, https:// www.fdrlibrary.org/budget.
82. Horwitz, "Herbert Hoover," 4–5.
83. Anthony Patrick O'Brien, "A Behavioral Explanation for Nominal Wage Rigidity During the Great Depression," *Quarterly Journal of Economics* 104 (November 1989): 719–35.
84. Jacob Viner, *Balanced Deflation, Inflation, or More Depression* (University of Minneapolis Press, 1933), 12.
85. See, for example, William G. Whittaker, *The Davis-Bacon Act: Institutional Evolution and Public Policy* (Congressional Research Service, 2007), https://crsreports.congress .gov/product/pdf/RL/94-408.
86. Horwitz, "Herbert Hoover," 5.
87. Douglas A. Irwin, *Free Trade Under Fire*, 5th ed. (Princeton University Press, 2020), 99. For a book-length treatment of the Smoot-Hawley Tariff, see Douglas A. Irwin, *Peddling Prosperity* (Princeton University Press, 2011).
88. Mark J. Perry, "The Economists' Tariff Protest of 1930," *AEI Ideas*, March 5, 2018, https://www.aei.org/carpe-diem/the-economists-tariff-protest-of-1930/.
89. St. Louis Federal Reserve Bank, "Unemployment Rate," FRED Economic Data, ac- cessed September 2024, https://fred.stlouisfed.org/graph/?g=jS05.
90. J. E. Meade, ed. *World Economic Survey, Eighth Year, 1938–1939* (League of Nations, 1939), 125–26.
91. Selgin, *False Dawn*, 188. A few pages later (p. 189), Selgin adds, "Although the Popular Front offered various excuses for this [poor economic] outcome, according to Eichengreen the most compelling explanation was that government's New Deal– inspired policies, which 'imparted to the economy a negative supply shock on a mas- sive scale.'" Selgin here quotes University of California, Berkeley, economist Barry

Eichengreen, "The Origins and Nature of the Great Slump Revisited," *Economic History Review* 45 (May 1992): 213–39.

92. Meade, *World Economic Survey*, 11–13.

93. A notable exception to the widespread neglect of these League of Nations' data is Folsom, who writes on page 248 that "other nations recovered from the Great Depression more quickly than did the United States. During the late 1930s, the League of Nations collected statistics from the United States and from many other nations on industrial recovery. Much of that data supports the idea that Roosevelt's New Deal created economic uncertainty and was in fact uniquely unsuccessful as a recovery program." See Folsom, *New Deal or Raw Deal?*

94. Selgin, *False Dawn*, 195.

95. Statista, "Monthly Value of the Dow Jones Industrial Average (DJIA) from January 1920 to December 1955," accessed September 2024, https://www.statista.com/statistics/1249670/monthly-change-value-dow-jones-depression/.

96. Selgin, *False Dawn*, 196.

97. Selgin, *False Dawn*, 193.

98. Harold L. Cole and Lee E. Ohanian, "New Deal Policies and the Persistence of the Great Depression: A General Equilibrium Analysis," *Journal of Political Economy* 112 (August 2004): 779–816.

99. Jason E. Taylor, *Deconstructing the Monolith: The Microeconomics of the National Industrial Recovery Act* (University of Chicago Press, 2019), 129–56.

100. Selgin, *False Dawn*, 185.

101. See Friedman and Schwartz, *A Monetary History*, 544; Douglas A. Irwin, "Gold Sterilization and the Recession of 1937–1938," *Financial History Review* 19 (December 2012): 249–67.

On top of these contractionary monetary policies, fiscal policy was also contractionary from 1936 through 1938. Beginning in the spring of 1936, Treasury Secretary Henry Morgenthau, along with President Roosevelt, worried about the growth of the federal government's debt. They acted on this concern. Federal expenditures in 1937 were 7.3 percent less than they'd been a year earlier and would fall by another 11 percent in 1938. Federal receipts, in contrast, rose. In 1937 receipts were 38 percent higher than they were in the previous year, and by 1938 these would rise by another 26 percent. See Gerhard Peters, "Federal Budget Receipts and Outlays: Coolidge-Biden," The American Presidency Project, last updated May 28, 2021, https://www.presidency.ucsb.edu/statistics/data/federal-budget-receipts-and-outlays.

However, like Irwin, Selgin argues in *False Dawn* that this fiscal retrenchment played, at best, a supporting role in causing the 1937–1938 downturn, not least because this retrenchment wasn't as large as it appeared. This is due to the government making a huge one-time "bonus payment" to WWI veterans in 1936—a payment that was never destined to be repeated. So the cut in expenditures from 1936 to 1937 looked to be fiscally more significant than it really was. On page 203, Selgin summarizes as follows: "It's therefore likely that the cutback in net government spending was to blame for less, and perhaps much less, than half of the '37 downturn."

102. Douglas A. Irwin, "What Caused the Recession of 1937–38?," *VoxEU*, September 11, 2011, https://cepr.org/voxeu/columns/what-caused-recession-1937-38. See also Friedman and Schwartz, *A Monetary History*, 545: "Though the decline may not seem large in absolute amount, it was the third largest cyclical decline recorded in our figures, exceeded only by the 1920–21 and 1929–33 declines."

103. Federal Reserve Bank of St. Louis, "Industrial Production."

104. Douglas A. Irwin, "Gold Sterilization and the Recession of 1937–1938," *Financial History Review* 19 (December 2012): 249–67.

105. Statista, "Monthly Value of the Dow Jones Industrial Average (DJIA)."

106. Federal Reserve Bank of St. Louis, "Unemployment Rate," FRED Economic Data, https://fred.stlouisfed.org/graph/?g=jS05.

107. Friedman and Schwartz, *A Monetary History*, 543–45.

108. Selgin, *False Dawn*, 198.

109. Price Fishback, "US Monetary and Fiscal Policy in the 1930s," *Oxford Review of Economic Policy* 26 (Autumn 2010): 385–413; see especially figure 4 on page 402.

110. Demian Brady, *Federal Spending in Historical Context* (National Taxpayers Union, 2022), table 3, https://www.ntu.org/library/doclib/2022/04/Government-Spending-in-Historical-Context-3.pdf.

111. Tax Foundation, "Historical U.S. Federal Individual Income Tax Rates & Brackets, 1862–2021," published August 24, 2021, https://taxfoundation.org/data/all/federal/historical-income-tax-rates-brackets/.

112. Tax Foundation, "Historical U.S. Federal Corporate Income Tax. Rates & Brackets, 1909–2020," Tax Foundation, August 24, 2021: https://taxfoundation.org/data/all/federal/historical-corporate-tax-rates-brackets/ .

113. Charles W. Calomiris and R. Glenn Hubbard, "Internal Finance and Investment: Evidence from the Undistributed Profits Tax of 1936–37," *Journal of Business* 68 (October 1995): 443–82; see especially pages 447–48.

114. Franklin D. Roosevelt, "Address at Boston, Mass.," The American Presidency Project, delivered October 21, 1936, https://www.presidency.ucsb.edu/documents/address-boston-mass.

115. Calomiris and Hubbard, "Internal Finance and Investment."

116. Franklin D. Roosevelt Presidential Library & Museum, Diaries of Henry Morgenthau Diary Jr., April 27, 1933–July 27, 1945 Collection, Microfilm Role no. 50, 3–4, http://www.burtfolsom.com/wp-content/uploads/2011/Morgenthau.pdf. In this 1939 testimony, Morgenthau describes the length of the Roosevelt administration as "eight years," but he almost surely meant "six years."

117. Amity Shlaes, "Introduction," in *New Deal Rebels* (American Institute for Economic Research, 2023), xiii.

118. Franklin D. Roosevelt, "Acceptance Speech for the Renomination for the Presidency," The American Presidency Project, delivered July 27, 1936, https://www.presidency.ucsb.edu/documents/acceptance-speech-for-the-renomination-for-the-presidency-philadelphia-pa.

119. H. W. Brands, *Traitor to His Class* (Doubleday, 2008), 448.

120. Franklin D. Roosevelt, "Annual Message to Congress," The American Presidency Project, delivered January 3, 1936, https://www.presidency.ucsb.edu/documents/annual-message-congress-2.

121. Brands, *Traitor to His Class*, 449.

122. Franklin D. Roosevelt, "Jackson Day Dinner Address," The American Presidency Project, delivered January 8, 1936, https://www.presidency.ucsb.edu/documents/jackson-day-dinner-address-washington-dc.

123. Roosevelt, "Jackson Day Dinner Address."

124. Brands, *Traitor to His Class*, 450.

125. As quoted in Brands, *Traitor to His Class*, 451.

126. Franklin D. Roosevelt, "Address at Madison Square Garden," The American Presidency Project, delivered October 31, 1936, https://www.presidency.ucsb.edu/documents/address-madison-square-garden-new-york-city-1.

127. Roosevelt, "Address at Madison Square Garden."

128. Meade, *World Economic Survey*, 16.

129. Winston Churchill, *Great Contemporaries*, 2nd ed. (Arcole Publishing, 1939; repr., 2017), 252–53.

130. Churchill, *Great Contemporaries*, 252–53.

131. Churchill, *Great Contemporaries*, 254.

132. Benjamin M. Anderson, *Economics and the Public Welfare* (Liberty Fund, 1949; repr., 1979), 478, 483.

133. Robert Higgs, *Depression, War, and Cold War: Studies in Political Economy* (Oxford University Press, 2006), 5.

134. Higgs, *Depression, War, and Cold War*, 9.

135. Meltzer, *A History of the Federal Reserve*, 570.

136. The "switch in time" came with the US Supreme Court's March 1937 ruling in West Coast Hotel Co. v. Parrish, 300 U.S. 379. In this ruling Justice Owen Roberts joined with pro-New Deal colleagues to create a 5–4 majority upholding a minimum-wage statute imposed by Washington state. Roberts's move was interpreted—justly so, it turns out—as a signal that the Supreme Court would, from there on in, look far more favorably upon New Deal economic controls. The earlier ruling that held parts of the NIRA to be unconstitutional is A. L. A. Schechter Poultry Corporation v. United States, 295 U.S. 495 (1935).

137. Higgs, *Depression, War, and Cold War*, 22. Consistent with these findings, economists Scott Baker, Nicholas Bloom, and Steven Davis, using a different measure of economic uncertainty, conclude that the highest level of economic uncertainty in the twentieth century occurred in the 1930s. See Scott R. Baker, Nicholas Bloom, and Steven J. Davis, "Measuring Economic Policy Uncertainty," *Quarterly Journal of Economics* 131 (November 2016): 1593–1636.

138. Higgs, *Depression, War, and Cold War*, 23.

139. Higgs, *Depression, War, and Cold War*, 23.

140. Quote in Higgs, *Depression, War, and Cold War*, 16.

141. J. R. Vernon, "World War II Fiscal Policies and the End of the Great Depression," *Journal of Economic History* 54 (December 1994): 850–68.

142. Robert J. Samuelson, "Great Depression," in *Concise Encyclopedia of Economics, First ed.*, ed. David R. Henderson (Liberty Fund, 1993), https://www.econlib.org/library/Enc1/GreatDepression.html. (Robert Samuelson is not related to the economist Paul Samuelson.)

143. Robert Higgs, *Depression, War, and Cold War*, table 3–4, 71. Steven Horwitz and Michael J. McPhillips offer further evidence that Americans' living standards during the war were hardly better than during the Depression. See Horwitz and McPhillips, "The Reality of the Wartime Economy," *Independent Review* 17 (Winter 2013): 325–47. Of course, military victory over an evil enemy is a public good, and the value of this good might make low living standards during wartime worthwhile to endure. Nevertheless, as far as they go, the facts offer no clear evidence of recovery of living standards or of the market economy's health during the war. Writing in 1943, Paul Samuelson admitted that "the war itself has meant a reversion to lower consumption standards." Paul A. Samuelson, "Full Employment After the War," in *Postwar Economic Problems*, ed. Seymour E. Harris (McGraw-Hill, 1943), 45.

144. From peak wartime spending in 1944, the US government slashed its spending by 75 percent by 1948. See David R. Henderson, "The U.S. Postwar Miracle," Working Paper No. 10–67 (Mercatus Center, November 2010), https://www.mercatus.org/research/working-papers/us-postwar-miracle. On page 1, Henderson adds that this spending reduction "brought federal spending down from a peak of 44 percent of gross national product (GNP) in 1944 to only 8.9 percent in 1948."

145. Samuelson, "Full Employment After the War," 51 (emphasis in original).

146. Kimberly Amadeo, "US Budget Deficit by Year Compared to GDP, the National Debt, and Events," *The Balance*, April 5, 2022, https://www.thebalancemoney.com/us-deficit-by-year-3306306.

147. Only two years in American history did the US government even come close to running peacetime budget deficits that were as large a percentage of GDP as Samuelson proposed be run at the end of WWII. The first year it did so was 1919, when the deficit was 16.6 percent of GDP; the second year was 2020, when the deficit was 14.5 percent of GDP. See US Government Spending, "Federal Deficit Analysis," accessed September 2024, https://www.usgovernmentspending.com/federal_deficit_percent_gdp.

     However, as Samuelson said, the budget for 1919 was really still a wartime budget. And, of course, 2020 was the first and worst year of the COVID-19 pandemic. See Samuelson, "Full Employment After the War," 48.

148. Quoted in David R. Henderson, "The U.S. Postwar Miracle," 4.

149. Selgin, *False Dawn*, 261.

150. Henderson, "The U.S. Postwar Miracle."

151. Henderson, "The U.S. Postwar Miracle," 1.

152. See Federal Reserve Bank of St. Louis, "Budget of the United States Government, 1921–2023," FRASER, https://fraser.stlouisfed.org/title/budget-united-states-government-54?browse=1920s#19001. In 1949—a year marked by a mild recession—the government again ran a small budget deficit.

153. Henderson, "The U.S. Postwar Miracle," 2.

154. Higgs, *Depression, War, and Cold War*, table 3–4, 71.

155. Among those who believe the "pent-up demand" theory is Nobel laureate economist Paul Krugman. See, for example, Paul Krugman, "Spending in Wartime," *The Conscience of a Liberal* (blog), January 23, 2009, https://archive.nytimes.com/krugman.blogs.nytimes.com/2009/01/23/spending-in-wartime/.

156. Henderson, "The U.S. Postwar Miracle," 17–18. Henderson argues that another reality at odds with the "pent-up demand" theory is the fact that, while the postwar years witnessed a fall in the savings *rate*, this rate remained positive. Americans continued to save rather than disgorge their savings to satisfy pent-up consumption demands.

157. Federal Reserve Bank of St. Louis, "Industrial Production."

158. Calculated from Bureau of Economic Analysis data. See Bureau of Economic Analysis, "National Data: National Income and Product Accounts," accessed September 2024, http://tinyurl.com/3r3vpk6a.

159. Higgs, *Depression, War, and Cold War*, 21.

160. Higgs, *Depression, War, and Cold War*, 21. On pages 22–23, Higgs argues that the sharp fall in the difference, following the war, between yields on long-term bonds and short-term bonds also testifies to investors' increased confidence that their property and contract rights were more secure.

Four: The Myth of Trade Hollowing Out American Manufacturing

1. The Statistical Office of the United Nations, "Manufacturing Exports for France, Japan, Germany, Italy, the United Kingdom and the United States," in *International Trade Statistics, 1900–1960* (United Nations, 1962), https://unstats.un.org/unsd/trade/imts/Historical%20data%201900-1960.pdf.
2. The Statistical Office of the United Nations, *International Trade Statistics*.
3. See The Wilson Center, "A Short History of America's Economy Since World War II," *The World's Economy and the Economy's World*, January 23, 2014, https://tiny url.com/3ebcekz6; Govind Bhutada, "The U.S. Share of the Global Economy Over Time," *Visual Capitalist*, January 14, 2021, https://www.visualcapitalist.com /u-s-share-of-global-economy-over-time/.
4. Federal Reserve Bank of St. Louis, "Industrial Production: Total Index (INDPRO)," FRED Economic Data, accessed September 2024, https://fred.stlouisfed.org/series /INDPRO.
5. YiLi Chien and Paul Morris, "Is U.S. Manufacturing Really Declining?" April 11, 2017, Federal Reserve Bank of St. Louis, https://www.stlouisfed.org/on-the -economy/2017/april/us-manufacturing-really-declining.
6. Calculated by dividing FRED Economic Data source "All Employees, Manufacturing" (MANEMP) by "All Employees, Total Nonfarm" (PAYNSA). Because in the 1940s more than ten percent of American workers were employed in agriculture, manufac- turing employment's share of *all* employment was somewhat lower. See Martin Wolf, "Manufacturing Fetishism Is Destined to Fail," *Financial Times*, November 12, 2024.
7. Richard E. Schumann, "Compensation from World War II Through the Great Society," U.S. Bureau of Labor Statistics, published January 30, 2003, 3, https://www .bls.gov/opub/mlr/cwc/compensation-from-world-war-ii-through-the-great -society.pdf.
8. Calculated from Federal Reserve Bank of St. Louis, "Unemployment Rate (UNRATE)," FRED Economic Data, accessed September 2024, https://fred.stlouis fed.org/series/UNRATE.
9. Federal Reserve Bank of St. Louis, "Nonfarm Business Sector: Real Hourly Compensation for All Workers (COMPRNFB)," FRED Economic Data, accessed September 2024, https://fred.stlouisfed.org/series/COMPRNFB.
10. U.S. Bureau of Labor Statistics, "Average Hourly Earnings, Manufacturing," accessed September 2024, https://www.bls.gov/data/#employment. Calculated based on the chain weighted CPI used for the federal tax indexing.
11. Our World in Data, "GDP per Capita," accessed September 2024, https://ourworldindata .org/grapher/gdp-per-capita-prados-de-la-escosura?tab=chart&country=~USA.
12. Brian Reinbold and Yi Wen, "Historical U.S. Trade Deficits," Federal Reserve Bank of St. Louis, published May 17, 2019, https://research.stlouisfed.org/publications/ economic-synopses/2019/05/17/historical-u-s-trade-deficits.
13. David Beniaminov and Michelle Cluver, "Sector Views: S&P 500 Sensitivity to Global Factors," *Global X*, October 3, 2022, https://www.globalxetfs.com/ sector-views-sp-500-sensitivity-to-global-factors/.
14. See, for example, Howard Gold, "The U.S. Economy Will Never Have Another Golden Age," *MarketWatch*, September 1, 2017, https://www.marketwatch.com/ story/the-us-economy-will-never-have-another-golden-age-2017-09-01.
15. Barack Obama, "Remarks by the President on Economic Mobility," The White House, published December 4, 2013, https://obamawhitehouse.archives.gov/the -press-office/2013/12/04/remarks-president-economic-mobility.

16. Joe Biden, "Remarks by President Biden at Signing of Executive Order on Strengthening American Manufacturing," The White House, published January 25, 2021, https://tinyurl.com/37hkpre4.

17. Jim Tankersley, "The Real Reason the American Economy Boomed After World War II," *New York Times*, August 6, 2020, https://www.nytimes.com/2020/08/06/sunday-review/middle-class-prosperity.html.

18. Ralph Nader, ed. *The Case Against Free Trade: GATT, NAFTA, and the Globalization of Corporate Power* (Earth Island Press, 1993), 1. NAFTA went into effect on January 1, 1994, and the GATT was transformed into the WTO on January 1, 1995.

19. Chris Cillizza, "Pat Buchanan Says Donald Trump Is the Future of the Republican Party," *Washington Post*, January 12, 2016, https://www.washingtonpost.com/news/the-fix/wp/2016/01/12/pat-buchanan-believes-donald-trump-is-the-future-of-the-republican-party/.

20. "Read Donald Trump's Speech on Trade," *Time*, June 28, 2016, https://time.com/4386335/donald-trump-trade-speech-transcript/.

21. Donald Trump, "The Inaugural Address," The White House, published January 20, 2017, https://trumpwhitehouse.archives.gov/briefings-statements/the-inaugural-address/.

22. Glenn Kessler, "Are Jobs Lost Due to 'Bad Trade Policy' or Automation?" *Washington Post*, October 17, 2019, https://www.washingtonpost.com/politics/2019/10/17/are-jobs-lost-due-bad-trade-policy-or-automation/.

23. See Michelle Fox, "Democratic Congresswoman Supports Trump's Tariffs: We Can't Afford to Lose US Steel Production," CNBC, published March 2, 2018, https://www.cnbc.com/2018/03/02/democratic-congresswoman-supports-trumps-tariffs-we-cant-afford-to-lose-us-steel-production.html; Sherrod Brown, *Myths of Free Trade: Why American Trade Policy Has Failed* (The New Press, 2006); Bernie Sanders, "Why I Oppose Free Trade," *Seven Days*, October 28, 1993, https://www.sevendaysvt.com/news/sanders-why-i-oppose-nafta-2435080.

24. David J. Lynch, "Biden's Course for U.S. on Trade Breaks with Clinton and Obama," *Washington Post*, August 27, 2023, https://www.washingtonpost.com/business/2023/08/27/biden-trade-trump/.

25. Robert Lighthizer, "Donald Trump's Former Trade Chief Makes the Case for More Tariffs," *The Economist*, March 8, 2024, https://www.economist.com/by-invitation/2024/03/08/donald-trumps-former-trade-chief-makes-the-case-for-more-tariffs.

26. Charles Schumer, "New Record Trade Deficit Indicates a Slow Bleeding at the Wrists for U.S. Economy, Shows Increasing Dependence on Countries like China, Japan," Senate Majority Leader Chuck Shumer, published July 25, 2006, https://www.schumer.senate.gov/newsroom/press-releases/schumer-new-record-trade-deficit-indicates-a-slow-bleeding-at-the-wrists-for-us-economy-shows-increasing-depend ence-on-countries-like-china-japan.

27. U.S. Census Bureau, "U.S. Trade in Goods and Services—Balance of Payments (BOP) Basis: 1960–2023," accessed September 2024, https://www.census.gov/foreign-trade/statistics/historical/gands.pdf. In nominal dollars the total excess of imports over exports is $15.9 trillion. We converted all nominal dollars into 2023 dollars using the Personal Consumption Expenditures Price Index.

28. Federal Reserve Bank of St. Louis, "All Employees, Manufacturing (MANEMP)," FRED Economic Data, accessed September 2024, https://fred.stlouisfed.org/series/MANEMP.

29. Robert E. Scott, "U.S. Trade Deficits: Causes, Consequences, and Policy Implications," Economic Policy Institute, published June 11, 1998, https://www.epi.org/publication/trade-deficits-consequences-policy-implications/.

30. John Komlos, "Why Trade Deals Hurt Americans," *PBS New Hour*, June 15, 2015, https://www.pbs.org/newshour/economy/trans-pacific-partnership-fast-track.

31. Amitrajeet A. Batabyal, "International Trade Has Cost Americans Millions of Jobs. Investing in Communities Might Offset Those Losses," *The Conversation*, August 3, 2020, https://theconversation.com/international-trade-has-cost-americans-millions-of-jobs-investing-in-communities-might-offset-those-losses-143406.

32. Oren Cass, "Why Trump Is Right About Tariffs," *Wall Street Journal*, October 27, 2023, https://www.wsj.com/economy/trade/why-trump-is-right-about-tariffs-3cad4097?mod=article_inline.

33. Lighthizer, "Donald Trump's Former Trade Chief."

34. Lighthizer, "Donald Trump's Former Trade Chief."

35. Charlie Savage, Jonathan Swan, and Maggie Haberman, "A New Tax on Imports and a Split from China: Trump's 2025 Trade Agenda," *New York Times*, December 29, 2023, https://www.nytimes.com/2023/12/26/us/politics/trump-2025-trade-china.html; Robert Schroeder, "Trump Suggests Tariffs Could Go Higher than 10%. Why One Economist Is Saying, 'Bonkers,'" *MarketWatch*, April 30, 2024, https://www.morningstar.com/news/marketwatch/20240430138/trump-suggests-tariffs-could-go-higher-than-10-why-one-economist-is-saying-bonkers.

36. Joe Biden, "Remarks by President Biden on American Manufacturing and Creating Good-Paying Jobs," The White House, published December 6, 2022, https://www.whitehouse.gov/briefing-room/speeches-remarks/2022/12/06/remarks-by-president-biden-on-american-manufacturing-and-creating-good-paying-jobs/.

37. On the politics and economic consequences of Smoot-Hawley, see Douglas A. Irwin, *Peddling Protectionism: Smoot-Hawley and the Great Depression* (Princeton University Press, 2011).

38. Douglas A. Irwin, *Free Trade Under Fire*, 5th ed. (Princeton University Press, 2020), 260.

39. Franklin D. Roosevelt, "The Great Arsenal of Democracy," Fireside Chat 16, radio broadcast on December 29, 1940, https://www.americanrhetoric.com/speeches/fdrarsenalofdemocracy.html.

40. Douglas A. Irwin, Petros C. Mavroidis, and Alan O. Sykes, *The Genesis of the GATT* (Cambridge University Press, 2009). Lower tariffs were seen also as an important instrument for increasing the prospects of lasting peace by encouraging greater economic integration across the globe.

41. See Federal Reserve Bank of St. Louis, "Shares of Gross Domestic Product: Exports of Goods and Services (B020RE1Q156NBEA)," FRED Economic Data, https://fred.stlouisfed.org/series/B020RE1Q156NBEA; Federal Reserve Bank of St. Louis, "Shares of Gross Domestic Product: Imports of Goods and Services (B021RE1Q156NBEA)," FRED Economic Data, https://fred.stlouisfed.org/series/B021RE1Q156NBEA.

42. Richard N. Langlois, *The Corporation and the Twentieth Century: The History of American Business Enterprise* (Princeton University Press, 2023), 20.

43. Here's Douglas Irwin, *Free Trade Under Fire*, 12–13:

> As countries around the world began to recover from the destruction and dislocation caused by World War II, and also began the gradual dismantling of their trade barriers, global commerce began to rise in importance

starting in the early 1970s. Further trade liberalization in the 1980s and 1990s, the opening of the previously closed economies of China and India, the end of Communism in Eastern Europe and the Soviet Union, and technological improvements in shipping such as containerization—all these developments pushed trade to record levels.

On the development and impact of containerized shipping, see Marc Levinson, *The Box: How the Shipping Container Made the World Smaller and the World Economy Bigger*, 2nd ed. (Princeton University Press, 2016).

44. Statistical Office of the United Nations, *International Trade Statistics, 1900–1960*, May 1962, table XXIII, https://unstats.un.org/unsd/trade/imts/Historical%20data%201900-1960.pdf.

45. Phil Gramm, Robert Ekelund, and John Early, *The Myth of American Inequality* (Rowman & Littlefield, 2022), 142.

46. In 1975 the total number of nonfarm jobs in the United States was 77.07 million; in October 2024, that number was 159.01 million. See Federal Reserve Bank of St. Louis, "All Employees, Total Nonfarm (PAYEMS)," FRED Economic Data, https://fred.st louisfed.org/series/PAYEMS#0; Federal Reserve Bank of St. Louis, "Unemployment Rate." COVID-19 began to affect the US economy in February 2020. It was finally declared, by the Biden administration, to have ended forty months later, in May 2023. The above calculation of average monthly unemployment rates thus excludes these forty months. The most recent five-year period (ending in October 2024) that excludes the forty pandemic months thus begins in August 2016 and runs through January 2020 (which is forty-two months) and then includes the eighteen months from May 2023 through October 2024.

47. Federal Reserve Bank of St. Louis, "Industrial Production: Manufacturing (NAICS)," FRED Economic Data, https://fred.stlouisfed.org/series/IPMAN.

Of course, manufacturing output plummeted with the onset of the pandemic, but it quickly recovered.

48. Lauren Lindstrom, "Trump Wants to Bring Jobs Back to Ohio," *The Blade*, October 14, 2016, https://www.toledoblade.com/Politics/2016/10/14/Donald-Trump-wants -to-bring-jobs-back-to-Ohio-Economy-is-Republican-s-focus-in-speech-in -Cincinnati.html.

49. World Bank Group, "Metadata Glossary," last updated 2024, https://databank.world bank.org/metadataglossary/world-development-indicators/series/NV.IND.MANF .ZS.

50. Calculated from data found in Scott Lincicome, "Manufactured Crisis: 'Deindustrialization,' Free Markets, and National Security," *Cato Institute*, January 27, 2021, figure 8; Federal Reserve Bank of St. Louis, "Real Value Added by Industry: Manufacturing (RVAMA)," FRED Economic Data, https://fred.stlouisfed.org/series /RVAMA.

Lincicome's dollar figures were converted into the 2017 dollars used by the St. Louis Fed with the GDP deflator calculator available here: https://spice-spotlight .scot/real-terms-calculator/. As of November 2024, the latest date for which manufacturing value-added data are available is the second quarter of 2024.

51. Colin Grabow, "The United States Remains a Manufacturing Powerhouse," *Cato at Liberty*, October 25, 2023, https://www.cato.org/blog/united-states-remains -manufacturing-powerhouse.

52. Board of Governors of the Federal Reserve System, "Industrial Production and Capacity Utilization—G.17," released August 9, 2023, https://www.federalreserve .gov/releases/g17/related_data/manuf_invest_capital.htm.

53. Board of Governors of the Federal Reserve System, "Industrial Production and Capacity Utilization—G.17—Manufacturing Investment and Capital, 4-digit NAICS," https://www.federalreserve.gov/releases/g17.

54. Scott Lincicome, "Manufactured Crisis," 10.

55. Federal Reserve Bank of St. Louis, "Industrial Capacity: Total Index (CAPB50001S)," FRED Economic Data, accessed September 2024, https://fred.stlouisfed.org/series/ CAPB50001S.

56. Robert Zoellick, "The Biden-Trump Economy of Nostalgia," *Wall Street Journal*, April 2, 2024, A17.

57. U.S. Bureau of Economic Analysis, "Shares of Gross Domestic Product: Personal Consumption Expenditures: Services [DSERRE1Q156NBEA], FRED Economic Data, accessed September 3, 2024, https://fred.stlouisfed.org/series/ DSERRE1Q156NBEA.

58. Esteban Ortiz-Ospina, "Manufacturing Accounts for a Relatively Small and Declining Share of Total Employment in Rich Countries," *Our World In Data*, November 5, 2024, https://ourworldindata.org/data-insights/manufacturing-accounts-for-a-rel atively-small-and-declining-share-of-total-employment-in-rich-countries. The BLS defines manufacturing employment as jobs held by employees of "establishments engaged in the mechanical, physical, or chemical transformation of materials, substances, or components into new products." See US Bureau of Labor Statistics, "Industries at a Glance: Manufacturing: NAICS 31–33," accessed September 2024, https://www.bls.gov/iag/tgs/iag31-33.htm#about.

59. Federal Reserve Bank of St. Louis, "All Employees, Manufacturing (MANEMP)," FRED Economic Data, accessed September 2024, https://fred.stlouisfed.org/series /MANEMP.

60. Calculated by dividing FRED Data source "All Employees, Manufacturing" (MANEMP) by "All Employees, Total Nonfarm" (PAYNSA). The footnote for figure A shows the trend line.

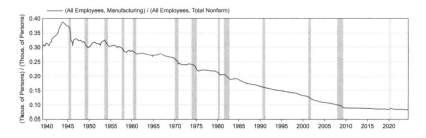

Figure A. (All Employees, Manufacturing) / (All Employees, Total Nonfarm)

61. Mark J. Perry, "Phenomenal Gains in Manufacturing Productivity," *AEI Ideas*, April 12, 2012, https://www.aei.org/carpe-diem/phenomenal-gains-in-manufactur ing-productivity/.

62. For data up through 2017 on the average weekly work hours of production workers in manufacturing industries, see John Pencavel, "The Future of Hours of Work?"

Stanford Institute for Economic Policy Research, published September 2018, https://siepr.stanford.edu/publications/policy-brief/future-hours-work.

63. Of course, it briefly turned negative during the pandemic. See Federal Reserve Bank of St. Louis, "Nonfarm Business Sector: Labor Productivity (Output per Hour) for All Workers (OPHNFB)," FRED Economic Data, accessed September 2024, https://fred.stlouisfed.org/series/OPHNFB.

64. Federal Reserve Bank of St. Louis, "Manufacturing Sector: Labor Productivity (Output per Hour) for All Workers (OPHMFG)," FRED Economic Data, accessed September 2024, https://fred.stlouisfed.org/series/OPHMFG.

65. Federal Reserve Bank of St. Louis, "A Plateau for Manufacturing?" *The FRED Blog*, May 24, 2018, https://fredblog.stlouisfed.org/?s=manufacturing+worker+productivity.

66. See Gramm, Ekelund, and Early, *The Myth of American Inequality*, 90–98.

67. Because worker pay closely tracks worker productivity, falling productivity lowers real wages and worsens Americans' standard of living.

68. Michael J. Hicks and Srikant Devaraj, *The Myth and the Reality of Manufacturing in America* (Ball State University Center for Business and Economic Research, 2017), 6, https://conexus.cberdata.org/files/MfgReality.pdf.

69. Colin Grabow, "The United States Remains."

70. Robert Z. Lawrence, "Recent US Manufacturing Employment: The Exception That Proves the Rule," Working Paper No. 17–12 (Peterson Institute for International Economics, November 2017), table 1, 13, https://www.piie.com/sites/default/files/documents/wp17-12.pdf.

71. Between 2012 and 2022, the share of China's workforce employed in services increased by 11 percentage points. Statista, "Distribution of the Workforce Across Economic Sectors in China from 2012 to 2022," accessed September 2024, https://www.statista.com/statistics/270327/distribution-of-the-workforce-across-economic-sectors-in-china/. According to International Institute for Management Development (IMD) Business School economist Richard Baldwin, the absolute number of workers employed in China's manufacturing sector peaked in 2013; in 2020, nineteen million fewer Chinese workers were employed in manufacturing than in 2013. See Policy Tensor (@policytensor), "Everyone seems convinced that the Chinese stole our MFG jobs," Twitter (now X), March 20, 2024, https://twitter.com/policytensor/status/1770615928788574474.

72. Our World In Data, "Manufacturing Jobs as a Share of Total Employment, 2000 to 2021," accessed September 2024, https://ourworldindata.org/grapher/manufacturing-share-of-total-employment?tab=chart&country= .

73. Mark J. Perry, "More Than 6 Americans Produce Services for Every Worker Producing Physical Stuff. And Yet, Trump Ignores Thriving US Service-Sector in Talks About Trade," *AEIdeas*, March 18, 2018, https://www.aei.org/carpe-diem/more-than-6-americans-produce-services-for-every-worker-producing-physical-stuff-and-yet-trump-ignores-thriving-us-service-sector-in-talks-about-trade/.

74. See Gramm, Ekelund, and Early, *The Myth of American Inequality*, 154, and U.S. Census Bureau, "Census Bureau Releases New Educational Attainment Data," published February 24, 2022, https://www.census.gov/newsroom/press-releases/2022/educational-attainment.html.

75. "Percent of the Labor Force Employed in Agriculture, United States, 1800 to 2000," in Ruggles et al., "The Decline of Intergenerational Coresidence in the United States, 1850 to 2000," *American Sociological Review* 72 (December 2007), https://www

.researchgate.net/figure/Percent-of-the-Labor-Force-Employed-in-Agriculture
-United-States-1800-to-2000-Sources_fig1_51117517.

76. See ZipRecruiter, "What Is the Average Technology Salary by State," accessed September 2024, https://www.ziprecruiter.com/Salaries/What-Is-the-Average-Tech nology-Salary-by-State; ZipRecruiter, "Manufacturing Salary," accessed September 2024, https://www.ziprecruiter.com/Salaries/Manufacturing-Salary.

77. Hillary Clinton supported NAFTA when she was First Lady, but later she criticized it. Jason Margolis, "Hillary Clinton's Stand on NAFTA and the TPP: It's Complicated, and Evolving," *The World*, July 28, 2016, https://theworld.org/stories/2016 -07-28/hillary-clinton-s-stand-nafta-and-tpp-it-s-complicated-and-evolving#. Ms. Clinton also, like President Trump, opposed US participation in the Trans-Pacific Partnership.

78. World Bank, "Weighted Average Tariff 2000 and 2014," World Integrated Trade Solutions, accessed September 2024, https://wits.worldbank.org/CountryProfile/en /Country/CHN/Year/2014/Summary.

79. For an example of someone who claims that China's entry into the WTO played a major role in destroying manufacturing jobs in the United States, see Matthew Schmitz, "There's One Person Trump Absolutely Needs in His Administration," *New York Times*, November 22, 2024.

80. Calculated by the authors from St. Louis Federal Reserve Bank, FRED Economic Data, "All Employees, Manufacturing (MANEMP)" divided by "All Employees, Nonfarm (PAYEMS)."

81. Lorenzo Caliendo and Fernando Parro, "Estimates of the Trade and Welfare Effects of NAFTA," NBER Working Series Paper No. 18508 (November 2012), 6, https:// www.nber.org/system/files/working_papers/w18508/w18508.pdf.

82. Federal Reserve Bank of St. Louis, "All Employees, Total Nonfarm (PAYNSA)," FRED Economic Data, accessed September 2024, https://fred.stlouisfed.org/series /PAYNSA;

Federal Reserve Bank of St. Louis, "Industrial Production: Manufacturing (NAICS)," FRED Economic Data, accessed September 2024, https://fred.stlouisfed .org/series/IPMAN.

83. Federal Reserve Bank of St. Louis, "All Employees, Manufacturing (MANEMP)."

84. See Mattias Busse, "Competition Intensity, Potential Competition and Transaction Cost Economics," *World Competition*, September 2002, figure 1, 11; WTO, "Tariffs Applied by WTO Members Have Almost Halved Since 1996," April 23, 2023, https:// ifcba.org/news/tariffs-applied-wto-members-have-almost-halved-1996.

85. World Trade Organization, "Evolution of Trade Under the WTO: Handy Statistics," last updated 2024, https://www.wto.org/english/res_e/statis_e/trade_evolution_e/ evolution_trade_wto_e.htm.

86. Kristen Hopewell, "Lessons from Trump's Assault on the World Trade Organization," Chatham House, published August 3, 2021, https://www.chathamhouse.org/2021 /08/lessons-trumps-assault-world-trade-organization.

87. James Bacchus, "The Biden Administration Continues to Be Wrong About the WTO," *Cato@Liberty*, September 26, 2023, https://www.cato.org/blog/biden -administration-continues-be-wrong-about-wto.

88. Donald J. Trump, "My Tariff Policies Were a Success," Letters, *Wall Street Journal*, August 30, 2023, https://www.wsj.com/articles/donald-trump-my-tariff-policies -were-a-success-foreign-markets-2ec33248.

89. Trump, "My Tariff Policies Were a Success."

90. From 1790 to 1896, the United States had a deficit in its trade balance on goods and services for some 75 percent of the years. See U.S. Department of Commerce, "Balance of International Payments, 1790–1970," in *Historical Statistics of the United States: Colonial Times to 1970* (U.S. Bureau of the Census, 1975), Series U 1-25, 867–68.

91. See William A. Niskanen, "The Determinants of U.S. Capital Imports," *Annals of the American Academy of Political and Social Science* 516 (July 1991): 36–49, who writes (on page 37) that "for about 300 years, from the first English settlements in Virginia and Massachusetts until World War I, foreigners invested more in the area that became the United States than Americans invested in other countries." See also Douglass C. North, "The United States in the International Economy, 1790–1950," in *American Economic History*, ed. Seymour E. Harris (McGraw-Hill, 1961), 181–206.

92. U.S. Department of Commerce, *Historical Statistics of the United States: Colonial Times to 1970*, Series U 1-20, 864, and U 26-39, 869.

93. Don Boudreaux, "If Trade Surpluses Are So Great, the 1930s Should Have Been a Booming Decade," *Café Hayek* (blog), December 21, 2006, https://cafehayek.com /2006/12/if_trade_surplu.html.

94. On the politics and economic consequences of Smoot-Hawley, see Irwin, *Peddling Protectionism*.

95. All of the above figures come from Macrotrends, "U.S. Trade Balance 1960– 2024," last updated 2024, https://www.macrotrends.net/global-metrics/countries /USA/united-states/trade-balance-deficit. We converted the nominal dollars into real dollars using this inflation adjustor: https://www.in2013dollars.com/ Personal-Consumption-Expenditures-Price-Index/price-inflation.

96. Federal Reserve Bank of St. Louis, "Capital Stock at Constant National Prices for United States (RKNANPUSA666NRUG)," FRED Economic Data, accessed September 2024, https://fred.stlouisfed.org/series/RKNANPUSA666NRUG.

97. Data on the current-dollar net worth of American households are found at Federal Reserve Bank of St. Louis, "Households; Net Worth, Level (BOGZ1 FL192090005Q)," FRED Economic Data, accessed September 2024, https://fred .stlouisfed.org/series/BOGZ1FL192090005Q. We converted the nominal dollars into real dollars using this inflation adjustor: https://www.in2013dollars.com/ Personal-Consumption-Expenditures-Price-Index/price-inflation.

We then divided the inflation-adjusted figures on household net worth by the number of households as reported at Statista, "Number of Households in the U.S. from 1960 to 2023," accessed September 2024, https://www.statista.com/ statistics/183635/number-of-households-in-the-us/.

98. Federal Reserve Bank of St. Louis, "Rest of the World; Foreign Direct Investment in U.S.: Equity; Asset (Market Value), Level (BOGZ1FL263092141A)," FRED Economic Data, accessed September 2024, https://fred.stlouisfed.org/series /BOGZ1FL263092141A. We converted the nominal dollars into real dollars using this inflation adjustor: https://www.in2013dollars.com/Personal-Consump tion-Expenditures-Price-Index/price-inflation.

99. Daniel Ikenson, *Will Deglobalization Dim the Gains from Global Investment? Lessons from US Manufacturing* (Hinrich Foundation, May 2022), https://tinyurl .com/yupttm6h. Ikenson found that the contribution (in 2019) of foreign direct

investment to manufacturing output in the United States might have been as much as $463 billion, or 20.9 percent of US manufacturing output.

100. As quoted in Thomas Cahill, *Sailing the Wine-Dark Sea: Why the Greeks Matter* (Anchor Books, 2003), 247.

101. Statista, "Daily Turnover of Global Foreign Exchange Market with 39 Different Currencies from 2001 to 2022," accessed September 2024, https://www.statista.com /statistics /247328/activity-per-trading-day-on-the-global-currency-market/.

102. See Macrotrends, "U.S. GDP Growth Rate 1960–2024," last updated 2024, https:// www.macrotrends.net/global-metrics/countries/USA/united-states/gdp-growth -rate#:~:text=. On the CBO blog, Fried states, "On balance, in CBO's projections, the trade barriers imposed since January 2018 reduce both real output and real household income. By 2020, they reduce the level of real U.S. GDP by roughly 0.3 percent and reduce average real household income by $580 (in 2019 dollars). Beyond 2020, CBO expects those effects to wane as businesses adjust their supply chains." Daniel Fried, "The Effects of Tariffs and Trade Barriers in CBO's Projections," Congressional Budget Office, published August 22, 2019, https://www.cbo.gov/publication/55576.

103. Veronique de Rugy, "Telling the Truth on Tariffs," Opinions, *Noozhawk*, March 16, 2018, https://www.noozhawk.com/veronique_de_rugy_telling_the_truth_on_tariffs/.

104. Douglas A. Irwin, "Trade Truths Will Outlast Trump," *Wall Street Journal*, November 19, 2020, https://www.wsj.com/articles/trade-truths-will-outlast-trump-11605828052.

105. Calculated by dividing FRED Economic Data source MANEMP by PAYNSA.

106. See Federal Reserve Bank of St. Louis, "Industrial Production: Manufacturing (NAICS) (IPMAN)," FRED Economic Data, accessed September 2024, https://fred .stlouisfed.org/series/IPMAN. See also Federal Reserve Bank of St. Louis, "Average Hourly Earnings of Production and Nonsupervisory Employees, Manufacturing (CES3000000008)," FRED Economic Data, accessed September 2024, https://fred .stlouisfed.org/series/CES3000000008; Federal Reserve Bank of St. Louis, "Average Hourly Earnings of Production and Nonsupervisory Employees, Total Private (AHETPI)," FRED Economic Data, accessed September 2024, https://fred.stlouis fed.org/series/AHETPI. We adjusted these data for inflation using this Personal Consumption Expenditures Price Index calculator: https://www.in2013dollars .com/.

107. Federal Reserve Bank of St. Louis, "Industrial Production: Manufacturing (NAICS)," FRED Economic Data, accessed September 2024, https://fred.stlouisfed.org/series/ IPMAN. From August 2016 through February 2018, the average monthly index value of American manufacturing output was 99.8908; from November 2022 through October 2024, the average monthly index value of American manufacturing output was 99.7593.

108. Lighthizer, "Donald Trump's Former Trade Chief."

109. See Patrick J. Buchanan, *The Great Betrayal* (Little, Brown, 1998), 222–26; Ha-Joon Chang, "Kicking Away the Ladder: How the Economic and Intellectual Histories of Capitalism Have Been Re-Written to Justify Neo-Liberal Capitalism," *Post-Autistic Economics Review*, no. 15 (September 2002), https://www.paecon.net/PAEtexts/ Chang1.htm; Michael Lind, "So What If Tariffs Are Taxes?" *American Compass*, July 24, 2024, https://americancompass.org/so-what-if-tariffs-are-taxes/. See particularly where Lind writes that "in the nineteenth century, the U.S. pursued a successful import substitution strategy that transformed it from an agrarian to an industrial economy with the help of tariffs that kept out manufactured goods from Britain

and other more advanced economies, reserving America's growing home market for American-made goods." See also Oren Cass, "Free Trade's Origin Myth," *Law & Liberty*, January 2, 2024, https://lawliberty.org/forum/free-trades-origin-myth/.

110. Douglas A. Irwin, *Clashing over Commerce* (University of Chicago Press, 2017), 140–47.

111. Irwin, *Clashing over Commerce*, 202.

112. Friedrich List, *The National System of Political Economy* (Australia: Imperium Press, 2022 [1841]. This book originally appeared in 1840 under the title *Das nationale System der Politischen Oekonomie*). It was an influential treatise that argued in support of infant-industry protection.

113. Douglas A. Irwin, "The Aftermath of Hamilton's 'Report on Manufacturing,'" NBER Working Paper No. 9943 (September 2003), 17, 18.

114. Irwin, *Clashing over Commerce*, 131: "The Tariff of 1816 was the first 'protectionist' tariff of the United States in the sense that it was mainly designed to provide assistance to domestic manufacturers facing foreign competition."

115. Irwin, *Clashing over Commerce*, figure 4.1, 190; U.S. Department of Commerce, *Historical Statistics of the United States: Millennial Edition* (U.S. Bureau of the Census, 2006), table Ee424-430.

116. Calculated by authors from the index figures on the U.S. annual industrial production reported by Joseph H. Davis, "An Annual Index of U. S. Industrial Production, 1790–1915," *Quarterly Journal of Economics* 119 (November 2004): 1177–215; see especially table III, 1189.

117. Calculated by authors from the index figures on U.S. annual industrial production reported by Davis, "An Annual Index of U. S. Industrial Production," 1177–215; see table III, 1189.

118. The population figures are from U.S. Census 1830 (population 12,866,020) and U.S. Census 1860 (population 31,443,321). See https://search.findmypast.com/search-world-records/us-census-1830#:~:text=.

119. Irwin, *Clashing over Commerce*, 196.

120. U.S. Department of Commerce, *Historical Statistics of the United States: Millennial Edition*, table Ee424-430.

121. Calculated by authors from the index figures on U.S. annual industrial production reported by Davis, "An Annual Index of U. S. Industrial Production," 1177–215; see table III, 1189.

122. U.S. Department of Commerce, *Historical Statistics of the United States: Millennial Edition*, table Ee424-430.

123. Calculated by authors from the index figures on U.S. annual industrial production reported by Davis, "An Annual Index of U. S. Industrial Production," 1177–215; see table III, 1189.

124. Albert Gallatin, "Gallatin's Memorial of the Free Trade Convention," in *State Papers and Speeches on the Tariff*, ed. Frank W. Taussig (Harvard University Press, 1892), 127–28.

125. Alfred Marshall, "Memorandum on the Fiscal Policy of International Trade (1903)," in *Official Papers by Alfred Marshall*, ed. J. M. Keynes (Macmillan, 1926), 365–420; the quotation in the text is found on page 394.

126. Marco Rubio, "The Case for Common-Good Capitalism," *National Review*, November 13, 2019, https://www.nationalreview.com/2019/11/the-case-for-common-good-capitalism/.

127. Oren Cass, "The Communal Power of a Real Job," Opinion, *New York Times*, August 4, 2019, https://www.nytimes.com/2019/08/03/opinion/sunday/workers-conserva tives.html. See also Oren Cass, "The Working Hypothesis," *The American Interest*, October 15, 2018, https://www.the-american-interest.com/2018/10/15/ the-working-hypothesis/.

128. Robert Lighthizer, "The Free Trade Folly," in *Rebuilding American Capitalism: A Handbook for Conservative Policymakers* (American Compass, 2023), https:// americancompass.org/rebuilding-american-capitalism/productive-markets/ the-free-trade-folly/.

129. We describe here what economists call "consumer sovereignty," a term first introduced by the economist W. H. Hutt in his 1936 book, *Economists and the Public* (Transaction Publishers, 1936; repr., 1990), 257–72. The classic and still-unsurpassed explanation of the role of prices in directing the allocation of resources is found in F. A. Hayek, "The Use of Knowledge in Society," *American Economic Review* 35 (September 1945): 519–30.

130. Gary Clyde Hufbauer and Sean Lowry, *U.S. Tire Tariffs: Saving Few Jobs at High Cost*, Economic Policy Brief No. PB 12-9 (Peterson Institute, April 2012). For more on average annual salary in manufacturing, see Talent.com, "Manufacturing Average Salary in the USA, 2024," last updated 2024, https://www.talent.com/ salary?job=manufacturing.

131. Stephen Morgan, Shawn Arita, Jayson Beckman et al., "The Economic Impact of Retaliatory Tariffs on U.S. Agriculture," U.S. Department of Agriculture, Economic Research Service, published January 2022, https://www.ers.usda.gov/publications/ pub-details/?pubid=102979.

132. Lauly Li, "TSMC Founder Morris Chang Backs U.S. on China Chip Curbs," *NikkeiAsia*, March 16, 2023, https://asia.nikkei.com/Business/Tech/Semiconductors/ TSMC-founder-Morris-Chang-backs-U.S.-on-China-chip-curbs.

133. Adam Smith, *An Inquiry into the Nature and Causes of the Wealth of Nations* (1776; repr., Liberty Fund, 1981), 463.

134. Leland B. Yeager, *Free Trade: America's Opportunity* (Robert Schalkenbach Foundation, 1954), 31.

135. Nina Pavcnik, "Trade Liberalization, Exit, and Productivity Improvements: Evidence from Chilean Plants," *Review of Economic Studies* 69 (January 2002): 245–76.

136. More specifically, as it has been amended over the years, the Jones Act today requires—as described by researchers at the Cato Institute—"that such ships be at least 75 percent U.S.-owned, at least 75 percent U.S.-crewed, and assembled entirely in the United States with all 'major components of the hull and superstructure' fabricated domestically." See Colin Grabow, Inu Manak, and Daniel J. Ikenson, "The Jones Act: A Burden America Can No Longer Bear," *Cato Institute*, June 28, 2018, https://www.cato .org/publications/policy-analysis/jones-act-burden-america-can-no-longer-bear.

137. For a defense of the Jones Act on national-security grounds, see, for example, Robert C. O'Brien, "The Jones Act Is Essential for U.S. National Security," Opinion, *American Maritime Partnership*, June 30, 2021, https://www.americanmaritimepart nership.com/articles/the-jones-act-is-essential-for-u-s-national-security/.

138. Lawrence H. Summers (@LH Summers), "This should be cautionary with respect to the possible long run," Twitter (now X), December 11, 2022, https://x.com/ LHSummers/status/1601920663727611905.

139. Frederick W. Smith, "The Business of America," Speech, Calvin Coolidge Presidential Foundation Gala, New York, NY, December 5, 2023.

140. Obama White House, *The Economic Benefits of U.S. Trade* (Executive Office of the President, May 2015) 3, https://obamawhitehouse.archives.gov/sites/default/files /docs/cea_trade_report_final_non-embargoed_v2.pdf.

141. Gary Clyde Hufbauer and Megan Hogan, "America's Payoff from Engaging in World Markets since 1950 Was Almost $2.6 Trillion in 2022," Peterson Institute for International Economics, published December 2023, https://www .piie.com/publications/policy-briefs/americas-payoff-engaging-world-markets -1950-was-almost-26-trillion-2022.

142. Thucydides, "Pericles' Funeral Oration," University of Minnesota, posted 1996, http://hrlibrary.umn.edu/education/thucydides.html.

143. Will Durant, *The Life of Greece* (MJF Books, 1939), 276.

144. William Bourke Cockran, *In the Name of Liberty: Selected Addresses by William Bourke Cockran*, ed. Robert McElroy (G. P. Putnam's Sons, 1925), 211.

Five: The Financial Crisis Myth

1. National Bureau of Economic Research, "US Business Cycle Expansions and Contractions," NBER, last updated 2024, https://www.nber.org/research/data/ us-business-cycle-expansions-and-contractions.

2. Robert Rich, "The Great Recession: December 2007–June 2009," Federal Reserve History, published November 22, 2013, https://www.federalreservehistory.org/ essays/great-recession-of-200709#:~:text=.

3. St. Louis Federal Reserve Bank, "Unemployment Rate (UNRATE)," FRED Economic Data, accessed September 2024, https://fred.stlouisfed.org/series/UNRATE.

4. Barack Obama, "Presidential Debate at Belmont University in Nashville, Tennessee," The American Presidency Project, delivered October 7, 2008, https://www.presidency .ucsb.edu/documents/presidential-debate-belmont-university-nashville-tennessee.

5. Barack Obama, "Remarks by the President at Signing of Dodd-Frank Wall Street Reform and Consumer Protection Act," The White House, released July 21, 2010, https://obamawhitehouse.archives.gov/the-press-office/remarks-president-signing -dodd-frank-wall-street-reform-and-consumer-protection-act.

6. Government Publications Office, "Remarks at a Campaign Rally in Roanoke, Virginia, July 13, 2012," in *Public Papers of the Presidents of the United States: Barack Obama, 2012, Book 2: July 1–December 31, 2012* (US Government Printing Office, 2017), 1003.

7. "25 People to Blame for the Financial Crisis," *Time*, 2009, https://content.time.com/ time/specials/packages/completelist/0,29569,1877351,00.html.

8. "25 People to Blame," *Time*.

9. Richard A. Posner, *A Failure of Capitalism: The Crisis of '08 and the Descent into Depression* (Harvard University Press, 2009).

10. Posner, *A Failure of Capitalism*, 23.

11. The Financial Crisis Inquiry Commission, *Final Report of the National Commission on the Causes of the Financial and Economic Crisis in the United States* (US Government Printing Office, January 2011), xvii–xviii. On page 94 the majority of the commission members criticized the Federal Reserve for not using "the legal system to rein in predatory lenders."

12. "Chris Dodd and Barney Frank interviewed by David Brancaccio," *Marketplace*, American Public Media, posted September 19, 2018, YouTube, 1:33, https://www .youtube.com/watch?v=pFHyx36qqhY.

13. Wayne Duggan and Michael Adams, "A Short History of the Great Recession," *Forbes Advisor*, June 21, 2023, https://www.forbes.com/advisor/investing/great-recession/.

14. Duggan and Adams, "A Short History of the Great Recession."

15. Charles W. Calomiris and Stephen H. Haber, *Fragile by Design: The Political Origins of Banking Crises & Scarce Credit* (Princeton University Press, 2014), 205.

16. Calomiris and Haber, *Fragile by Design*, 207.

17. Bill Clinton and Al Gore, *Putting People First: How We Can All Change America* (Three Rivers Press, 1992), 144, 114.

18. "Statement of the Honorable Robert Reich, Secretary, U.S. Department of Labor," in *Hearing Before the Joint Economic Committee, Congress of the United States June 22, 1994* (US Government Printing Office, 1994), 6–10, https://www.jec.senate.gov/ reports/103rd%20Congress/Targeted%20Pension%20Fund%20Investment%20 for%20Economic%20Growth%20and%20Development%20(1635).pdf.

19. "Statement of the Honorable Henry Cisneros, Secretary, U.S. Department of Housing and Urban Development," in *Hearing Before the Joint Economic Committee*, 19–24.

20. See Calomiris and Haber, *Fragile by Design*, 208–48.

21. "Statement of Alan Greenspan," *Hearing Before the Committee on Oversight and Government Reform, House of Representatives, October 23, 2008* (US Government Printing Office, 2010), https://www.govinfo.gov/content/pkg/CHRG -110hhrg55764/html/CHRG-110hhrg55764.htm.

22. Calomiris and Haber, *Fragile by Design*, 209.

23. Federal Housing Finance Agency, "The Housing Goals of Fannie Mae and Freddie Mac in the Context of the Mortgage Market: 1996–2009," Mortgage Market Note 10-2 (February 1, 2010), https://tinyurl.com/4uk7v5u8.

24. See Peter J. Wallison, "Dissenting Statement," in *Final Report of the National Commission on the Causes of the Financial and Economic Crisis in the United States* (U.S. Government Printing Office, 2011), 511.

25. National Community Reinvestment Commission, *CRA Commitments* (NCRC, 2007), 5, https://fcic-static.law.stanford.edu/cdn_media/fcic-docs/2007-09-00%20 NCRC%20CRA%20Commitments.pdf.

26. See Wallison, "Dissenting Statement," 489.

27. Edward Pinto, "Memo from Edward Pinto to the FCIC Staff re Triggers of the Financial Crisis," memorandum sent to FCIC staff, March 15, 2010, 20, https://elischo lar.library.yale.edu/cgi/viewcontent.cgi?article=6327&context=ypfs-documents.

28. Pinto, "Memo from Edward Pinto," vii, 1.

29. Harold Uhlig, "Mortgage-Backed Securities and the Financial Crisis of 2008: A Post Mortem," University of Chicago, published May 1, 2018, https://bfi.uchicago.edu/ insight/research-summary/mortgage-backed-securities-and-the-financial-crisis -of-2008-a-post-mortem/. Mortgage-backed securities were rated AAA, just as US Treasury bonds.

30. Barack Obama, "Remarks by the President on Financial Reform," The White House, released January 21, 2010, https://obamawhitehouse.archives.gov/the-press-office /remarks-president-financial-reform.

31. Obama, "Remarks by the President on Financial Reform."

32. FDIC, "Quarterly Banking Profile, Fourth Qurter 2007," *FDIC Quarterly* 2, no. 1 (2008): table III-A; FDIC, *1978 Annual Report of the Federal Deposit Insurance Corporation* (Federal Deposit Insurance Corporation, 1979), table 106.

33. Federal Reserve Bank of St. Louis, "World Bank, Bank Capital to Total Assets for United States [DDSI03USA156NWDB]," FRED Economic Data, accessed July 25, 2024, https://fred.stlouisfed.org/series/DDSI03USA156NWDB; Federal Reserve Bank of St. Louis, "FRED Graph," FRED Economic Data, accessed July 25, 2024, https://fred.stlouisfed.org/graph/?g=inaS.

34. FDIC, *2007 Annual Report* (Federal Deposit Insurance Corporation, 2008), https://archive.fdic.gov/view/fdic/633. "At the end of September 2007, more than 99 percent of all FDIC-insured institutions met or exceeded the highest regulatory capital standards." See where the footnote identifies this category as "well capitalized."

35. FDIC, *2007 Annual Report*.

36. Rep. Barney Frank (D-Massachusetts) said the following during a September 25, 2003, hearing of the House Financial Services Committee: "I do think I do not want the same kind of focus on safety and soundness that we have in OCC [Office of the Comptroller of the Currency] and OTS [Office of Thrift Supervision]. I want to roll the dice a little bit more in this situation towards subsidized housing." See "What They Said About Fan and Fred," *Wall Street Journal*, October 2, 2008.

37. Congressional Research Service, "Major Financial Services Legislation, The Gramm-Leach-Bliley Act (P.L. 106-102): An Overview," accessed September 2024, https://www.policyarchive.org/handle/10207/972.

    See page CRS-3: "Primary supervision of all components, be they banking, insurance, or securities firms, remains with their federal or state line supervisor"; page CRS-3, "securities regulators will generally regulate securities activities no matter where they occur"; and pages CRS 8–9, "the Act provides for functional regulation of insurance sales by state regulators who have traditionally understood the nature of the independent agency system."

38. Federal Reserve History, "Financial Service Modernization Act of 1999 (Gramm-Leach-Biley)," published November 12, 1999, https://www.federalreservehistory.org/gramm-leach-bliley-act.

39. Congressional Budget Office, "S. 900, Gramm-Leach-Bliley Act," published November 23, 1999, www.cbo.gov/publication/12033.

40. William J. Clinton, "Statement on Signing the Gramm-Leach-Bliley Act," The American Presidency Project, delivered November 12, 1999, https://www.presidency.ucsb.edu/documents/statement-signing-the-gramm-leach-bliley-act.

41. Lauren Carroll, "Bill Clinton: Glass-Steagall Repeal Had Nothing to Do with Financial Crisis," *Politifact*, August 19, 2015. https://www.politifact.com/factchecks/2015/aug/19/bill-clinton/bill-clinton-glass-steagall-had-nothing-do-financi/.

42. Andrew Ross Sorkin, "Reinstating an Old Rule Is Not a Cure for Crisis," *New York Times*, May 21, 2012.

43. See Tom Harkin, "Senate," *Congressional Record* 146, no.155 (December 2000): S11896; "The language of the bill clarifies what is already the current state of the law. The Commodity Futures Trading Commission does not regulate traditional banking products." Also see, in the same comments on page S11897, a letter to Tom Harkin from Treasury Secretary Lawrence Summers, US Securities and Exchange Commission (SEC) Chairman Arthur Levitt, Federal Reserve Chairman Alan Greenspan, and CFTC Chairman William Rainer: "The Members of the President's

Working Group on Financial Markets strongly support the Commodities Future Modernization Act."

44. See Lawrence H. White, "How Did We Get into This Financial Mess?" *Cato Institute Briefing Papers*, no. 110 (November 2008), https://search.issuelab.org/resources/2479/2479.pdf. Also see Federal Reserve Bank of St. Louis, "Board of Governors of the Federal Reserve System (US), Real Estate Loans, All Commercial Banks (REALLN)," FRED Economic Data, accessed July 24, 2024, https://fred.stlouis fed.org/series/REALLN. During 2001–2007, real estate loans grew an average of 12.6%.

45. Federal Reserve Bank of St. Louis, "US Census Bureau and US Department of Housing and Urban Development, Median Sales Price of Houses Sold for the United States [MSPUS]," FRED Economic Data, accessed June 27, 2024, https://fred.stlouis fed.org/series/MSPUS.

46. Fannie Mae Foundation, *Case Study: Countrywide Home Loans, Inc.* (Fannie Mae Foundation, 2000), 121, https://fcic-static.law.stanford.edu/cdn_media/fcic -docs/2000-00-00%2Fannie%20Mae%20Foundation%20Making%20New%20 Markets.pdf.

47. For example, in 2014, Princeton economist Alan Blinder wrote that "the financial crisis provided several examples of 'bailouts' in which it seemed sensible to swallow some moral hazard in order to prevent or limit a financial catastrophe (e.g., Bear Stearns, AIG, and others)." Alan S. Blinder, "What Did We Learn from the Financial Crisis, the Great Recession, and the Pathetic Recovery?" Working Paper No. 243 (Griswold Center for Economic Policy Studies, Princeton University, November 2014), https://spia.princeton.edu/system/files/research/ documents/Blinder_What_Did_We_Learn_from_the_Financial_Crisis_the _Great_Recession_and_the_Pathetic_Recovery.pdf. See also Alan S. Blinder and Mark Zandi, "The Financial Crisis: Lessons for the Next One," Center on Budget and Policy Priorities, published October 15, 2015, https://www.cbpp.org/research/ the-financial-crisis-lessons-for-the-next-one.

48. Avi Lerner, Zunara Naem, Theresa Gullo, and Christina H. Anthony, *Report on the Troubled Asset Relief Program—May 2022* (Congressional Budget Office, 2022), 2, https://www.cbo.gov/system/files/2022-05/58029-TARP.pdf.

    Note these CBO statements: "CBO estimates an overall net gain to the government of $9 billion from those transactions—a net gain of about $24 billion from assistance to banks and other lending institutions, partially offset by a cost of $15 billion for assistance to AIG," and "General Motors (GM) and Chrysler, along with their asso- ciated financing intermediaries and suppliers, received about $80 billion in TARP funds, all of which has been repaid by the companies or written off by the Treasury. The total subsidy cost recorded was $12 billion."

49. Office of Management and Budget, *Analytical Perspectives—Budget of the U.S. Government, FY 2011* (US Government Printing Office, 2010), 13; Congressional Budget Office, *The Budget and Economic Outlook: Fiscal Years 2010 to 2020* (CBO, 2010), 122; and Joshua Galin, "Minutes of the Federal Open Market Committee," Board of Governors of the Federal Reserve System, released October 9, 2024; see table 1.

50. Bureau of Economic Analysis, "National Income and Product Accounts, Average Real GDP Growth Rates from 2011 Through 2016," accessed September 2024, table 1.1.1, https://tinyurl.com/37uuewp4.

51. Bureau of Economic Analysis, National Data: National Income and Product Accounts, "Supplemental GDP Data," table 7.1, line 10, https://tinyurl.com/nm95f2k6; Bureau of Labor Statistics, "Labor Force Statistics from the Current Population Survey, 1948 to 2013," interactive data source available here: https://data.bls.gov/pdq/SurveyOutputServlet.

52. Calculated by the authors by using the Bureau of Economic Analysis's "Interactive Data Application" page, https://www.bea.gov/itable/. Matching the postwar average percent of real per capita growth twenty quarters after the recession began would have increased such incomes by 10.7 percent versus the drop of 0.8 percent, which would have increased them by $6,417; see Bureau of Labor Statistics. Matching the postwar average percentage growth in jobs sixty months after the recession began would have increased jobs by 6.5 percent versus the actual drop of 2 percent, adding 12.5 million more jobs.

53. Barack Obama, "Remarks by the President in Twitter Town Hall," The White House, released July 6, 2011, https://obamawhitehouse.archives.gov/the-press-office/2011/07/06/remarks-president-twitter-town-hall.

54. Robert Higgs, "Wartime Prosperity? A Reassessment of the U.S. Economy in the 1940s," *Journal of Economic History* 52 (March 1992): 41–60.

55. The figures in this and the previous paragraph are found at and calculated from Federal Reserve Bank of St. Louis, "Real Gross Domestic Product," FRED Economic Data, accessed September 2024, https://fred.stlouisfed.org/series/GDPC1; and Federal Reserve Bank of St. Louis, "Unemployment Rate."

56. Sarah Foster, "Fed's Interest Rate History: The Federal Funds Rate from 1981 to the Present," Bankrate, published December 13, 2023, https://www.bankrate.com/banking/federal-reserve/history-of-federal-funds-rate/.

57. Federal Reserve Bank of St. Louis, "All Employees, Total Nonfarm," FRED Economic Data, accessed September 2024, https://fred.stlouisfed.org/series/PAYEMS.

58. Federal Reserve Bank of St. Louis, "Real Median Personal Income in the United States," FRED Economic Data, accessed September 2024, https://fred.stlouisfed.org/series/MEPAINUSA672N.

59. Calculated by the authors by using the Bureau of Economic Analysis's "Interactive Data Application" page, https://www.bea.gov/itable/. From the fourth quarter of 1982 to the fourth quarter of 1986, real per capita GDP grew from $31,337 to $36,931, an increase of 17.8 percent. From the second quarter of 2009 to the second quarter of 2013, real per capita GDP grew from $53,017 to $55,914, an increase of 5.4 percent. Matching the Reagan recovery would have generated real per capita income of $62,481, or an additional $6,567. For a family of four, that would be $26,268. From the fourth quarter of 1982 to the fourth quarter of 1986, the number of jobs grew from 99.1 million to 110.5 million, an increase of 11.4 percent. From the second quarter of 2009 to the second quarter of 2013, the number of jobs grew from 140.3 million to 143.8 million, an increase of 2.5 percent. Matching the Reagan recovery would have meant generating 156.4 million jobs, an extra 12.5 million jobs.

60. Calomiris and Haber, *Fragile by Design*, 204.

61. Mitra Toosi, "Employment Outlook: 2006–16, Labor Force Projections to 2016: More Workers in Their Golden Years," *Bureau of Labor Statistics Monthly Labor Review* (November 2007): table 3, 29, https://www.bls.gov/opub/mlr/2007/11/art3full.pdf.

62. US Bureau of Labor Statistics, "Labor Force Statistics from the Current Population Survey, Household Data Historical, Table A-1, Employment Status of the Civilian Noninstitutional Population," BLS, last modified November 1, 2024, https://www .bls.gov/web/empsit/cpseea01.htm.

63. Phil Gramm, "Reagan and Obama: A Tale of Two Recoveries," *Wall Street Journal*, August 29, 2012, https://www.wsj.com/articles/SB100008723963904448127045776 09863412900388.

64. Gramm, "Reagan and Obama."

65. Gramm, "Reagan and Obama."

66. See Casey B. Mulligan, *The Redistribution Recession: How Labor Market Distortions Contracted the Economy* (Oxford University Press, 2012), 41–118.

67. Congressional Budget Office, "Troubled Asset Relief Program," published April 17, 2009, https://www.cbo.gov/publication/24884; Congressional Budget Office, "Estimated Impact the American Recovery and Reinvestment Act on Employment and Economic Output in 2013," published February 21, 2014, https://www.cbo.gov/ publication/45122.

68. Office of Management and Budget, *Historical Tables, FY 2025* (US Government Printing Office, 2024), table 1.2.

69. Winston Churchill, "Roosevelt and the Future of the New Deal," *The Daily Mail*, April 24, 1935.

70. See BBC News Staff, "State of the Union: Obama to Seek Tax Raises on Wealthy," BBC News, published January 18, 2015, https://www.bbc.com/news/world-us -canada-30869190; Barack Obama, "Weekly Address: Passing the Buffett Rule So That Everyone Pays Their Fair Share," The White House, released March 31, 2012, https://obamawhitehouse.archives.gov/blog/2012/03/31/weekly-address-passing -buffett-rule-so-everyone-pays-their-fair-share.

71. Scott R. Baker, Nicholas Bloom, and Steven J. Davis, "Measuring Economic Policy Uncertainty," *Quarterly Journal of Economics* 131 (November 2016): 1593–1636.

Six: The Myth and Reality of Income Inequality in America

1. National Archives, "Declaration of Independence," accessed November 2024, https://www.archives.gov/founding-docs/declaration-transcript.

2. Abraham Lincoln, "Speech to the One Hundred Sixty-Sixth Ohio Regiment," Abraham Lincoln Online, last updated 2018, https://www.abrahamlincolnonline .org/lincoln/speeches/ohio.htm.

3. Will and Ariel Durant, *The Lessons of History* (MJF Books, 1968), 20.

4. "Have the Top 0.1% of Americans Made Out Like Bandits since 2000?," *The Economist*, May 7, 2020, https://www.economist.com/united-states/2020/05/07/ have-the-top-01-of-americans-made-out-like-bandits-since-2000.

5. Quoted in William Voegeli, "Leveling, Up and Down," *Claremont Review of Books*, Fall 2022, https://claremontreviewofbooks.com/leveling-up-and-down/.

6. Colin Gordon, *Growing Apart: A Political History of American Inequality*, Inequality.org, last updated April 6, 2020, https://scalar.usc.edu/works/growing -apart-a-political-history-of-american-inequality/index

7. Gordon, *Growing Apart*, "Introduction."

8. Thomas Piketty, *Capital in the Twenty-First Century*, trans. Arthur Goldhammer (Harvard University Press, 2014), 265.

9. Hannah Brockhaus, "Pope Francis: Catholics Should Combat 'Dismal' Economic Inequality with Hope," Catholic Diocese of Raleigh, published August 26, 2020, https://dioceseofraleigh.org/news/pope-francis-catholics-should-combat-dismal-economic-inequality-hope#:~:text=."

10. Brockhaus, "Pope Francis."

11. Aimee Picchi, "Why 200 Millionaires Want Higher Taxes: Inequality Is 'Eating Our World Alive,'" CBS News MoneyWatch, published January 18, 2023, https://www.cbsnews.com/news/millionaires-higher-taxes-on-rich-davos-inequality/.

12. Greg Rosalsky, "A Nobel Prize-Winning Immigrant's View on American Inequality," *Planet Money*, September 26, 2023, https://www.npr.org/sections/money/2023/09/26/1199422599/a-nobel-prize-winning-immigrants-view-on-american-inequality.

13. Rosalsky, "A Nobel Prize-Winning Immigrant's View."

14. Rosalsky, "A Nobel Prize-Winning Immigrant's View."

15. Bridget O'Brian, "Nobel Laureate Joseph Stiglitz on the Price of Inequality," *Columbia News*, June 14, 2012, https://news.columbia.edu/news/nobel-laureate-joseph-stiglitz-price-inequality.

16. Paul Krugman, "The Undeserving Rich," *New York Times*, January 19, 2014, https://www.nytimes.com/2014/01/20/opinion/krugman-the-undeserving-rich.html.

17. US Census Bureau, "Table H-3. Mean Household Income Received by Each Fifth and Top 5 Percent, All Races: 1967 to 2022," and "Table H-4. Gini Indexes for Households, by Race and Hispanic Origin of Householder," last updated August 30, 2024, https://www.census.gov/data/tables/time-series/demo/income-poverty/historical-income-households.html; and US Census Bureau, "Table 2. Poverty Status of People by Family Relationship, Race, and Hispanic Origin: 1959 to 2022," last updated September 10, 2024, https://www.census.gov/data/tables/time-series/demo/income-poverty/historical-poverty-people.html.

18. Phil Gramm, Robert Ekelund, and John Early, *The Myth of American Inequality* (Rowman & Littlefield, 2022), 48–51, and footnote 10, 215–16. Derived from US Census Bureau, "Table H-4. Gini Indexes for Households." The years 1947–1967 were computed from the archived tables of income distributions for individual years provided by the Census Bureau.

19. Organisation for Economic Co-operation and Development, "Income Inequality," OECD Data, accessed September 2024, https://data.oecd.org/inequality/income-inequality.htm; Organisation for Economic Co-operation and Development, "Income Inequality," in *Society at a Glance 2016: OECD Social Indicators* (OECD Publishing, 2016), https://read.oecd-ilibrary.org/social-issues-migration-health/society-at-a-glance-2016/income-inequality_soc_glance-2016-16-en#page1.

20. See Gramm, Ekelund, and Early, *The Myth of American Inequality*, chapter 2, for a detailed accounting of the undercounting in the Census measure of household income.

21. Congressional Budget Office, "Revenues in 2017: An Infographic," published March 5, 2018, https://www.cbo.gov/publication/53627#:~:text=; US Census Bureau, "2017 Quarterly Summary of State & Local Tax Revenue Tables," last updated October 8, 2021, https://www.census.gov/data/tables/2017/econ/qtax/historical.Q4.html#list-tab-1553017079.

22. Matthew Gardner, "Who Pays Taxes in America in 2017?" Institute on Taxation and Economic Policy, published April 13, 2017, https://itep.org/who-pays-taxes-in-america-in-2017/.

23. On the derivations of the dollar amount of transfer payments ($1.9 trillion) excluded from the Census Bureau's calculation of household income, see Gramm, Ekelund, and Early, *The Myth of American Inequality*, chapter 2; for tax data, see pages 25–28.

24. US Bureau for Economic Analysis, "Table 3.12. Government Social Benefits," and "Table 1.1.9. Implicit Price Deflators for Gross Domestic Product," US Bureau for Economic Analysis, National Income and Product Accounts, last updated September 27, 2024, https://apps.bea.gov/iTable/?reqid=19&step=3&isuri=1&nipa_table_list=110&categories=survey. For a more complete set of sources, see the notes to table 2.2 of Gramm, Ekelund, and Early, *The Myth of American Inequality*, 20.

25. Gramm, Ekelund, and Early, *The Myth of American Inequality*, 35.

26. See Juliana Menasce Horowitz, Ruth Igielnik, and Rakesh Kochhar, "Trends in Income and Wealth Inequality," Pew Research Center, published January 8, 2020, https://www.pewresearch.org/social-trends/2020/01/09/trends-in-income-and-wealth-inequality/; Statista, "Percentage Distribution of Household Income in the United States in 2022," published September 16, 2024, https://www.statista.com/statistics/203183/percentage-distribution-of-household-income-in-the-us/.

27. Gramm, Ekelund, and Early, *The Myth of American Inequality*, 31.

28. Gramm, Ekelund, and Early, *The Myth of American Inequality*, table 2.4, 29.

29. Gramm, Ekelund, and Early, *The Myth of American Inequality*, 32.

30. Gramm, Ekelund, and Early, *The Myth of American Inequality*, table 5.1, 63.

31. Gramm, Ekelund, and Early, *The Myth of American Inequality*, 62–68.

32. Note: Net transfers are transfer payments minus taxes when transfer payments are greater than taxes. Net taxes are taxes minus transfer payments when taxes are greater than transfer payments. Real dollars are calculated using the Consumer Price Index for All Urban Consumers.

33. Comparative rates of growth for these aggregates were calculated from the National Income and Product Accounts; see US Bureau for Economic Analysis, "Table 2.1. Personal Income and Its Disposition," "Table 3.12. Government Social Benefits," and "Table 3.1. Government Current Receipts and Expenditures," National Income and Product Accounts, last updated September 27, 2024, https://tinyurl.com/2ex9bwub.

34. Kayla Fontenot, Jessica Semega, and Melissa Kollar, "Income and Poverty in the United States: 2017," US Census Bureau, published September 12, 2018, https://tinyurl.com/39crc2pc.

35. Gloria Guzman and Melissa Kollar, *Income in the United States: 2022* (US Census Bureau, 2023), table A-4b, 34.

36. Shuaizhang Feng, Richard V. Burkhauser, and J. S. Butler, "Levels and Long-Term Trends in Earnings Inequality: Overcoming Current Population Survey Censoring Problems Using the GB2 Distribution," *Journal of Business & Economic Statistics* 24 (January 2006): 57–62, especially page 58, https://www.jstor.org/stable/27638852.

37. US Census Bureau, Current Population Reports, Series P60-188, "Appendix C. Conversion to a Computer-Assisted Questionnaire," in *Income, Poverty, and Valuation of Noncash Benefits: 1993* (US Government Printing Office, 1995), C-2. https://www.census.gov/library/publications/1995/demo/p60-188.html

38. US Census Bureau, Current Population Reports, "Appendix C. Conversion," in *Income, Poverty, and Valuation*.

39. See notes 38 and 29 from the US Census Bureau, "Table H-4. Gini Indexes for Households." See also Carmen DeNavas-Walt and Bernadette D. Proctor, *Income and Poverty in the United States: 2014* (US Census Bureau, 2015), Appendix D,

https://www.census.gov/content/dam/Census/library/publications/2015/demo/
p60-252.pdf.

40. Gramm, Ekelund, and Early, *The Myth of American Inequality*, 50.

41. In the United States, Medicare and Medicaid—including the Children's Health Insurance Program (CHIP)—are transfer payments, as the benefits go only to people who specifically qualify based on their income, age, or disability. Medicaid is paid for by the general taxpayer. With Medicare, the federal government pays the portion not covered by beneficiary-paid Medicare premiums. While the OECD does not dispute adding some one hundred federal programs that the Census Bureau does not count in its submission, it challenges counting Medicare and Medicaid, as other OECD countries have socialized medicine, and therefore, everybody is covered. In the case of these other countries, the redistribution is captured in taxes, which the OECD counts in its measure of income inequality, unlike the Census. But in America, Medicare and Medicaid *are*, in fact, transfer payments. They are not available to everybody, and they clearly fit in the OECD definition of transfer payments. See Martine Durand, "Many Data Sets Show High U.S. Inequality," *Wall Street Journal*, August 23, 2018. See also Phil Gramm and John Early, "The OECD's View of U.S. Inequality Is Mistaken," *Wall Street Journal*, August 28, 2018.

42. See Gramm, Ekelund, and Early, *The Myth of American Inequality*, 56–57.

43. Thomas Piketty, *Capital in the Twenty-First Century* (Harvard University Press, 2014).

44. Piketty, *Capital in the Twenty-First Century*, 300.

45. Gerald Auten and David Splinter, "Income Inequality in the United States: Using Tax Data to Measure Long-Term Trends," *Journal of Political Economy* 132 (July 2024): 2179–27.

46. Hugh Rockoff, "Great Fortunes of the Gilded Age," NBER Working Paper No. 14555 (December 2008), table 6, 37.

47. See Gramm, Ekelund, and Early, *The Myth of American Inequality*, 54.

48. Emmanuel Saez and Gabriel Zucman, *The Triumph of Injustice: How the Rich Dodge Taxes and How to Make Them Pay* (W. W. Norton, 2019).

49. Robert Faturechi, "ProPublica's Tax Revelations Lead to Calls for Reforms—and Investigation," ProPublica, June 9, 2021, https://www.propublica.org/article/propub licas-tax-revelations-lead-to-calls-for-reforms-and-investigation#:~:text= .

50. Ted Late, "Who Owns Microsoft? Biggest MSFT Stockholders in 2024," *Coincodex*, April 22, 2024, https://coincodex.com/article/29185/who-owns-microsoft/.

51. William D. Nordhaus, "Schumpeterian Profits in the American Economy: Theory and Measurement," NBER Working Paper No. 10433 (April 2004), https://www .nber.org/papers/w10433.

52. Gloria Guzman and Melissa Kollar, *Income in the United States: 2022*, table A-2, 16, 60–279.

53. Gramm, Ekelund, and Early, *The Myth of American Inequality*, figure 9.1, 142.

54. Gramm, Ekelund, and Early, *The Myth of American Inequality*, figure 8.3, 131.

55. The Pew Charitable Trusts, *Pursuing the American Dream: Economic Mobility Across Generations* (The Pew Charitable Trusts, 2012), 6, https://www.pewtrusts .org/~/media/legacy/uploadedfiles/wwwpewtrustsorg/reports/economic_mobility/ pursuingamericandreampdf.pdf.

56. Raj Chetty, Nathaniel Hendren, Patrick Kline, and Emmanuel Saez, "Where Is the Land of Opportunity? The Geography of Intergenerational Mobility in the United

States," *Quarterly Journal of Economics* 129, no. 4 (2014): 1553–624, see the online appendices, https://academic.oup.com/qje/article/129/4/1553/1853754.

57. Michael R. Strain, *The American Dream Is Not Dead (But Populism Could Kill It)* (Templeton Press, 2020), figure 16, 83.

58. The Maryland Statehouse, "George Washington's Resignation," accessed November 2024, https://msa.maryland.gov/msa/mdstatehouse/html/gwresignation.html.

Seven: The Myth That Poverty Is a Failure of American Capitalism

1. Lyndon B. Johnson, "Special Message to Congress Proposing a Nationwide War on the Sources of Poverty," The American Presidency Project, delivered March 16, 1964, https://www.presidency.ucsb.edu/documents/special-message-the-congress-proposing-nationwide-war-the-sources-poverty. For the decline in the postwar poverty rate, see Phil Gramm, Robert Ekelund, and John Early, *The Myth of American Inequality* (Rowman & Littlefield, 2022), 35–36.

2. Gramm, Ekelund, and Early, *The Myth of American Inequality*, table 5.1, 62–65.

3. Franklin D. Roosevelt, "Annual Message to Congress," The American Presidency Project, delivered January 4, 1935, https://www.presidency.ucsb.edu/documents/annual-message-congress-3.

4. Thomas Piketty, *Capital in the Twenty-First Century*, trans. Arthur Goldhammer (Harvard University Press, 2014), 26.

5. Matthew Desmond, *Poverty, by America* (Crown, 2023).

6. Matthew Desmond, "Why Poverty Persists in America," *New York Times Magazine*, March 9, 2023, https://www.nytimes.com/2023/03/09/magazine/poverty-by-america-matthew-desmond.html.

7. Samuel Moyn, "Poverty, By America by Matthew Desmond Review—How the Rich Keep the Poor Down," *The Guardian*, March 22, 2023, https://www.theguardian.com/books/2023/mar/22/poverty-by-america-by-matthew-desmond-review-how-the-rich-keep-the-poor-down.

8. Joel Blau, "Review of One Nation, Underprivileged: Why American Poverty Affects Us All," *Journal of Sociology & Social Welfare* 32 (December 2005): 165–67, https://scholarworks.wmich.edu/cgi/viewcontent.cgi?article=3120&context=jssw; the quotation in the text appears on page 166.

9. Matt Bruenig, "Tired of Capitalism? There Could Be a Better Way," *Washington Post*, September 30, 2015, https://www.washingtonpost.com/news/in-theory/wp/2015/09/30/tired-of-capitalism-lets-try-basic-income/.

10. United Nations Human Rights Office of the High Commissioner, "Summary," in *Report of the Special Rapporteur on Extreme Poverty and Human Rights on His Mission to the United States of America—Note by the Secretariat* (United Nations, 2018), https://www.ohchr.org/en/documents/country-reports/ahrc3833add1-report-special-rapporteur-extreme-poverty-and-human-rights.

11. International Monetary Fund, Western Hemisphere Dept. "United States: Staff Report for the 2017 Article IV Consultation," *International Monetary Fund* 2017, no. 239 (2017): 14.

12. Rakesh Kochhar, "Middle Class Fortunes in Western Europe," Pew Research Center, published April 24, 2017, appendix D.

13. See Gramm, Ekelund, and Early, *The Myth of American Inequality*, 35–36.

14. Matthew Desmond, "Why Poverty Persists in America."

15. Desmond, *Poverty, by America*, 184.

16. Gramm, Ekelund, and Early, *The Myth of American Inequality*, 36–37.

17. Gramm, Ekelund, and Early, *The Myth of American Inequality*, 37.

18. Gramm, Ekelund, and Early, *The Myth of American Inequality*, 13–34; data summary shown in figure 2.1, page 31.

19. Emily A. Shrider and John Creamer, "Poverty in the United States: 2022, Current Population Reports," US Census Bureau, published September 2023, table A-3, 23, https://www.census.gov/content/dam/Census/library/publications/2023/demo/p60-280.pdf.

20. Shrider and Creamer "Poverty in the United States: 2022."

21. Gramm, Ekelund, and Early, *The Myth of American Inequality*, 19–25.

22. Gramm, Ekelund, and Early, *The Myth of American Inequality*, 19–25.

23. Gramm, Ekelund, and Early, *The Myth of American Inequality*, 62–64.

24. Gramm, Ekelund, and Early, *The Myth of American Inequality*, table 2.4, 29.

25. Gramm, Ekelund, and Early, *The Myth of American Inequality*, 37.

26. Gramm, Ekelund, and Early, *The Myth of American Inequality*, 37.

27. Gramm, Ekelund, and Early, *The Myth of American Inequality*, 37–38.

28. Gramm, Ekelund, and Early, *The Myth of American Inequality*, 37–38.

29. Gramm, Ekelund, and Early, *The Myth of American Inequality*, 38.

30. National Alliance to End Homelessness, "Health and Homelessness," last updated December 2023, https://endhomelessness.org/homelessness-in-america/what-causes-homelessness/health/.

    According to the US Department of Housing and Urban Development, people living in shelters are more than twice as likely to have a disability compared to the general population. On a given night in 2023, 31 percent of the homeless population reported having a serious mental illness, 24 percent of those conditions related to chronic substance abuse, and nearly 11,000 people had HIV/AIDS. Conditions such as diabetes, heart disease, and HIV/AIDS are found at high rates among the homeless population, sometimes three to six times higher than that of the general population. See US Department of Housing and Urban Development, "AHAR Reports," HUD Exchange, last updated 2024, https://www.hudexchange.info/homelessness-assistance/ahar/#2023-reports.

31. Bruce D. Meyer and James X. Sullivan, *Annual Report on U.S. Consumption Poverty: 2017* (University of Chicago and University of Notre Dame, 2018), https://tinyurl.com/3k739per.

32. Richard V. Burkhauser, Kevin Corinth, James Elwell, and Jeff Larrimore, "Evaluating the Success of President Johnson's War on Poverty: Revisiting the Historical Record Using a Full-Income Poverty Measure," *Social Science Research Network* (March 17, 2019), https://ssrn.com/abstract=3353906 or http://dx.doi.org/10.2139/ssrn.3353906.

33. Data on housing of poor households are taken from the US Census Bureau, "American Housing Survey for the United States: 2011," and "Current Housing Reports H150/11, September 2013," accessed September 2023, https://www.census.gov; additional analysis by Robert Rector and Rachel Sheffield, "The War on Poverty After Fifty Years," in *Backgrounder No. 2955* (Heritage Foundation, 2014).

34. Feeding America, "No One Can Thrive on an Empty Stomach," accessed July 10, 2024, https://www.feedingamerica.org/#:~:text=No%20One%20Can%20Thrive%20on,more%20than%2014%20million%20children.

35. Alisha Coleman-Jensen, Matthew P. Rabbitt, Christian A. Gregory, and Anita Singh, *Household Food Security in the United States in 2017* (Economic Research Service, US Department of Agriculture, 2018), table 1A, 1.

36. Gramm, Ekelund, and Early, *The Myth of American Inequality*, 41, footnote 22.

37. Gramm, Ekelund, and Early, *The Myth of American Inequality*, 41, footnote 19.

38. Gramm, Ekelund, and Early, *The Myth of American Inequality*, 40–42.

39. See Gramm, Ekelund, and Early, *The Myth of American Inequality*, 57; Kochhar, "Middle Class Fortunes in Western Europe."

40. Bruce D. Meyer, Derek Wu, Victoria R. Mooers, and Carla Medalia, "The Use and Misuse of Income Data and Extreme Poverty in the United States," *Journal of Labor Economics* 39 (January 2021): S5–S58; the quoted passage appears on page S5.

41. Meyer, Wu, Mooers, and Medalia, "The Use and Misuse of Income Data," S5–S58; the quoted passage appears on page S5.

42. Organisation for Economic Co-operation and Development, "Net Social Expenditures Aggregated Data in Percentage of Gross Domestic Product, 2015," OECD Data Explorer, accessed September 2024, https://stats.oecd.org/Index.aspx ?datasetcode=SOCX_REF. Net social expenditures are approximately the same as transfer payments.

43. Piketty, *Capital in the Twenty-First Century*, 26.

44. Gigi Zamora, "The 2023 Forbes 400 Self-Made Score: From Silver Spooners To Bootstrappers," *Forbes*, October 3, 2023, https://www.forbes.com/sites/gigi zamora/2023/10/03/the-2023-forbes-400-self-made-score-from-silver-spooners -to-bootstrappers/.

45. Steven M. Rosenthal and Lydia S. Austin, "Tax Notes, "The Dwindling Taxable Share of U.S. Corporate Stocks," *Tax Notes*, May 16, 2016, 923–34.

46. See Gramm, Ekelund, and Early, *The Myth of American Inequality*, table 5.2, 71.

47. See Gramm, Ekelund, and Early, *The Myth of American Inequality*, table 5.1, 63.

48. Gramm, Ekelund, and Early, *The Myth of American Inequality*, 28–32.

49. Personal Responsibility and Work Opportunity Reconciliation Act of 1996, Pub. L. No. 104-193, 110 Stat. 2105.

50. Robert Rector and Patrick F. Fagan, "The Continuing Good News About Welfare Reform," *The Heritage Foundation Backgrounder*, no. 1620 (February 2023).

51. Gramm, Ekelund, and Early, *The Myth of American Inequality*, 66.

52. Gramm, Ekelund, and Early, *The Myth of American Inequality*, 66.

53. See Rector and Fagan, "The Continuing Good News."

54. Gramm, Ekelund, and Early, *The Myth of American Inequality*, 28–32.

55. Gramm, Ekelund, and Early, *The Myth of American Inequality*, table 2.4, 29, and figure 2.1., 31.

56. Gramm, Ekelund, and Early, *The Myth of American Inequality*, 173–77.

57. See Thomas Sowell, *Charter Schools and Their Enemies* (Basic Books, 2020); National Center for Education Statistics, "NAEP Technical Documentation: Achievement Levels," National Assessment of Educational Progress, accessed November 2024, https://nces.ed.gov/nationsreportcard/tdw/analysis/describing_achiev.aspx.

58. Gramm, Ekelund, and Early, *The Myth of American Inequality*, 42.

59. See US Census Bureau, *Current Population Survey, Annual Demographic* File (US Census Bureau, 1968); US Census Bureau, *Current Population Survey, Annual Social and Economic (ASEC) Supplement* (US Census Bureau, 2018), https://www2.census

.gov/programs-surveys/cps/techdocs/cpsmar18.pdf. This data is also summarized in Gramm, Ekelund, and Early, *The Myth of American Inequality*, table 5.2, 71.

60. US Census Bureau, "Housing Survey 1974," last updated November 10, 2021, https://www.census.gov.

61. Gramm, Ekelund, and Early, *The Myth of American Inequality*, 146; calculated from US Census Bureau, "Decennial Census of 1960 and 1970," interpolating between 1960 and 1970. See US Census Bureau, "Decennial Census of 1960" and "Decennial Census of 1970," last updated August 4, 2023, https://www.census.gov.

62. Gramm, Ekelund, and Early, *The Myth of American Inequality*, 37–38.

63. See Nicholas Eberstadt, "Post-Pandemic Recovery for America's Prime Age Labor Force: A Tale of Two Sexes," *AEIdeas*, June 9, 2024.

64. See Casey Mulligan, *The Redistribution Recession: How Labor Market Distortions Contracted the Economy* (Oxford University Press, 2012), 41–118.

Eight: Lessons and Conclusions

1. See David McCord Wright, "Letters to the Editor," *Wall Street Journal*, September 12, 1961.

2. Edith Hamilton, *The Ever-Present Past* (W. W. Norton, 1964), 37.

3. Office of Management and Budget, *FY 2025 Budget Submission* (US Government Printing Office, 2024), table 13.1.

INDEX

INDEX